T0288590

'Once again, Reitano and Shaw are ahead of the pack. While criminals were initially wrong-footed by Covid-19, within weeks they readjusted their strategies to profit from the unprecedented government funds entering the economy. Criminal Contagion explains what has been happening in the world of organized crime, what we must do about it and what will happen if we don't. Clear, pithy and satisfyingly comprehensive, it should be read by everyone concerned about the consequential threats we will face post-pandemic. A gem of a book.'

Misha Glenny, author of *McMafia: Seriously Organised Crime*

'While the world has reeled under the impact of Covid-19, organized criminals have thrived. This meticulously researched book shows clearly and convincingly how and why criminality boomed. A call for concerted and serious action against a contagion just as serious as coronavirus.'

Oliver Bullough, author of *Moneyland: Why Thieves and Crooks Now Rule the World* and *How to Take It Back*

'A timely book that rigorously assesses how criminals are taking advantage of the pandemic to boost illicit businesses. A must-read and an indispensable reference for policy-makers, analysts and academics.'

Moisés Naím, Distinguished Fellow, Carnegie Endowment for International Peace, and author of *Illicit* and *The End of Power*

'A brilliant tour d'horizon of how local and global criminal organizations have responded, and in many cases thrived, amid the Covid-19 pandemic, refactoring deviant supply chains and backfilling services where governments have failed. Reitano and Shaw's reporting is riveting.'

Nils Gilman, Vice President of Programs, Berggruen Institute, and author of *Deviant Globalization: Black Market Economy in the 21st Century*

'It's a truism that of all entrepreneurs, criminals are the fastest to spot new opportunities. This timely, readable and thoroughly shocking book demonstrates how even a global pandemic can be good for (criminal) business.'

Mark Galeotti, author of *The Vory: Russia's Super Mafia*

'Criminal Contagion is a tour de force, combining meticulous research with a global perspective, and highlighting how the pandemic created novel opportunities for expanding illicit markets and enriching criminal organizations. Congratulations to the authors on this timely and important book.'

Phil Williams, Professor of International Security,
University of Pittsburgh

'Not all have suffered from Covid-19. This well-illustrated analysis explains that criminals, by exploiting human vulnerability, have been major beneficiaries of the pandemic. Critical reading for those seeking to understand and address the diverse and costly human consequences of Covid-19.'

Louise Shelley, University Professor, George Mason University, and
Director, Terrorism, Transnational Crime and Corruption Center

'An engaging analysis of organized crime, corruption, and the political economy in the face of the global pandemic. The multiple impacts and lessons moving forward make this a compelling read.'

Jay Albanese, Professor in the Wilder School of Government & Public
Affairs, Virginia Commonwealth University, and author of
*Organized Crime: From the Mob to Transnational Organized Crime*

'Covid-19 has transformed not only the world, but also the underworld. Reitano and Shaw are the perfect guides for this vivid and eye-opening journey through a global criminal landscape reshaped by pandemic and response. A tour de force.'

James Cockayne, author of
*Hidden Power: The Strategic Logic of Organised Crime*

'This timely book shows how criminals have exploited the disruption of the pandemic. While packed with up-to-date facts, it is also accessible and engaging. The lessons drawn here go beyond just Covid-19, with broader implications for understanding the dynamics of criminal networks.'

Richard Wortley, Professor of
Crime Science, University College London

# CRIMINAL CONTAGION

TUESDAY REITANO
MARK SHAW

# Criminal Contagion

## *How Mafias, Gangsters and Scammers Profit from a Pandemic*

HURST & COMPANY, LONDON

First published in the United Kingdom in 2021 by
C. Hurst & Co. (Publishers) Ltd.,
83 Torbay Road, London NW6 7DT

Printed in Great Britain by Bell and Bain Ltd, Glasgow

Distributed in the United States, Canada and Latin America by
Oxford University Press, 198 Madison Avenue, New York, NY 10016,
United States of America.



A Cataloguing-in-Publication data record for this book
is available from the British Library.

ISBN: 9781787384460

This book is printed using paper from registered sustainable
and managed sources.

www.hurstpublishers.com

To our families

And in memory of Eitan Silkoff (1991–2020)

# CONTENTS

*List of Acronyms* xi

1. Introduction 1
2. Disruption 11
3. Between Cold War and Covid 27
4. No Escape, No Way Home 47
5. Business as Usual 65
6. Criminal Commodities 83
7. Wildlife's Revenge? 97
8. It's Virtual 115
9. The Fish Rots from the Head 133
10. Covid and Punishment 151
11. Gangland Rules 169
12. Who's Going to Pay? 187
13. Prevention, Treatment and Cure 205

*Notes* 217
*Acknowledgements* 289
*Index* 293

# LIST OF ACRONYMS

| | |
|---|---|
| BEC | Business Email Compromise |
| BRI | Belt and Road Initiative |
| CBP | (United States) Customs and Border Patrol |
| CITES | Convention on International Trade in Endangered Species of Wild Fauna and Flora |
| CND | Commission on Narcotics Drugs |
| CSAM | Child sexual abuse material |
| CV | Comando Vermelho (Brazilian crime group) |
| DRC | Democratic Republic of Congo |
| EMCDDA | European Monitoring Centre for Drugs and Drug Addiction |
| FDN | Famila do Norte (Brazilian crime group) |
| FinCEN | US Treasury Financial Crimes Enforcement Network |
| FTZ | Free Trade Zone |
| GCC | Gulf Cooperation Council |
| ILO | International Labour Organization |
| IOM | International Organization for Migration |
| IUU | Illegal, unreported and unregulated fishing |
| MDMA | Methylenedioxymethamphetamine (commonly known as ecstasy) |

| | |
|---|---|
| NRW | North Rhine-Westphalia |
| OCCRP | Organized Crime and Corruption Reporting Project |
| OECD | Organization for Economic Co-operation and Development |
| PPE | Personal Protective Equipment |
| PPP | Paycheck Protection Program |
| SAR | Suspicious Activity Report |
| SEZ | Special Economic Zone |
| TCM | Traditional Chinese Medicine |
| UK | United Kingdom |
| UNESCO | United Nations Educational, Scientific and Cultural Organization |
| UNHCR | United Nations High Commissioner for Refugees |
| UNODC | United Nations Office on Drugs and Crime |
| UNTOC | United Nations Convention Against Transnational Organized Crime |
| WHO | World Health Organization |

1

# INTRODUCTION

Sometime in December 2019, an unknown virus crossed over from an animal—mostly likely a bat—to humans. Several people in Wuhan, a city in China where transmission of the virus seems to have first occurred, were hospitalised with severe pneumonia, but medical staff quickly realised that something else was at play. Further research identified a novel coronavirus—formally labelled SARS-CoV-2—which caused a disease in humans called Covid-19.

The virus was highly infectious and lethal. Uniquely, many people who contracted the disease showed no symptoms, while others did not display them immediately, making it difficult to ascertain infection rates. On 1 January 2020, the Chinese authorities closed the wholesale food market where the virus was first identified, and on 20 January they confirmed human-to-human transmission—and warned that the virus was spreading fast.[1] In order to contain the virus, all movement and business were halted, and people had to stay inside. Wuhan had entered lockdown.

This was a term that was rapidly to become common parlance as the virus surged around the world. By April 2020, it was estimated that around two billion people globally were in some form of lockdown aimed at containing the spread of the virus. Commercial airlines reduced or suspended services, while border closures and social distancing measures were put in place by the vast majority of countries to reduce the rate of infection and prevent public health systems from being overwhelmed.

But this suspension of economic and social activity came at a heavy cost. Whole sectors collapsed in a matter of days, triggering the loss of millions of jobs across the tourism, entertainment, hospitality, travel and services industries. Everyone was affected, from giant multinationals to those working in the gig economy, although some felt the impact far more than others. The relentless march of the coronavirus—which was declared a pandemic by the World Health Organization (WHO) on 11 March[2]—had brought our busy world to a screeching halt.

Billions of words have already been written about the impact of the virus on the legal economy, and rightly so. The pandemic is a defining moment in history, a major disruption to the overall trajectory of globalisation, and a significant accelerator of some trends already under way, especially in the virtual sphere. It is likely to shape lives and livelihoods for years to come. Leading economies have been driven into recession, and developing economies are seeing ever greater numbers of people fall further into poverty. In June 2020, the International Monetary Fund (IMF) anticipated a 4.3% drop in global

GDP for the year.[3] That may not sound significant until you compare it with the 2008–9 recession, which triggered only a 0.1% contraction in the global economy, with devastating results.[4]

Far fewer words have been written about the impact of the pandemic on the illegal economy of organised crime. As the pandemic hit, these criminals were faced with the same set of challenges as everyone else: disrupted businesses, risks of infection, life under lockdown. But, unlike ordinary people, many found ways to carry on working, and even thrived.

Understanding how the coronavirus impacted on this world of organised crime, and how organised crime in turn affected the social and economic fallout of Covid-19, is the aim of this book.

### *Covid and crime*

We work in an organisation, the Global Initiative Against Transnational Organized Crime, established to understand illicit markets and their effects. When the virus began to spread in early 2020, we mobilised our field network and analysts and began to collect as much information as we could about the changes that seemed to be under way in criminal markets.

Like those of many analysts, our views changed over time. At first we thought there was more disruption in some markets, notably illicit narcotics, than turned out to be the case. Meanwhile, some areas, particularly the cyber sphere, exceeded expectations as to the speed and breadth of criminal growth. In some cases, the relationship between the pandemic and crime was relatively straightforward: with fewer commercial flights in operation, drug couriers were unable to travel and deliver their products. In other cases, the impact was more indirect: fears of contracting Covid-19, for example, changed consumer demand for illegal wildlife products in Asia.

But a common theme emerged: criminal tactics were evolving and crime was continuing—even flourishing—while law enforcement struggled to keep up, hamstrung by the necessity of responding to the pandemic and weakened by droves of personnel falling sick. Although we have spent years studying organised crime issues, nothing lessens our surprise at the ability of criminals to adapt or the resilience of criminal markets and actors. What we have observed with the coronavirus is extraordinary and has renewed our belief in the importance of understanding the changing dynamics of organised crime and developing new responses to it.

We begin this book with an overview of the disruption caused by the pandemic, then step back to examine the rise of organised crime since the early 1990s and the advent of globalisation. Interestingly, many of the same causes that have facilitated the spread of the coronavirus—greater interconnectedness and trade, rising urbanisation, and a booming global population—also contributed to the growth of organised crime across the globe in the pre-pandemic period. Indeed, this dispersion of criminal groups and networks—as well as the violence they engendered—was often described in terms of disease. In 2007, for example, Antonio Maria Costa, head of the United Nations Office on Drugs and Crime (UNODC), referred to the 'drug epidemic' which must be contained, and claimed that organised crime had metastasised, or spread uncontrollably.[5] Taking the metaphor literally, some analysts have even explored how the principles of epidemiology could be applied to the response to organised crime.[6] At the same time, the threat posed by organised crime was largely discounted in this period. Global responses were weak and fragmented, and the nature and extent of the growth of illicit markets were poorly understood.

As a result, by the time the pandemic hit, organised crime and illicit markets were well established across the globe, dealing in a range of illicit commodities from narcotics and people to wildlife and gold. We explore the impact of the pandemic on the various individual criminal markets before turning to the broader implications of the coronavirus for forms of criminal governance and the challenges that state actors faced during the pandemic. We conclude with some ideas for the prevention, treatment and cure of illicit markets and organised crime in a post-pandemic world.

Our book makes three conclusions regarding the impact of Covid-19 on crime. Firstly, the consequences of the pandemic differed from market to market, although several criminal markets are now tightly intertwined, resulting in knock-on effects. Secondly, the pandemic has in many cases accelerated changes that were already under way in the criminal economy, especially online. Thirdly, we need in the case of each market to distinguish between the immediate disruption caused, on the one hand, by lockdowns and the same general uncertainties that have plagued the legal economy and, on the other hand, by the longer-term economic crisis or depression that the pandemic is likely to cause and the future prospects of the criminal economy as global economic and trade dynamics change.

### *A note on terms*

In assessing the impact of the coronavirus on crime, it is important to be clear about the terms we use. When we talk of organised crime, we mean those organised groups or networks that are active in controlling or benefiting from illicit markets. In this study, we cover a range of criminal-style organisations, from drug cartels, historical mafias, newer gangs and loose networks of dynamic criminal actors, including those within the state who offer protection to criminals and criminal markets. In different ways, all these organisations and outfits engage in corruption and violence to achieve their objectives. We recognise that there are differences between these organisational phenomena, but we see them as a spectrum of linked actors deeply embedded in the business of making criminal markets operate. Almost without exception, they also have a foot in the legal economy, and legal and illegal commercial activities are frequently interwoven.

When we refer to criminal or illicit markets, we mean those that states have generally determined to be outside the law, such as the trafficking of drugs, human beings or wildlife products, or those in which licit products are obtained by illegal means, such as gold. But it is worth emphasising at the outset that states have different legal frameworks and what is illegal in one place may not be so in another, or may be enforced differently, or with different emphases, depending on political decisions, political will or questions of state capacity and legitimacy.

Criminal markets can be hard to understand because the information that guides legitimate economies—the basis for determining prices, for example—is hidden or uncollected in the case of illicit economies. Analysts work around this dearth of data by piecing together information from multiple sources to ascertain what might be going on. Some of this is conjecture, but the study of illicit markets has improved greatly, even if it is far from perfect. Our objective here is to assemble as much information as we can to take a first stab at understanding what happened to illicit markets during the pandemic. We think that is important because the defining nature of the pandemic may itself shape the nature of illicit market activity, and by implication organised crime, for decades to come. It is a subject likely to occupy researchers for at least as long.

### *A better response*

The coronavirus presents extraordinary challenges to global governance, the economy and social order. Where we go from here is an open question: there is no agreed plan, no guiding ideology to steer us through the chaos and disruption that the pandemic has brought. Yet there will be change. As Ivan Krastev, one of Europe's leading political and social thinkers, says: 'The world will be transformed, not because our societies want change or because there's consensus for the direction of change—but because we cannot go back.'[7]

Political economies are being visibly reshaped across the globe at all levels. The volume, nature and direction of global trade will shift. The policy space, as so often in periods of crisis, is more open than ever: fixed ideas are up for debate.

Our view is that the pandemic may provide a long-overdue opportunity to rethink how several illicit markets are regulated; to build more effective institutions to fight organised crime; and to improve the life and livelihood of people often caught in a web of criminal governance.

But the window of opportunity is likely to be brief and chances have already been lost. Instead of investments in legitimate state institutions, civil society action or local communities, the responses of many leaders around the world have tended towards heavy-handed lockdowns, coupled with failures to effectively counter disinformation and provide social safety nets to the most vulnerable. Some political and economic elites have even exploited the disruption to profit or to enhance discreet agendas, including the state protection of illicit markets. In other cases, state action has actually created new illicit markets through prohibiting the sale of goods and services, such as alcohol.

If action is not forthcoming, criminal actors will continue to operate. Illicit markets and networks are always adapting to find new routes for established illicit commodities so as to meet existing as well as new demand. While of a different order, the challenges posed by the pandemic are, for criminals, also arguably nothing out of the ordinary: just another barrier to overcome in the relentless pursuit of profit. Demand and supply of illicit products may have fluctuated through the pandemic, but neither is going away anytime soon.

And the global turmoil may actually play into the criminals' hands. The economic devastation of the pandemic has caused many people's livelihoods to shrink or disappear, and this is offering new opportunities for illicit money to enter new geographies and speculate on new sectors as businesses collapse. The swelling ranks of vulnerable and excluded people are also an enormous potential resource for criminal groups. Such people are susceptible to recruitment as the tools and commodities of criminal markets, including those for violence and exploitation (for sex or labour); as a potential market for illegal products; and as the labour force for many illegal markets (in drug production or illegal mining, for example). Criminals have proved extraordinarily resilient during the pandemic—in part because illegal markets often weed out lesser actors—and many will emerge even stronger than before.

Barbara Tuchman concluded her classic study of the Black Death—the 14th-century plague, which was estimated to have killed from one-third to two-thirds of Europe's population—with an assessment of what had changed as a result: 'Consciousness of wickedness made behaviour worse. Violence threw off restraints. It was a time of default. Rules crumbled. Institutions failed in their functions … The times were not static. Loss of confidence in the guarantors of order opened the way to demands for change, and miseria gave force to the impulse.' 'Mankind,' she ends, 'was not improved by the message.'[8]

Tuchman's medieval pandemonium may appear far removed from our twenty-first-century lives, but the stirrings of similar forces are now at play. The shifts and adaptations that took place in the underworld and upperworld during the pandemic pose real challenges to the rule of law, institutions and social cohesion. Violence is endemic in many areas of the world where criminal organisations hold sway.

As we argue in the following pages, our world is suffering not just from one pandemic, but two: coronavirus and crime. And while the coronavirus pandemic has done incalculable damage, it is crime that may shape our longer-term trajectory. The globalised, connected nature of the illicit now touches on all aspects of human existence, from human rights and health, the economy, poverty, inequality and social exclusion, the environment, climate change and the future of species, urbanisation and peace, to the very nature of politics and governance itself. It is as important a challenge as any faced by the global community, and one where we are not clearly succeeding. Rather than accelerating this downward trajectory, could the pandemic offer us an opportunity to reshape our response?

# 2

# DISRUPTION

It is a story now well known to the world, but, in retrospect, it is still astonishing to see how quickly the coronavirus spread in those early months of the year, and how quickly things changed. For those living in the Western hemisphere, the news articles that appeared on New Year's Day about an unknown, pneumonia-like disease in central China were barely blips on the radar of an already congested news picture. Our attention was dominated, we thought, by more pressing issues, like climate change, migration, the fate of the so-called liberal international order, Donald Trump. Whatever this disease was, it was happening far away.

And then it wasn't. In a matter of weeks, the coronavirus spread rapidly through China and beyond, with the first overseas case reported in Thailand in mid-January. The epicentre soon shifted, moving from China to Iran, then to northern Italy and Spain, and thereafter more broadly across continental Western Europe. Italy declared a state of emergency on 31 January and suspended all flights to and from China, but the virus continued to spread across the country, and on 8 March the Italian Prime Minister, Giuseppe Conte, declared a lockdown, which affected more than 60 million people.[1] But the virus still found a way out. Two holidaymakers returning from Italy brought the pandemic to South Africa, and on 15 March President Cyril Ramaphosa declared a state of national disaster.[2] Hotspots emerged in different parts of Africa, though only South Africa saw significant rates of infection and death, prompting the imposition of a fierce lockdown.

As Europe's first wave peaked in March and April, a virus cluster sparked in New York. At first it was just a few dozen cases, all linked to international travel, but the spring break and national holiday weekends taught the world about 'superspreader' events, which transmitted the virus in expanding clusters across North America over the summer[3] and across the southern border to Mexico and South America. In Brazil, President Jair Bolsonaro proudly embraced his role as one of the most prominent virus deniers, claiming that the coronavirus was only 'a little flu'.[4] Before long, however, Brazil, together with Mexico, Argentina, Colombia and Peru, was battling a major outbreak.[5]

During those early months, governments moved quickly, though unevenly, to put in place measures to limit the spread of the outbreak, to support public health systems, to try to bolster the economy and ensure public order and safety. The first thing to stop was air travel. Travellers proved the primary vector for transmission, and so in March governments started to close airports and cancel flights. Pre-pandemic, the number of commercial flights per day typically hovered around 170,000—in just two weeks, this fell to around 25,000.[6]

By the end of March, 91% of people worldwide—7.1 billion people in total—were living in countries with travel restrictions relating to Covid-19; almost 40% lived in countries whose borders had closed completely to non-residents.[7] By May, more than 60% of all global passenger jets were sitting idle, and 25 million aviation industry jobs and 100 million travel and tourism jobs had been abruptly lost.[8] Alongside border closures came social distancing measures: by early June, these had been employed by more than 100 countries, to varying degrees.

Governments attempted to mitigate the economic impact of these measures by granting relief payments to the unemployed or those furloughed and injecting subsidies into flagging industries, while trying to fight the pandemic through the massive procurement of medical supplies and equipment. But damage was unavoidable. Entire industries were shuttered overnight, triggering the loss of millions of jobs across multiple sectors of national economies. Office buildings went dark when staff were sent to work from home, furloughed or laid off. Regular trade decreased significantly, with Shanghai, the world's busiest port, witnessing a 20% drop in container volume between January and February 2020.[9] The price of oil—a key indicator of the global economy before the pandemic—even turned negative for the first time in history, in April 2020, as the economic arrest sent demand plummeting.[10]

As governments across the world intervened dramatically in the lives of their citizens, the pandemic became a litmus test of trust in government, institutions and expertise. Countries that offered subsidies and the safety net of state assistance found compliance easier, but in nations where the right to govern is still contested and the state provides little in terms of service delivery to significant portions of the population, getting people to comply with stringent lockdowns was an uphill battle. The challenge of compliance was also complicated by disinformation and partisan politics in many countries—a situation often not helped by the leaders themselves. Mexico's president, Andrés Manuel López Obrador, like President Donald Trump over the border, stubbornly refused to wear a face mask.

Law enforcement agencies—and, in some places, the military—were deployed onto the streets to police lockdowns, sometimes at the expense of human rights.[11] In Uganda, there were numerous reports of police brutality in enforcing the curfew that had been imposed at the beginning of April. In one particularly egregious incident, an officer approached a street vendor who was in the process of packing away in time for the curfew and kicked over a saucepan filled with boiling oil, leaving her with burns across her face, chest, arms and legs.[12] In Nigeria, the country's human-rights body reported that police had killed 18 people during the first two weeks of lockdown—a third more deaths than those attributable to the virus.[13] In Honduras, military police killed a man who had left his home in contravention of the lockdown restrictions, while there were other reports of the police using electric shock weapons and tear gas.[14] In Europe, videos circulated showing the French police using excessive force, harassment, verbal abuse and humiliation in some of the country's poorer neighbourhoods, which Amnesty International called 'violations of international law relating to human rights'.[15] In South Africa, a man was beaten to death by soldiers over the minor lockdown violation of drinking after curfew.[16]

Amid all this upheaval, the logisticians of global crime scrambled to adapt their businesses to a new and volatile reality. Inevitably, criminal opportunists quickly saw that there was money to be made.

### *Disruption in the underworld*

In the early months of the pandemic, there was discussion in the media and in policing circles that the anti-Covid measures being taken by governments could trigger significant ruptures in the global illicit economy. We suggested as much in some of our initial coverage of the pandemic.[17]

Organised crime requires mobility and infrastructure—the flow of people and goods on roads and through seaports and airports—in order to conceal illicit activities. So, optimistically, we hoped that if legitimate flows were stopped or reduced, the space of the illicit economy would also be constrained. And there is little question that, at least initially, organised crime and criminal groups did share some of the pain of the upperworld. All over the world, restaurants, shops, hotels, theatres and nightclubs declared bankruptcy.[18]

The closure of many of those night-time and entertainment economies was a critical hit to organised-crime groups, which frequently own bars and nightclubs as front companies and money-laundering hubs, and use them to provide 'security' services, extort patrons and owners, sell drugs, and run networks of prostitutes.[19] The cessation of professional sports also hit the sports betting, match-fixing and gambling operations that are often run by mafia and criminal networks, being a favoured way to launder money from other criminal trades.[20] The Japanese Yakuza was so badly hurt that one branch even offered to help disinfect a cruise liner quarantined in late February so as to pick up some extra money and sympathy.[21]

The imposition of strict lockdowns between March and May also reduced the space for criminal actors to hide and led to some serendipitous successes for law-enforcement agencies. In Italy, a long-sought mafia boss of the 'Ndrangheta was finally caught by police, not for his crime dealings, but for having contravened Italy's strict lockdown restrictions.[22]

Lockdown also impacted on other areas of criminal activity, such as illicit manufacturing. During their lockdown, Chinese companies were operating at 50% capacity or less (if they were not closed altogether), and Chinese manufacturers and sellers of drug ingredients reported delays in production and shipment.[23] In an interview, one Chinese manufacturer of fake garments lamented: 'Staff can't go back to factories, so factories can't actually open yet. Furthermore, the fabrics markets are all closed so we can't get any fabrics. The impact means delays to our shipment and production of goods. Right now, we can't produce anything at all!'[24]

Border controls also disrupted human smuggling and trafficking operations, as well as freezing migrant flows in general. Not only were the police and border forces determined to stop the journeys of undocumented migrants and refugees, but towns of transit also became inhospitable, as they feared migrants might be carrying the virus. Smugglers themselves feared the health risks of being on the move.[25] That Iran was one of the first hotspots of the virus proved a major disruption along the significant migrant route from Central and West Asia towards Europe. Tensions rose in early May when it appeared that Iranian guards had forced around 55 Afghan migrants to jump into the fast-moving Harirud River, causing at least 17 of them to drown.[26]

Facing border closures, human smugglers abandoned their clients (including pregnant women and children), turned to more dangerous routes, or found new ways to squeeze cash out of their now-immobile clients, including labour and sex trafficking, and extorting ransom money from their families.[27]

The adaptability shown by smugglers and traffickers soon manifested in other criminal sectors, especially once it became clear that the pandemic was also creating opportunities for organised crime groups. This was evident in the sphere of shipping, where food, fuel, medicines and medical equipment were typically expressed through the ports as governments tried to ensure that basic needs would be met.[28] Meanwhile, lockdowns and health protocols reduced the availability of manpower to unload ships, perform inspections and control customs, with the result that there was much less inspection of goods moving through ports to confirm that their contents were indeed what was stated on the waybills. In some countries, physical inspections by port officials were suspended completely to limit movement and contacts. Criminals quickly recognised the potential of this situation, smuggling drugs and other contraband in the expedited shipments. In mid-April, the UK Border Force discovered 14 kg of cocaine hidden within boxes of face masks in a van that was attempting to enter the UK through the Channel Tunnel.[29]

At the same time, counterfeiters (always alert to the hottest trends) quickly began to capitalise on the explosion of new demand for virus-mitigating products such as face masks, coronavirus test kits, personal protective equipment (PPE) worn by frontline workers, or medicine and medical equipment used for treating patients with Covid-19. The scams ranged from opportunistic street corner sales to the illicit mass production of substandard goods by unscrupulous corporations changing supply lines. Health NGOs in Kenya issued warnings about the distribution of counterfeit hand sanitisers, after local gangs had slapped a convincing label on small plastic containers that contained nothing more potent than tap water,[30] and arrests were made in Nairobi at an outlet selling fake coronavirus testing kits.[31] In a one-week operation in March 2020, the WHO and INTERPOL made 121 arrests across 90 countries, resulting in the confiscation of Covid-related fake pharmaceuticals worth over US$14 million. The operation also closed down more than 2,500 websites, social-media pages and online marketplace sites selling fake and fraudulent medical products.[32]

Doorstep scammers and organised thieving rings also adapted their usual modus operandi to scout houses or commercial properties as potential targets of robbery by posing as tradesmen and ringing prospectively at doorbells.[33] As early as March, reports emerged from Switzerland of criminal groups scouting out homes to loot, claiming to be from official state agencies and requesting access to properties under the guise of disinfecting buildings. In one notorious example in South Africa, criminals posing as state officials went around houses collecting cash which they claimed was contaminated with the virus and needed to be taken away for cleaning. (Unsurprisingly, neither they nor the cash ever returned.)[34] Other countries reported doorstep scammers peddling fake products and cures.[35] But the window for these kinds of physical scams was relatively short-lived in most places, as more widespread and stricter social distancing and mobility restrictions were imposed and enforced.

For the neighbourhood drug dealer in Europe, the first days of lockdown and social distancing were tough. Lingering on street corners had suddenly become impossible, making drop-offs harder and fraught with risk, both from the increasing police presence and from the virus itself. But the dealers quickly adapted, following the shifting market. Interest in party drugs like cocaine and synthetics such as Ecstasy fell, since parties were now few and far between, but cannabis use went up as people had more time to smoke. Demand for highly addictive substances like heroin, meth and fentanyl also rose as anxious addicts stocked up to ensure their stash would last when dealers disappeared off the street.[36] The quality of drugs was diluted and prices began to climb.

Informal surveys of drug users suggested that their dealers were taking careful precautions to keep themselves healthy, wearing PPE, making no-contact drops, and even disinfecting the cash they received in exchange.[37] Police forces in the UK reported that dealers were also disguising themselves as essential workers, wearing hospital scrubs, NHS badges, workout gear, and parcel, grocery and fast-food delivery uniforms as cover for being out on the streets and to avoid being questioned.[38] Many dealers also shifted quickly to online drug retailing—by March, the European Monitoring Centre for Drugs and Drug Addiction (EMCDDA) was already reporting a notable rise in activity on three popular darknet drug markets, relating particularly to cannabis sales, which is interesting as cannabis is a drug whose consumption is legal in much of Europe.[39]

In some cases, states gave a gift to organised crime by creating new shortages in normally legal goods, providing an easy alternative form of income. At the end of March, the South African government declared a moratorium on the sale of tobacco products, alcohol[40] and, somewhat mysteriously, hot pies and roast chicken.[41] Almost immediately, media sources across South Africa began to report increased criminal activity relating to alcohol and tobacco. As prices soared,[42] South African gangs moved into this market as suppliers to local communities, providing a massive boost to organised crime.[43] Interviews with smugglers operating across the border with Zimbabwe, Malawi and Botswana showed that they had seized the opportunity to capitalise on increased demand for cigarettes in neighbouring South Africa by smuggling the product across the border.[44] In a similar way, Panama's prohibition on alcohol sales led to increased smuggling of beer and spirits from Costa Rica, and Argentina's decision to stop tobacco production led to an increase of contraband from Paraguay.[45]

In other places where states fell short and people were desperate, mafia groups and gangs were the fastest to fill the void. In Rio de Janeiro's *favelas*, it was drug-trafficking groups who imposed and policed curfews;[46] and in Manenberg in Cape Town (one of the areas worst affected by gang violence in South Africa), rival gangs briefly appeared to call a truce and distributed food parcels to their communities.[47] In Mexico, the family of notorious drug trafficker Joaquín 'El Chapo' Guzmán went around distributing food boxes and bottles of water with the now-incarcerated drug lord's face stencilled on them.[48]

### *Crime thrives online*

Where the illicit economy really flourished was online, as organised crime used technology to appeal to a uniquely bored, immobile and isolated clientele who were thirsty for information and supplies. Industry data from all over the world showed meteoric rises in internet usage—50% to 60% higher than in the previous year[49]—as people avidly followed the news of the outbreak, entertained themselves, communicated with family members, and shopped, worked and schooled online.[50] E-commerce boomed: in April 2020, US and Canadian retailers reported that online orders were 146% higher than the previous year.[51] Even Africa, which has the lowest levels of online e-commerce in the world, saw web use grow dramatically, with companies reporting a 500% increase month-on-month during lockdown.[52]

Criminals were quick to surf the wave. They used the Covid-19 crisis to bombard individuals and businesses with misinformation, distribute malware and conduct phishing attacks and scams. One particularly shocking example was the 'Corona-Antivirus' email scam that promised to provide an internet anti-virus protection that, if the app was running on their computer, would protect users from coronavirus.[53] A website, Self.inc, is currently maintaining a list of coronavirus scams, and at the time of writing it details more than 144 ways in which criminals and fraudsters are trying to take money from the naive and gullible. These include e-commerce sites looking to sell fake equipment, miracle remedies and cures, and promises of products that will never be delivered. Between May and July, the purchase of coronavirus-related domain names, such as 'freecoronavaccine.net', exploded; around 115,000 virus-themed domains were registered in 2020 alone.[54]

Another set of online scams that proliferated during lockdowns used misinformation to mimic government agencies and other trusted institutions to steal personal information, credit card data or solicit funds. Business email compromise (BEC) schemes are a form of low-tech financial fraud in which emails are sent to employees of large companies from their CEOs, suppliers or other authoritative figures, instructing them to take actions such as transferring large sums of money. They assumed (almost certainly correctly) that with most employees working from home—often in situations where they were grappling with challenging personal circumstances—their level of vigilance was lower. Data-security company reports showed that BEC scams directed at US companies had increased by 200% between April and May 2020—coinciding exactly with the lockdown period in the United States—and that cybercriminals were targeting larger dollar amounts than was normal.[55]

The lockdown also proved a boon for another prominent organised crime enterprise—online sexual exploitation. Even before lockdown, estimates suggested that 30% of the internet's bandwidth was devoted to porn. Porn sites get more visitors each month than Netflix, Amazon and Twitter combined,[56] and this trend exponentially increased during the protracted lockdowns in Europe and the Americas. There was a massive hike in subscriptions to online porn sites during lockdown, not to mention the development of an interesting new kink in 'pandemic porn' that got more than 9 million hits in March. Pornhub, the global number one online pornography site which had 42 billion hits in 2019, gave free access to its premium services to everyone under lockdown, causing an 18% rise in global subscriptions in a single month.[57] But Pornhub has a long-documented and extensive problem managing non-consensual online abuse, including revenge porn, child pornography, videos of rape and sexual abuse, as well as videos involving missing persons. More than two million people have signed a petition to hold Pornhub executives to account for aiding trafficking in persons.[58]

Organised crime groups operating in the real-life (often involuntary) flesh trade were well positioned to use the people under their control—sex workers, drug users, drug mules and their usual victims of extortion—for forced online sexual exploitation. The confinement period also allowed those with more deviant tastes to find each other. Europol members reported increased online activity by those seeking child abuse material, as well as parallel postings in dedicated forums and boards by offenders welcoming opportunities to engage with children, whom they expected to be more vulnerable because of isolation, less supervision and greater time spent online.[59] In June, Thailand reported a record high in online child sex abuse cases: the police task force recovered more than 150,000 files of sexual abuse material and investigated more than 280 cases of internet-facilitated child sexual exploitation (of which at least 80 were confirmed cases of human trafficking).[60] It is now an acknowledged reality by law enforcement officials that during lockdown the peer-to-peer groups with an interest in child sexual exploitation have grown in size; and having found those online communities, the newly active members are unlikely to disengage.

*Problems for another day?*

There is little doubt that the coronavirus pandemic has hit vulnerable groups the hardest and greatly increased their vulnerability arising from both the public health crisis and its second-order impacts on the economy and security. This population, too, often includes those who are implicated in criminal markets, such as sex workers, victims of human trafficking, drug users and low-level street pushers. It also includes those in the process of moving or migrating irregularly with the aid of smugglers, or those beholden to loan sharks after their businesses closed down or dried up in lockdown.

While interest groups and the media did sound alerts about these risks at the time, the attention of government was elsewhere, its resources mobilised to meet the humanitarian imperative of prevailing medical needs. Safeguarding measures were harder to achieve as enforcement officers, social workers and communities were themselves afflicted by social distancing and restricted from moving, while potential victims and the vulnerable were isolated from seeking assistance.

When the entire global population was caught up in anxiety and fear for their lives and their employment, it was hard to summon up sympathy for an aspiring drug mule, or for a drug-addled prostitute being beaten for someone's online pleasure. The slums, where criminal groups reign with extreme violence, were already a problem too complex to solve before the pandemic. Any aspiration to stop criminal groups inserting themselves further into local governance and the economy was optimistic, although few in those intense early weeks of lockdown were looking that far ahead. The issue of organised crime and its victims was, for the most part, a problem for another day.

# 3

# BETWEEN COLD WAR AND COVID

To understand the full extent of how the pandemic affected crime—and how crime responded—we need to wind the clock back to the early 1990s. It was during this period that the phenomenon of what is termed 'transnational organised crime' came into being and grew rapidly, feeding off the wreckage of the old Soviet order and the boom in global trade. Between the end of the Cold War in 1991 and the 2020 coronavirus pandemic, crime actors became vastly more sophisticated, powerful and influential. Local mafias turned into global networks; profits boomed to unheard-of levels; the tide of illicit products rose higher and higher. And for the most part, the criminals faced few challenges along the way.

## *New actors, new networks*

23 May 1992: a bomb shatters a highway bridge in Palermo, the blast so powerful that it registers on earthquake monitors around the city. Giovanni Falcone, an Italian anti-mafia magistrate who was instrumental in

jailing several high-profile Sicilian mafia figures, was killed in the explosion, his assassination ordered by those he had imprisoned.

One month later, Paolo Borsellino, Falcone's partner in investigating and prosecuting the mafia, was also killed in a massive bomb blast, together with five police bodyguards. Borsellino had been waiting for his turn to die, slipping out to buy cigarettes in the hope he would be killed alone. At the funeral of the bodyguards, tens of thousands of people protested at the mafia's actions, chanting, 'Justice! Justice! Justice!'

The murders of Falcone and Borsellino are seminal events in the story of organised crime, but why do we need to go back to the early 1990s to understand the impact of the pandemic on organised crime? There are three reasons. Firstly, the early 1990s marked the beginning of a period of global economic growth that coincided with a boom in global criminal activity. Secondly, the assassinations occurred at about the same time as the end of the Cold War, an event with far-reaching implications for security threats. And finally, Falcone's and Borsellino's deaths ultimately galvanised an international response to the growing phenomenon of organised crime that continues to shape policy today.

Before the 1990s, organised crime had largely been considered to be the purview of several relatively well-known sets of groups: the Italian mafias both home and abroad, the Chinese Triads, the Japanese Yakuza, the Russian Vory, and the Latin American cartels of the 1970s and 1980s. Academic studies focused on the particular characteristics of each of these groups, and there was little if any focus on the broader expansion and growing diversification of illicit markets. At the policy level, the experience of countering the Italian mafia in particular shaped the international debate on organised crime.

But times were changing. The Cold War ended abruptly, and the 1990s saw several countries undergo profound economic, social and political upheavals, all of which provided new opportunities for criminal groups while established systems of state control weakened. Prominent examples of this include Nigeria, Brazil, Colombia, South Africa, Albania and most notably Russia, where the implosion of the Soviet Union spawned criminal groups and networks that quickly seized control of large sectors of the newly privatized economy. Some 70% to 80% of all private business and banking in Russia is now said to be connected to organised crime.[1] The fragility of states in the post-Cold War period also facilitated an expansion of historical forms of organised crime that exploit absent or weak governance, such as maritime piracy in Somalia and the Gulf of Guinea.

Two widely read books published in the mid- and late 2000s vividly captured this sense of enormous growth in illicit trade and the organised criminal groups that controlled them. In his study *Illicit*, Moisés Naím, a former finance minister of Venezuela, tracked the growth of the illicit economy, dramatically concluding that illicit markets would be a key, if under-appreciated, feature in shaping power in a new world order. The journalist Misha Glenny's *McMafia*, which later spawned a television series, traced the expansion of criminal networks across the planet. Glenny's title implied the rapid growth, franchising and everyday use of the products of organised crime.

An important academic study of the phenomenon neatly labelled the emerging trend as 'deviant globalization',[2] an idea that was reinforced by the migration of some Italian mafia figures in the 1990s and 2000s to new global territories, where they set up 'mafia outposts'. The reality, however, was much more complicated. The dramatic rise of organised crime networks has been as much a story of the development of local criminal networks and groups as it has been about the movement of established groups. Local groups have made connections with those elsewhere, such as through the presence of growing diaspora populations. The best example of this is the highly networked system of West African organised crime, which remains poorly understood but is a key vector of global illicit markets. Indeed, many major criminal markets now operate without the involvement of what might be referred to as 'traditional organised crime'. In the first global assessment of organised crime, published in 2010, UNODC concluded that 'most trafficking flows are driven more by the market than by the groups involved in them'.[3]

The increasing primacy of the market during this period spoke to another dramatic development sweeping the world; that of globalisation. This worldwide boom in economic growth saw the rise of new illicit customers, such as those among the newly monied Asian middle class, who became an important driver of markets in the wildlife sector (especially as they did not suffer significantly during the 2008 financial crisis, unlike their Western counterparts).[4] But globalisation also profoundly transformed how illicit markets themselves operated, and at what scale. Technology, too, played a part, resulting in a brave new world for criminal expansion and profit.

*Game changers: Globalisation and technology*

The phenomenon of globalisation is critical to understanding the rise in global criminal networks during the 1990s and 2000s. Globalisation saw unprecedented movements of money, goods, people and contraband around the world, and this expansion of trade and advances in communication technology brought enormous opportunities for both licit and illicit markets.

Despite attention-grabbing news coverage of covert submersibles carrying drugs, criminal networks knew that integrating their operations into the global trading system, rather than circumventing it, would allow them to scale up their business to unprecedented levels. In this regard, the phenomenal growth in trade using containers aided and abetted the illicit movement of goods. By 2016, some 38.4 million twenty-foot containers were in service around the world, up from a figure of some 145,000 in the 1970s.[5] The number of commercial airlines and flights also experienced similar growth: by 2018 the International Civil Aviation Organization reported that the total number of passengers being carried on scheduled services had risen to 4.3 billion—a figure that (prior to the pandemic) was expected to double every fifteen years.[6] Air travel has been a key conduit for the movement of illicit goods, most of which go undetected. The occasional news reports of sensational seizures of contraband (mainly drugs but also wildlife products) at major international airports represent only a small proportion of the illicit movements that take place on commercial airlines.

The globalisation boom ran alongside a technological revolution which saw the advent of an entirely new sphere of human activity: the internet. Here the trend has been astonishing. By 2019, an estimated 4.1 billion people—53% of the population of the globe—had access to the internet. The number of internet users grew between 2005 and 2019 at a rate of 10% a year.[7] In 1994, there were fewer than 3,000 websites; by 2014, there were more than one billion—a 33,000,000% increase in just twenty years.

The growth of commercial activity in cyberspace—a key feature of the virtual economy—has provided enormous opportunities for fraud, identity theft and cyber extortion. The internet has also provided a platform for illegal advertising and sales, most specifically in relation to drugs on the dark web, but also in relation to a variety of other criminal services and products which are advertised and discussed on social media groups, such as highly sought-after wildlife species.

Technology has also provided criminals with increasingly sophisticated tools to conduct business and escape interdiction. Mobile phones and then encrypted communication technologies on mobile platforms have been a particular boon to criminal groups. Some research suggests that such communication tools literally changed the structure of criminal organisations, making them more network-based and dynamic than clearly ordered and hierarchical. In July 2020, European police announced that they had arrested nearly a thousand suspected criminals after an operation managed to breach the encrypted chat platform EncroChat, illustrating how widely the app had been used by an array of criminal groups. In regions such as Central America, the spread of cheap mobile-phone technology and messaging platforms such as WhatsApp was one of the major factors that expanded widespread extortion rackets—many of them run by the notorious and feared *mara* street gangs.[8]

The rise of an increasingly sophisticated (and opaque) financial system also helped facilitate criminal enterprise. A study in the early 2000s noted that the liberalisation of the financial global infrastructure directly 'increases the channels of communications between legal and illegal activities through the intermediary of painless banking'.[9] These shifts not only provided important new openings for corporations and wealthy individuals to avoid their tax obligations, but they also offered enormous opportunities for the laundering and investment of illegal profits in a number of locations globally. The US$1.9 billion fine imposed on HSBC in 2012 for laundering a river of Mexican drug money, among other banking transgressions, gives some indication of the scope of illicit money moving through the system.

The rapid expansion of cryptocurrencies also provided new and secure ways in which criminal proceeds could be banked anonymously. Over a decade since the establishment of Bitcoin, the first and most widely known of the cryptocurrencies, digital money has shown that it is around to stay, despite regular predictions of its demise. By November 2019, there were an estimated 3,000 cryptocurrencies worldwide, offering a range of options for criminal actors working to secure profit across multiple markets.

But for all the focus that has been placed on the movement of illicit proceeds of crime throughout the last two decades, there have been remarkably few prosecutions, and these have often been the result of media exposures, as in the case of the Panama Papers. Even though new laws were introduced to help investigate suspect money (by such means as unexplained wealth orders of court to compel people to reveal the sources of their wealth), they were thwarted by a lack of skills and resourcing (as well as by the well-paid lawyers of the wealthy), as a July 2020 report from the Intelligence and Security Committee of the UK Parliament highlighted.[10] Requirements introduced by the intergovernmental Financial Action Task Force to tackle money laundering, while onerous for banks, have often served only to increase the charges that are levied by expert money launderers.

Despite much political rhetoric about the need to act against dirty cash, illicit money quickly found its way into London real estate and has provided an important part of the political economy of financial centres such as Dubai and multiple places in between.

### *Evolving illicit markets*

During this period, illicit markets rarely stood still. As demand changed, interdiction efforts intensified and geopolitical shifts took place, criminal actors had to react. Indeed, the history of the past three decades is one of astonishing criminal adaptation, expansion and innovation. Every sector of illicit enterprise evolved, while those trying to stop such activities were often left playing a hopeless game of catch-up.

Drugs have been a steady and spectacular earner for criminal groups for a long time, but it was perhaps the emergence of kingpins such as Pablo Escobar and his Medellín Cartel in the 1970s that really brought the trade into the global limelight. Although Escobar and many of his fellow drug lords have since been toppled, by the time the pandemic hit, the drug business was stronger than ever. The UNODC's 2020 *World Drug Report* concluded that there has been an overall expansion and diversification in the global illicit drug market over the past two decades,[11] with increases in cocaine production in the Andean region, a surge in heroin poppy production in Mexico and Central Asia, and the growth in production of an impressive array of new synthetic drugs.

These new drugs perhaps best show the dynamic nature of the drugs trade and how it responds to supply and demand. Take the case of fentanyl, the synthetic drug at the heart of the United States' opioid crisis. When prescription painkiller addicts in the US ran out of pills, at first they turned to Mexican heroin, and then fentanyl. It soon became known that fentanyl was much more potent than heroin, and, increasingly, some users began skipping the heroin phase altogether. Predictably enough, given the larger profit margins of fentanyl, the

Mexican cartels embraced the drug with gusto, either exporting it or producing it themselves. Aside from supply and demand, interdiction efforts have also spurred the development of new drugs that are harder to detect and easier to transport, such as synthetic cannabinoids.

The hunger of drug traffickers for greater profits and market dominance has driven the expansion of the industry across the world. This development has resulted in important shifts in the nature of criminal groups and networks engaged in the drugs trade, such as the extraordinary growth in violence associated with some drug markets. This can be seen most notably, but not exclusively, in Mexico, where the market has become vast and contested, triggering hyper-violent turf wars and competition.

Apart from drugs, the pre-pandemic period also saw the rise or dramatic expansion of a dizzying number of other criminal markets. Human smuggling, for example, has increased significantly, and migrant smugglers have taken advantage of instability in several countries, notably Syria and some parts of Central America, to offer paid passage for people desperate to leave. Between 2014 and 2016, the European 'migration crisis' and the surge of smuggling of children on the US southern border precipitated political ructions in both regions. But the major factor generating demand for the services of organised criminal smugglers (and driving up the prices they could charge) lay with the failure to provide safer and more secure legal alternatives for movement. Those who resorted to smugglers often risked their lives: between June 2014 and July 2017, the death or disappearance of some 22,500 migrants was recorded by the

International Organization for Migration (IOM).[12] The images of boatloads of migrants left to their fate by smugglers in the Mediterranean harrowingly captured the gravity of the crisis, but long-term coordinated action to help migrants has not only remained elusive, but has become politically unpalatable.

In parallel, human trafficking witnessed a noticeable uptick in the two decades before the pandemic. 'More victims of trafficking in persons were reported to UNODC in 2016', noted the organisation's 2019 global report on the subject, 'than at any previous time over the past 13 years', with some 40% more victims being detected. This development, too, had links to the growing restrictions on regular migration, as those eager to seek a better life often found themselves working in bonded servitude with questionable employment agencies, forced to seek work in illicit industries such as sex work, or held by smuggling groups for ransom and extortion. Greater reporting was a clear sign that the issue of human trafficking was very much on the global agenda, but without necessarily being closer to resolution.

Meanwhile, extortion grew in regions around the world, from Karachi to New York to San Salvador. Forms of extortion ranged from traditional 'protection' payments through to *la renta* on the streets of Central America, where huge swathes of people and businesses pay regular instalments to the brutally violent street gangs just to enable them to go about their daily lives. Many of the leaders running these rackets often operate out of prison.

The trade in illegal wildlife products was another criminal sector that accelerated dramatically from 2000 onwards. Demand increased in China and Vietnam for products sourced from big animals like rhino horn, pangolin scales, and lion and tiger bones, as well as an enormous number of other smaller species, such as tortoises, lizards and birds. The rate of change was phenomenal. The number of poached rhinos was negligible in the early 2000s, but in 2008 some 260 animals were victims of poaching, a soaring trend that peaked in 2015 with over 1,300 cases.[13] By that time, illegal wildlife products were regularly being advertised and traded on social media. Criminals, in a process of 'commodity swapping', sought to build new markets to replace those of species that were seen as likely to be depleted: lion bones were substituted for tiger parts, and hippo teeth for elephant ivory.

Criminal operations also contributed to dramatic deforestation across the globe. Species like the much-prized rosewood fetched high prices, and even individual trees became targeted by criminal groups. Meanwhile, a boom in illicit gold mining saw vast swathes of the Amazon basin destroyed. In Somalia, highly organised charcoal smuggling to the Gulf is having the same effect.[14] Despite reductions in some countries, the problem is now a global phenomenon, and individuals such as journalists, activists or community leaders who attempt to oppose the decimation of natural forests have become regular targets of assassination.

By 2019 there was also a series of emerging markets in commodities which attracted premium prices because of their scarcity: sand in India (where a 'sand mafia' is now active), and water in Kenya (controlled by water cartels). One of the most sophisticated and profitable criminal operations globally, about which little has been written, has been fuel smuggling.

It is hard to overestimate the importance of this diversification of criminal markets over the past twenty years. The proliferation of illicit commerce has pulled more and more countries into illicit trade, and more people have been influenced by global illicit flows.

### *Blurring lines*

As illicit markets continued to boom, diversify and spread geographically in the pre-pandemic period, the old definitions used in studying organised crime quickly became outdated. Ideas of 'source', 'transit' and 'destination' states became increasingly redundant as the lines between them started to blur. In East Africa, once a heroin transit zone, large numbers of people are now hooked on cheap heroin, while the development of synthetic drugs has enabled a single region to become both source and lucrative destination.

The ties between crime and states also became more entrenched, with the regional political economy shaped in important ways by drugs. In West Africa, for example, cocaine flows have an enormously damaging impact on local governance and conflict, most notably in Guinea-Bissau.

A critical trend that accompanied the growth of criminal markets through the first two decades of the new millennium was the degree to which state actors themselves became important vectors of the criminal economy. The wave of democratisation after the end of the Cold War provided unprecedented opportunities not only for the growth of illicit markets, but also for criminal actors to embed themselves in political systems in ways that mean they are now protected and harder to remove. Democracy has proved to be expensive, and political party funding has been an open invitation for business, both legal and illegal, to secure influence in many places. In Russia, for example, the rapid growth of the illicit economy and criminal entrepreneurs in the wake of the collapse of the Soviet Union evolved into a system whereby the state itself became complicit in organised crime and its gatekeeper—a fact unforeseen when 'Russian organised crime' was first debated in the 1990s.

Conflicts also proved fertile ground for organised crime, again challenging the established understanding of how war (and crime) function. Immediately after the end of the Cold War, a set of 'resource conflicts' broke out. Closely associated with the campaign to end the sale of 'blood diamonds' (gems which had their origin in conflict zones such as Sierra Leone and the Congo), these conflicts were not considered to be cases where organised crime (as traditionally understood) was involved, but the facts on the ground soon made it clear that war and crime were natural partners. The growing awareness of this relationship has in recent years been reflected in the analysis of war. The UN Security Council, for example, which concerns itself with issues of peace and security, referred to organised crime or illicit markets in a remarkable 64% of its resolutions in 2015.[15]

While criminals were involving themselves in new areas of activity, new actors hitherto unconnected to organised crime also began engaging in illicit trade. After state structures collapsed in Libya in the wake of the 2011 civil war, for instance, a migrant-smuggling economy developed in which often loosely organised militia groups took charge of the smuggling routes and ran quasi-official detention centres.

All of these features complicated the contested discussion around what constitutes 'organised crime'. Can a militia group be a criminal organisation, or a commercial company a mafia operation? The simple answer is yes. What has emerged in many places is a nexus between criminal, business and political actors, with states themselves becoming key actors. Given this messy reality, it is hardly surprising that attempts to foster a coherent response were slow to gain traction, and legitimate questions were asked whether they were fit for purpose at all.

### *A (flawed) response emerges*

During the early days of globalisation, it slowly dawned that the problem of organised crime had evolved beyond the traditional concepts dating from the Cold War. In a seminal article published in 1995, analyst Phil Williams noted that 'organised crime has traditionally been seen as a domestic problem bedevilling a relatively small number of states such as Italy, the United States and Japan. In the last few years, however, there has been a recognition that the problem is no longer limited to a few states and can no longer be treated as something that falls within a single jurisdiction.'[16]

Looking back from the vantage of 2020, Eduardo Vetere, a senior UN official, reported that by the late

1980s and early 1990s, wider concerns had developed about the growth of organised crime, primarily in relation to Eastern Europe, but blind spots still remained: 'These concerns though were focussed quite geographically and excluded for example Africa and other places, which was not seen as affected. Member states were still undecided at this point how to move forward—there was no consensus how to respond.'[17]

A ministerial conference in Naples in November 1994 resolved to negotiate a global convention on organised crime to match a 1988 convention which had sought to reduce drug trafficking. The UN negotiations, and the general policy debate, was driven by the notion—emphasised by the UN secretary general, Kofi Annan, on several occasions—that organised crime was (or would increasingly become) a global phenomenon that required a global solution. While attempts stalled for a period, the initiative of Poland, the United States and in particular Italy, in the wake of the assassination of Falcone, pushed forward the negotiations and brought about the signing by many states of the United Nations Convention Against Transnational Organized Crime (UNTOC). (The parties famously could not agree on the definition of 'organised crime', only on what constituted an organised crime group.) Fittingly, the convention was opened for signature in Palermo, in December 2000.

It is important to emphasise that in this period the debate was dominated by two important factors. The first was confidence in the UN and the multilateral system to address a new set of intersecting security threats. The second was that the discussion around organised crime, and illicit markets more generally, was still driven by the outlook and interests of a relatively small number of states. Nevertheless, negotiating a convention on what was a non-traditional threat to state security was still an important achievement.

But a few months after the signing of UNTOC, and as the UN bureaucracy was gearing up to facilitate its implementation, the terrorist attacks of 11 September 2001 took place. As a result, the global political order shifted dramatically and the issue of organised crime, which had been rising up the international policy agenda, was rapidly displaced. While implementing a UN convention is always more of a long haul than a short sprint, the advent of the global 'war on terrorism' had important implications. Resources and political bandwidth had effectively moved elsewhere.

The UN convention itself is little known outside a small group of state experts and UN officials who meet regularly to negotiate global policy matters on organised crime and illicit markets. One of the core challenges of our age has been dealt with in a series of meetings over two decades that seldom if ever receives press coverage. The discussion on drugs has been held in a separate forum, despite the degree to which finding solutions to the 'illegal drug problem' and the profits it generates for criminal groups would also have an immediate impact on the organised crime discussion. Unlike UN negotiations on, for example, climate change or human rights, those on organised crime have assumed little prominence given the scale of the challenge.

While states have been eager to ratify the convention as a symbolic gesture that they are responding to organised crime (at the time of writing an impressive 190 states are parties to UNTOC), there is much less evidence that the convention has been implemented or used as a system of law enforcement cooperation between states. The convention's provisions for prevention—critical in theory for reducing opportunities for crime—have barely been referred to. A review mechanism to ensure that implementation is in fact taking place was only agreed to in the year before Covid-19 struck. It is not very robust.

Discussions around the convention have increasingly and unsurprisingly been bogged down in the emerging geopolitical tensions, characterised in particular by heated exchanges between the Western democracies and Russia and China, and by an overall sense that the multilateral system is unable to deliver an effective solution.

For its part, INTERPOL has faced its own challenges. While INTERPOL's brand as the 'global police force' is a feature of crime fiction, the reality is more prosaic. The organisation's law enforcement brief is wider than merely that of organised crime, although illicit markets increasingly occupy much of its work. The results remain mixed, though, because of the uncertainties of funding, the vagaries of politics, and the reality that law enforcement cooperation globally is much less effective and often much slower than most people assume.

### *On the eve of Covid-19*

By 2019, the debate on how to respond to organised crime was proceeding in fits and starts. Responses tended to be driven by individual cases and isolated high-volume incidents where there was a particular visibility or impact on human lives. But the larger system and the sheer size of the illicit economy required a systematic and structural response, for which there seemed little political momentum.

Accordingly, the years before the pandemic struck were marked by some notable firsts in the area of illicit markets, as the power of organised crime continued to grow. These seemed a portent of the growing influence, and the astonishing size, of criminal markets.

Take the case of illicit narcotics. June 2019 saw the largest cocaine seizure in the history of the United States, when just under 16 tonnes of the drug were seized from a ship in Philadelphia. In the same month, the largest methamphetamine seizure in Australian history took place, when 1.6 tonnes (with an estimated street value of over a billion Australian dollars) were found in a Melbourne port. August 2019 saw the largest cocaine seizure in German history: 5 tonnes in a shipping container in a Hamburg port. In September 2019, the United Kingdom (UK) recorded its largest-ever heroin seizure when officers of the National Crime Agency intercepted a 1.3 tonne shipment. Malaysia saw its largest drug seizure in September 2019 (involving 12 tonnes of cocaine), while Brazil had a record year in 2019, with 50% more drug seizures than previously.

The number of refugees hit a global high in 2013, and has continued to climb since then, breaking new records year-on-year.[18] Their escape from conflict zones has been perilous and deadly. The liberal media have regularly declared their outrage over the loss of lives and the violent exploitation that migrants suffer, while the right-wing media have been equally outraged by the influx of yet more people across their sovereign borders and into their communities. Some states readily demonised migrants as economic and social parasites, while others appeared unable (or unwilling) to formulate an effective response, paralysed between fear of appearing 'soft' on the problem and the political cost of appearing inhumane. This played into the hands of human smugglers and traffickers, who thrived off the fractured politics, militarised borders and confusion, enabling them to grow their industry to an unprecedented size.

Looking back, the news in 2019 contained a drumbeat of signs that illicit markets—across a diversity of products—had reached unparalleled proportions. There seemed little opportunity to act decisively to undercut the torrent of illicit trade. Then the pandemic struck.

In the following chapters, we trace, market by illicit market, how this sophisticated and entrenched system of transnational organised crime met one of the biggest challenges in its existence. To begin, we turn to the industry most affected by the closing of borders: the movement of people.

# 4

# NO ESCAPE, NO WAY HOME

We live in an era of unprecedented mobility. Before the pandemic, the number of commercial flights taken was growing at a rate of between 5% and 7% per year,[1] with over 175,000 commercial flights a day filling the skies.[2] The number of cars was powerfully accelerating to the two billion mark as rising aspirations and GDP saw people the world over buying their own vehicles.[3] People were on the move, towards cities, towards larger economies and better livelihoods, or merely for pleasure. More people than ever before live in countries other than the ones in which they were born. In 2019, there were 272 million migrants globally—some 51 million more than ten years before.[4]

To the uniquely mobile generations used to moving around freely at will, the barriers and restrictions imposed during the pandemic seemed extraordinary and exceptional. Not being able to plan a holiday, drive to visit family or meet up in public places without fear brought alien emotions and novel frustrations. But for irregular migrants, asylum seekers, refugees and the internally displaced, the coronavirus represented the brutal *coup de grâce* on a trajectory that had been in place for some time: the reduction of safe and legal pathways for people on the move, and a growing hostility to migrants in transit and destination countries.

The confinement measures put in place to prevent the spread of the coronavirus also worsened the lives of victims of labour trafficking, forced marriage and domestic abuse—all forms of human trafficking. Exploitative criminal groups, and unethical and immoral corporations, individuals and even family members all have a hand in the practice, which can be transnational in scope or committed behind the closed doors of one's own home.

### *The migrant's plight: From crisis to crisis*

Over the past two decades, Europe, North America and Asia have all been dealing with migrant 'crises' as people in desperate circumstances resort to smugglers of various types to circumvent increasingly stringent immigration policies in the developed world. Many have been fleeing life-threatening situations: by the end of 2019, there were nearly 80 million people who had been forcibly displaced globally as a result of conflict, natural disaster or climate-necessitated relocation.[5]

During this period, human smuggling swelled to become an enormous criminal industry. In 2010, the UNODC estimated that the smuggling of migrants along two of the world's principal smuggling routes—from East, North and West Africa to Europe, and from

South America to North America—generated around US$6.75 billion for criminal groups in Africa and Latin America.[6] At the peak of Europe's migration crisis in 2015, Europol, the European police agency, reckoned that smugglers were earning between $5 billion and $6 billion by just bringing people to Europe alone.[7]

But when the pandemic hit, all that movement came to a sudden halt. As the coronavirus raced around the world, governments imposed border controls, lockdowns and contact tracing; untracked human movement was now seen as a weakness in the war against the disease. This unleashed, in the words of the UN secretary general, António Guterres, a 'tsunami of hate and xenophobia, scapegoating and scare-mongering'.[8]

Some politicians portrayed migrants as synonymous with infection—a gambit calculated to cement anti-immigration policies that predated the pandemic. 'We are doing everything in our power to keep the infection and those carrying the infection from entering the country,' declared President Donald Trump at a packed campaign rally in South Carolina in late February 2020.[9] On 21 March, the US closed its shared border with Mexico and introduced new coronavirus-related border rules, which resulted in 159,000 migrants—including nearly 9,000 unaccompanied migrant children and 7,600 families—being expelled without due process in the period to September 2020.[10]

Echoing his transatlantic ideological ally, the prime minister of Hungary, Viktor Orbán, announced to the national media in March: 'We are fighting a two-front war: one front is called migration, and the other one belongs to the coronavirus—there is a logical connection between the two, as both spread with movement.'[11] In a breach of EU and international refugee law, Orbán indefinitely sealed the borders of Hungary in March, making it impossible for any asylum seeker to enter the country legally and seek protection. Migrants attempting to cross into the country were pushed back into Serbia, blocked from entry or held in police custody.[12]

While few heads of state were as explicit as Trump and Orbán, many took similar steps. In March, Canada closed its land border with the US for the first time since the country became an independent nation. The prime minister, Justin Trudeau, announced that with the border closed, they would not hear asylum claims from those who entered by land from the US and would turn back any migrants who entered through unofficial points of entry.[13]

Some EU member states also closed their borders, stopped the registration and lodging of asylum applications, and curtailed the freedom of movement for refugees in and out of reception centres.[14] Italy—the country that had been the primary reception point for most of the migrants coming across the Mediterranean from Africa—passed a decree stating that for the duration of Covid-19, Italian ports could not be classified as 'places of safety' for people rescued at sea, thereby allowing the authorities to push back boats full of hundreds of Africans coming from Libya.[15] Cypriot authorities, having enacted a similar policy, were reported to have pushed back a boat with 175 Syrians, including 69 children, refusing them permission to land and seek asylum.[16] The Maltese government were restocking boats with fuel and giving life jackets to migrants but then escorting boats out to international water at gunpoint. According to one migrant quoted in *The Guardian*, the coastguard justified their actions by saying, 'Malta has a virus called corona if you've heard about it. We can't take you there because everyone is sick in Malta.'[17] Even in European countries where there was no official edict to halt the asylum system, the reality was that most government departments were closed, and officials began working from home or were furloughed, thus in effect preventing claims from being processed. By March, a combination of travel bans and other emergency measures led to a 43% decline in asylum applications in Europe.[18]

Turkey has been using migrants as political leverage with the EU for a number of years. This culminated in an agreement negotiated at a summit in November 2015 in terms of which the EU pledged more than €3 billion in aid to Turkey, as well as a range of political concessions, in exchange for Turkey clamping down on smugglers ferrying people across the Aegean.[19] But since the start of the pandemic, there has been a sharp and dangerous escalation in the Eastern Mediterranean linked to long-standing maritime disputes, drilling rights over natural gas reserves, and the eternal Cyprus question, after rival warships were deployed and fighter jets strategically sent to conduct exercises in the area.[20] Though negotiations brought the issue back from the brink of military conflict, Turkey again began instrumentalising its large population of Syrian refugees—estimated at between three and four million people—to pressure European governments for political and economic concessions. In late February, Turkey openly bused thousands of migrants to the Greek land border; over the course of March, it relaxed its clampdown on the sea smugglers working the coastline. Smugglers working in Turkey are a combination of criminal entrepreneurs and established organised crime groups who cheat, defraud, extort and entrap their clients,[21] and for political ends the Turkish government gave them free rein to do as they wished with their most vulnerable charges. In response, and with the pandemic as political cover, Greece has taken a hard line over migrants, refusing them asylum, towing their boats out to sea, and, according to some reports, actually expelling migrants physically from camps on the islands and putting them on rafts at sea.[22]

The majority of countries have stopped their resettlement programmes, leaving refugees stranded in camps in conflict zones across the world. The United Nations High Commissioner for Refugees (UNHCR) has charge of 1.4 million refugees looking for resettlement, but with embassy staff who usually manage the process recalled and most arrangements suspended, vulnerable migrants have been left in limbo. In the first half of 2020, refugee resettlements fell by nearly 69% compared with the same period in 2019.[23]

The repeated mention in public discourse of migrants as potential carriers of Covid-19 has also fuelled anti-migrant sentiment and xenophobia at the community level. Mexican locals in Chiapas state, for example, took to social media to voice their resistance to the conversion of a community centre into an emergency hostel for Central American migrants. In Ciudad Juárez, on the US–Mexico border, a poster containing threats against Cuban migrants was placed in a Cuban restaurant only a few days after restrictions were imposed on movement.[24] As well as facing local hostility, migrants trapped in transit countries also had to contend with the diversion of local social services and aid budgets towards the urgent needs of citizens associated with the pandemic. Stricter border controls and greater on-street enforcement heightened tensions for the marginalised and persecuted.

In order to prevent hostilities between migrants and the local populations, migrants were sometimes corralled into densely populated camps, although migrant activists feared that these settlements could become potential infection hotspots. Overcrowded, makeshift camps with insufficient medical assistance or the capacity to impose preventive measures were perfect breeding grounds for the virus, and many migrants lived in fear of an outbreak. These measures to prevent infection seemed to work initially, but steadily, as the first wave of lockdowns passed, the infections began to spark and grow.[25] In June, three asylum seekers tested positive for Covid-19 in a sprawling border encampment hosting 2,000 migrants living in tents in Matamoros, Mexico—just one of many such camps on the US–Mexico border.[26] By September, infections were rising sharply in the camps of people displaced by the Syrian civil war, both those trapped in the north-west corner of the country and those in its neighbours, Turkey, Iraq, Lebanon, Palestine and Jordan.[27]

Makeshift camps also sprang up in Bosnia and Herzegovina when the International Organization for Migration (IOM) sealed their official refugee camps and refused to let residents out or new migrants in. These camps consisted of tents and containers inside former factories, with no lighting, no hygiene facilities and limited services. Local police started rounding up migrants and forcibly bringing them to the new camp, where they were confined for the duration of the lockdown.[28]

*A smuggler's market*

Before the pandemic, a large body of research (including work of our own organisation) had shown that the reduction of legal avenues for movement and the securitisation of the migration landscape were driving more people into the hands of smuggling networks. But at the same time, the greater challenges of completing journeys were pushing smugglers to adopt more dangerous routes and to charge more for passage, which was rarely safe.[29]

This situation has only been exacerbated by the pandemic. A survey in the spring of 2020 conducted with migrants across a wide range of global routes by the Mixed Migration Centre found that half of the respondents reported increasing smugglers' fees since Covid, while 61% indicated that smugglers have been using more dangerous routes since the outbreak. In West Africa, a region where smugglers are rarely needed because of a regional (ECOWAS) freedom of movement treaty, 79% cited greater difficulties in moving around the region because of Covid, and 44% said they were more likely to use the services of a smuggler as a result.[30]

But the pandemic made life harder for smugglers too. The almost complete cessation of air travel meant that both migrant smuggling by air and intercontinental smuggling stopped entirely, and the suspension of most maritime passenger transport also put a short-term freeze on smuggling routes by sea. Our network in North Africa found that smugglers in Algeria were initially concerned that migrants would be more likely to have the virus or to carry it into new regions, and so had become more hesitant to supply their services. In Libya, smugglers who sought to continue operations faced significant resistance, not just from local communities and armed groups, but also from one another. We received reports of Libyan human smugglers attacking their Egyptian counterparts who were trying to bring migrants into Libya in contravention of the border control restrictions.[31]

Ultimately, though, in the words of the INTERPOL secretary general, Jürgen Stock, the pandemic did not blunt 'the determination of organised crime to prey on the vulnerable and make a profit from these crimes'.[32] As both INTERPOL and UNODC have observed in their reports, human smugglers looked for and (relatively quickly) found ways to overcome the lockdowns and border controls, and cater to the growing demand.

In some cases, routes shifted. Before the pandemic, migrants seeking passage into the UK typically came by truck, car or train. With the borders closed, this was impossible, and so smugglers developed the English Channel sea route from France—a route which has boomed since the lockdowns began. Thousands of migrants report being forced onto small boats at gunpoint or knifepoint and threatened with having their fingernails ripped out if they do not follow the orders of smugglers. In June alone, 2,000 people used this route, with boats landing in batches, ten or twenty at a time. More people landed in a single day in June than had arrived along the same Channel route in the entire previous year.[33]

Where smugglers could not find another route, they sought new ways to profit from their clients while keeping them in place. Irregular migrants using a smuggler are frequently subjected to abuse and exploitation—either being forced into working in order to pay for their passage or upkeep during the journey or being sexually exploited by their smugglers or forced into prostitution. Some are subjected to kidnapping for ransom or extortion. In September 2020, nearly 300 Rohingya refugees landed in Indonesia, having been at sea for around six months and were turned back by both Malaysian and Thai authorities.[34] Their long journey had been facilitated by smugglers who extorted money from their charges and disguised the death of a dozen migrants over the course of the months-long voyage.[35]

In Mexico, thousands of migrants trapped in border cities like Tijuana and Matamoros were described by one expert in a media report as 'a string of pearls along the border for the cartels to exploit'.[36] Kidnapping and extortion rackets run by the cartels are big business at the border during normal times, and the closure of the international lines made those criminal markets even more profitable. The harder the border is to cross, the more the cartels can charge to move people across it. Jobless, unemployed and desperate migrants in these border cities are also ripe for recruitment by organised crime.

*No way home*

Not all organised crime takes the form of shady people working on the edges of society. Criminality is also perpetrated by corporations, working seemingly within the law, that benefit from exploitative practices. One of the most prevalent forms of organised crime is human trafficking for the purposes of forced labour. The International Labour Organization (ILO) estimates that 24.9 million people globally are trapped in forced labour situations.[37]

Mass labour contracts to support tourism sectors, agriculture, construction and low-wage service industries have become a major feature of the global labour market, particularly in the states of the Gulf Cooperation Council (GCC). The companies that organise labour from places like the Philippines, Indonesia, India or Pakistan recruit locals on the promise of large wages, arrange their transport, and match them to employers overseas. But often these promises are false, and the employment agencies that facilitate these contracts have been documented as trapping workers into bonded labour by charging them several months' salary for visas, air tickets, other recruitment costs, and then for their substandard living arrangements while on site. These types of agreements contravene international labour law and are considered a form of human trafficking.[38] It has long been shown that migrant workers are far more likely to be exploited by their employers and have little or no recourse to voice their grievances about their treatment, making them more vulnerable to human trafficking and labour exploitation.

Some 23 million migrant workers live in the GCC countries and endure systematic abuse (involving unpaid wages, forced labour, dangerous working conditions, and unsanitary or inadequate housing) under the 'kafala' sponsorship system, which ties the legal right to residence in the host country to their employment contracts. As a result of the economic downturn caused by the pandemic, hundreds of thousands of migrant workers from India and Pakistan lost their jobs across the Gulf States. Many wanted to return home, but commercial flights had stopped, and their home states seemed disinclined to help them return. More than 60,000 Pakistani nationals in the United Arab Emirates registered to be repatriated, but only 9,000 of them were actually returned home on flights organised by the government.[39] More than 200,000 Indians also requested a return, but only a small fraction received it.[40] For the remainder, there is little sense of their fate—many have lost their jobs, and will have to eke out a living in the informal or illicit economies.

Allegations of forced labour and trafficking also dog the very industries responding to the pandemic—the garment and manufacturing companies making personal protective equipment (PPE). The largest rubber glove manufacturer, Top Glove, is based in Malaysia, and has an annual revenue of nearly US$100 million.

The company is the principal supplier of the UK's National Health Service. But in 2018 and 2019, investigations revealed that the company routinely used abusive labour practices, including forced labour, withheld wages, confiscated passports and debt bondage through recruitment fees.[41]

Rather than being furloughed, having their basic needs met and securing medical care, migrant workers are vulnerable to being forced to work in unsafe conditions. (Despite the lockdowns, the Malaysian factories making PPE maintained 100% production.)[42] Reports circulated of migrant workers being forced to work to compensate for pandemic-driven labour shortages or enduring further exploitation because of the need to lower production costs when the businesses themselves faced financial difficulty.[43] Some migrant workers were locked down and held in insufferable conditions while their employers waited to reopen.

### *No escape*

For many victims of human trafficking—included those trapped in forced marriages and victims of domestic abuse—the lockdown measures gave their persecutors even more power, particularly when victim and persecutor lived in the same space. Evidence suggests that the perpetrators of human trafficking all over the world used the risk of contagion to threaten and coerce vulnerable people, warning that they might throw their victims out on the street, where they would be exposed to the virus, if they did not comply. Many victims were denied medical assistance or had their sense of moral obligation not to put others at risk preyed upon in an effort to prevent them from leaving their situations of abuse.[44] The virus took children out of school and adults from their workplaces: this made it harder for them to escape from their captors and put them out of reach of the social workers, educators and health workers who are usually on the front line of identifying and responding to such abuse.[45] It also increased the number of people likely to find themselves in these terrible situations.

The United Nations Educational, Scientific and Cultural Organization (UNESCO) estimated that more than 89% of students enrolled in education globally, including 743 million girls, were out of school because of Covid closures.[46] The UN predicts that some 24 million may never return but will instead be sucked into work, particularly in the informal sector or illicit industries.[47] The cancellation of the academic year in countries across the world also increased those risks. Pressure was put on women and children to find ways to bring in additional money, including risky behaviours such as drug couriering, begging, prostitution or taking high-risk 'job opportunities' overseas that led them into exploitative work or human trafficking. Transactional sex was also widely reported as vulnerable girls and their families struggled to afford basic needs.[48] Polaris, an American NGO that operates the national human-trafficking hotline, identified an emerging form of sexual exploitation in which landlords force their tenants into sex when they cannot pay the rent.[49]

The incidence of forced marriage—a form of modern slavery and human trafficking practised most often by the families of girls themselves—also rose during the pandemic. In cultures where daughters are a burden on the family or can command a dowry, the indefinite closure of schools and dramatic constriction of incomes led some families to force their children to marry early.[50] The United Nations Population Fund has warned that the virus could lead to 13 million more child marriages over the next decade.[51]

Children in areas afflicted by a high concentration of gangs and criminal governance risk being recruited in greater numbers into criminal groups. From Manchester to Medellín, to Montego Bay to Mombasa, school closures meant that kids from lower-income families lost not only the structure that kept them out of trouble, but also often their primary meal of the day. Bored and hungry, both boys and girls have been easy pickings for gangs who like to have kids as messengers, lookouts, and couriers for drugs and other contraband, and in some instances as shooters, all because they are far less likely to attract police attention. Girls are being recruited and groomed into soliciting and prostitution. Our research networks in Kenya documented how kids were being recruited, at 600 Kenyan shillings (US$6) per day, to participate in phone-based virtual kidnapping and lottery scams—a mechanical process of repeated cold calling to announce over the phone either that the lucky recipient has won a prize and needs to provide account details (and a small deposit) for transfer, or that a family member has been picked up and held hostage for a small ransom. Both are lies, but the amount requested is small, and so anxious people pay rather than take the risk.[52] Child labour in itself is a form of human trafficking, but child labour impressed into criminal industries is also a human rights violation.

Night-time economies—not only bars, clubs and restaurants, but also sexual services like gentlemen's clubs, massage parlours, brothels and sex work—were some of the hardest hit by the pandemic. The human proximity and intimacy of activity in those establishments, combined with alcohol and drugs that reduce inhibitions, made them a priority vector for transmission of the virus, and thus the first to close and the slowest to reopen. But these places are also where some of the most vulnerable people work: low-skilled migrant workers and women and girls who cannot find legitimate employment elsewhere. Many work under threat and coercion, and nearly all such workers are stigmatised and shamed. A good deal of these businesses run predominantly on tips or fees for services, not salaries, and so even in the countries where government unemployment or furlough schemes are provided, workers may not qualify or receive enough to cover their living costs.

Even in developed countries where prostitution is legal, sex workers were afraid to apply for emergency funding or assistance, out of fear that the police might take advantage of their registration once the outbreak ends.[53] In the developing world, where there is no such assistance and even more stigma and fear, the picture is dire.[54] When there are bills to pay, mouths to feed, and money that needs to be sent home, it is all too easy to slide into illegal work. Legal sex workers the world over have expressed concern about the precariousness of their situation and the grim prospects they face as they look at the long-term decline of their industries and the choices that this will force them to make. These might include offering their services illegally and becoming more vulnerable to extortion and abuse, or taking loans or help from the rich (though often dangerous and criminal) owners of brothels, bars and clubs.[55] Their need now could trap them into trafficking later, yet there is precious little being done to help them.

As levels of mobility start to rise again, many will be thankful for the rediscovered joys of something resembling pre-pandemic life: a trip to visit a friend, a holiday. But for a vast majority of people, the pandemic's suspension of travel and its long-term consequences will have changed life forever, pushing them into the hands of traffickers, making journeys more dangerous, and exposing them to infection and destitution. In their precarious situations, they will have become even more profitable targets for and victims of organised crime.

5

# BUSINESS AS USUAL

The abrupt cessation of air travel when the global pandemic hit also spelt serious trouble for drug-trafficking groups, whose astronomical profits require a legion of recruited flight couriers (also known as mules) to travel on commercial airliners—the sheer number of mules ensuring that even if some are arrested, the drugs always get through.

Our own reporting network close to Nigerian drug traffickers, who are acknowledged experts in the flight drug-courier business, suggested some panic at the rapidly unfolding course of events. Flights were cancelled and couriers were reluctant to travel for fear of becoming sick. When flights did operate, there seemed to be more official scrutiny. When couriers managed to depart but didn't make their final destination, consignments had to be recovered and anxious couriers rerouted and subsequently persuaded or compelled to return their stash. All in all, it became a management and logistical nightmare.

For the drug mules, this loss of income was potentially devastating. On average, a drug mule's share of the load he or she carries on international passenger aircraft—woven into hair, swallowed, forced up the rectum or riskily concealed in hand luggage—is usually just short of half the street value of the drugs. These several thousand ingested dollars might not seem much to those in the developed world who are earning good salaries, but for the mule it often pays for education for children, medicines for relatives or just the basics of life for people in poor villages across Africa, Latin America and Asia. Without it, whole families will struggle to get by.

Much of the news and policy narrative around drug trafficking in the early days of the pandemic suggested that the experience of the Nigerian drug courier coordinators and their mules was merely one part of a larger upheaval. The general impression was that there were unprecedented disruptions in this global mega-industry, which has an estimated profit margin of anywhere between 26% and 58% and turnover running into the trillions of dollars.[1]

Further reporting revealed that the pandemic did have a disruptive effect on each of the three 'cogs' of the industry: the point of production or supply; the trafficking or transportation of drugs (including through transit states); and the markets where they are consumed. But while these disruptions were real, it also became clear that they were relatively minor and short-lived. Of all the actors in the drug-trafficking industry, the drug mules may have suffered the most. For many others in the illicit trade, the pandemic brought a few, usually localised shocks, but it was quickly back to business as usual.

*Production stays strong*

Before the pandemic struck, drug production was at a record high. The world was being flooded with cocaine and heroin, with surges in production recorded from 2013–14 onwards.[2] The output of synthetic drugs, particularly methamphetamine, has also increased significantly over the past decade. The pandemic merely brought a short-term jolt to drug production before business roared back to life.

In the case of cocaine, the spread of the virus combined with state actions to reduce the production of the drug in Latin America—but only temporarily. Cocaine is produced from the leaves of the coca bush and production occurs in Colombia, Peru and Bolivia. In Colombia (the global leader in cocaine production), forced eradication programmes continued despite the virus and in some cases the authorities entered areas where they had not regularly been before. However, overall levels of crop eradication declined in the country: between January and April 2020, 17,300 hectares were eradicated, 6,500 less than in the same period in 2019.[3] In Peru, which was badly affected by Covid-19, production fell as local communities imposed lockdowns to restrict activities and movement, but it crept up again after the Peruvian government suspended eradication efforts in mid-March 2020. In Bolivia, production actually increased, as state institutions had limited ability to intervene.[4]

There were other challenges, such as the reported shortage of gasoline (which is required for the production of the coca base) when stricter border controls with Venezuela reduced the quantities that could be smuggled out of that country.[5] And, at least in the early days of the pandemic in Latin America, there were fewer workers available given widespread fears of contracting the virus. However, part of the reason that production was able to rebound so quickly is that the coca bush is a perennial plant which grows and is harvested throughout the year, making it less vulnerable to short-term disruptions. In any case, the short jolt to production did not result in empty warehouses or a shortage of product on the street, as drug traffickers simply drew on their accumulated reserves to feed the market.[6]

In the case of methamphetamine, our network reported a slowdown in the purchase and delivery of chemical precursors when communities in Latin America refused to allow supplies into their territories. (It was said that shipments of chemicals from China and South East Asia were seen as possible sources of the virus by drug-producing workers.) Mexican drug cartels initially complained that the chemical precursors used to make methamphetamines and illicit fentanyl, which are usually sourced from China, had become harder and more complicated to procure, although those supply issues turned out to be very short-lived.[7] There is some indication that these complaints were manufactured to give the impression to the authorities that production had slowed or halted when in fact it continued apace. Suggestions that the cartels turned to US and Mexican manufacturers were also misleading—the diversion of supplies from these companies was already a regular occurrence before the advent of the pandemic.[8]

In any case, disruptions to the supply of precursors would probably not have affected operations: it is likely that large-scale meth labs had significant quantities of precursors in stock and were in little danger of running out as long as supply disruptions were short-lived. Mexican law-enforcement seizures of meth provide a useful indicator that production in fact continued and may even have grown during the pandemic. Fentanyl seizures in Mexico increased from 184 kg in the period from January to mid-September 2019 to just over one tonne (a 465% increase) for the same period in 2020. Seizures of methamphetamines increased from just under 13 tonnes between January and mid-September 2019 to just over 19 tonnes (a 33% increase) for the same period in 2020.[9]

As in the case of cocaine, the vast majority of opiates (opium, morphine and heroin) originate in three countries, with Afghanistan responsible for some 80% of supply. Unlike coca, however, opium poppy production is seasonal and so is much more susceptible to short-term disruptions. The harvesting period in late March or early June takes place over two weeks when the poppy capsules are 'lanced' repeatedly to extract opium. The harvest relies on large numbers of workers who travel to the districts where poppy is grown. Once the opium has been collected, morphine is extracted and converted into heroin, a process which requires access to chemicals such as acetic anhydride.

Pandemic-related disruptions seemed to be minimal, however. While a shortage of poppy lancers was reported during the pandemic, women in poppy-growing households were said to have joined the harvest to fill the labour gap. The payment price for lancing was also increased to provide greater incentives for workers to travel. The UNODC, which closely monitors the opium harvest in Afghanistan, was unable to draw clear conclusions as to whether the pandemic, and government and community responses to it in Afghanistan, had made any difference to production levels. The Taliban, which has a significant presence in poppy-growing areas, was said to be engaged in enforcing social-distancing measures, but it is unclear whether this was of any consequence for the harvest. One more concrete measure—the price of acetic anhydride—did fluctuate in early 2020, but not enough to suggest significant shortages.[10]

Alongside the traditional cultivation of opium poppies, Afghanistan has recently witnessed a boom in methamphetamine production, facilitated by the cultivation of a local shrub, the ephedra plant, from which ephedrine (one of the key precursor chemicals for crystal meth) can be produced. It is unclear what impact Covid-19 had on the production of meth in Afghanistan. Reports from mid-2020 suggest that there was little impact on—in fact, there was a growth in—the trafficking of meth into drugs markets in East Africa and southern Africa.[11]

### *The resilience of drug trafficking*

All the available evidence suggests that, despite some regional and national differences, and notwithstanding an initial 'shock' as the pandemic struck and resulting lockdowns were implemented, drug cultivation and production continued without significant change. This also appeared to be the case with the next cog in the system: trafficking.

While the data are fragmentary, declines in price for coca leaf and paste seemed to occur in several places. The national drug control agency in Peru reported a 46% drop in the price of coca leaf from January to April 2020. This was said to be the result of decreasing demand from traffickers, who were initially having difficulties in transporting drugs out of the country. But these disruptions, too, proved to be short-lived.

The ability to adapt and change methods and routes seems to have occurred on many drug-trafficking lanes. It was reported, for example, that when the Friendship Bridge (Ponte da Amizade) linking Brazil and Paraguay was closed for individual crossings, the movement of drug mules stopped. But the border is porous, and so mules simply took different, albeit less convenient, routings. And while individual travel was curtailed, cargo vehicles continued to cross borders between different Mercosur countries (Brazil, Argentina, Uruguay and Paraguay).[12]

But in the majority of cases, there was no need to adapt. While by May 2020 over 60% of all global passenger jets were sitting idle,[13] the fall in seagoing trade was much less serious.[14] This particularly benefited criminals, given that the majority of illicit trade—everything from narcotics to counterfeit goods—moves predominantly by sea. In drug trafficking, for example, some two-thirds of all seizures are made at ports and at sea.[15]

Container trade is critical for moving not only consignments of drugs but also the precursor chemicals to manufacture them. India and China are the largest producers and shippers of these, and Asian meth syndicates reported that they had not experienced any problem in accessing the required chemicals.[16] While there was some decline in container trade and an increase in 'blanked sailings' (temporally suspended shipping services), container ship sailings were still running at rates of at least 80% for all the routes out of Asia in March and April.[17]

Aside from seaborne trade, other means of international distribution continued throughout the pandemic. In a May 2020 report, Europol asserted that 'drug trafficking by air freight appears to be continuing'.[18] Chinese rail freight, which is now connected to European markets, showed an all-time-high cargo tonnage in January and February as local lockdowns were coming into effect.[19]

If anything, the pandemic restrictions made it easier for trafficking groups to get their product through points of entry. There was a decline in the capacity to search air freight and containers—usually around 2% of all containers are searched—because of social-distancing measures, sick personnel or the assignment of staff to other duties related to managing the pandemic. The need to keep trade moving and food and medicines supplied was also prioritised, with the result that searching and intelligence-led enforcement were reduced in some seaports. Some authorities created 'green lanes' at ports of entry and at border crossings to accelerate the processing of cargo shipments and to ensure their swift movement onto roads for distribution.[20] That kept drugs moving too.[21]

But how much was moving? Judging from drug seizures by law enforcement authorities, it seems a lot. While such seizures should not be regarded as a definitive source of data overall, they do provide some indication of both where trafficking continued to occur and what volumes were involved. Given the scale of drug consumption in Europe (the second-largest market for cocaine, heroin and methamphetamines), seizures of goods destined for that market provide some indicator of the vigour of trafficking activity.

Europol reported that a number of significant seizures were made in the first six months of 2020. At the end of March, Dutch authorities seized two tonnes of cocaine at Rotterdam Port, while in May half a tonne of cocaine was seized from a Montenegrin-flagged ship, sailing from Brazil and bound for Europe.[22] From January to May 2020 there were also at least ten seizures of cocaine at Colombian ports, half of which were destined for Antwerp in Belgium.[23] Colombian media reported that seizures of cocaine between January and June 2020 were in fact 8% higher—involving some 212 tonnes—than those for the same period in 2019, which totalled 197 tonnes.[24]

From our own research, we were also very aware that trafficking to Europe had ramped up during the pandemic. A clear case was provided by the small West African state of Guinea-Bissau, which has been an important transit point for cocaine trafficked to European markets since the mid-2000s.[25] Our interviews in Bissau indicate that key actors within the local trafficking economy, with support from the military and government, used the lockdown period to scale up business. 'Things have got much worse and the cocaine is flowing,' reported a prominent civil society leader in April 2020.[26] One reason that the drug transit trade through Guinea-Bissau continued is that the logistics of drug movement in the country are controlled almost entirely by traffickers, which meant that they could continue operating with little disruption. Even in the midst of the pandemic, ships continued to bring drugs close to the shore, where the drugs were offloaded onto smaller boats to bring them into the country.[27]

It also seemed to be business as usual on the US–Mexico border—or even business booming. Between January and August 2020, the US Customs and Border Patrol (CBP) seized more than twice as much meth (141,663 lb, or more than 64,000 kg) than it did during the whole of 2019 (68,585 lb, or 31,109 kg).[28] While this surge in meth seizures could be partly explained by increased enforcement by the CBP, the figure still suggests that both production and trafficking were functioning well, and potentially growing exponentially, despite the restrictions on the border that only allowed for essential and business travel across the line. (Local wisdom has it that seizures of drugs represent only some 10% of what gets through the official crossing points.) Marijuana and fentanyl seizures also grew, although seizures of cocaine dropped significantly during the same period for reasons that are not clear.

*View from the street*

To explore how the pandemic was affecting local drug markets, the EMCDDA and Europol conducted a survey in April 2020 across European states (see Figure 1).[29] The report found that across seven types of illicit drugs—methamphetamine, MDMA (Ecstasy), amphetamine, cocaine, heroin, cannabis resin and cannabis—and the twenty countries where government experts responded to the survey,[30] there were increases or strong increases of price in a third of all cases. No change was recorded in a quarter of all instances. Experts did not or were unable to answer in the majority of cases.

In the case of cocaine, only France reported a 'strong increase' in the price of the drug and a 'strong decrease' in availability. The remaining reports (ten in all) show decreases in availability and some increases in price, although the correlation between price and avail-

Figure 1: Summary of expert opinion on drug price changes during the Covid-19 lockdown across twenty EU states and seven drug types. (Source: https://www.emcdda.europa.eu/publications/joint-publications/eu-drug-markets-impact-of-covid-19_en)

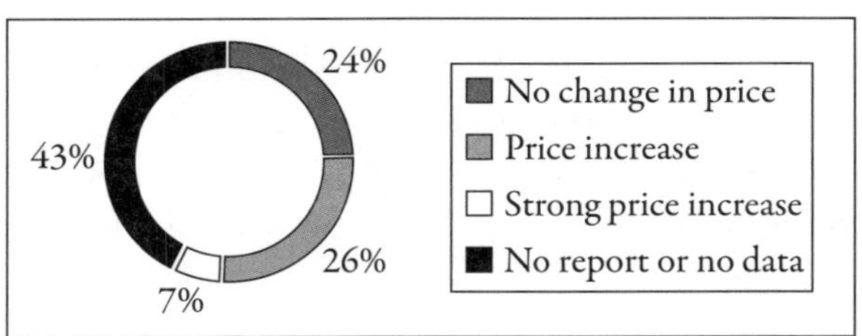

ability is often inconsistent, suggesting the greater likelihood of a sharp shock than any longer-term impact. What was noteworthy was that, of those countries reporting, a significant proportion (eight) indicated no changes in the availability of cocaine during the first months of the pandemic.[31]

In the case of heroin, France and Norway reported strong increases in the retail price of the drug, while several other countries (Croatia, Cyprus, Denmark, Luxembourg, Romania and Spain) reported some increases. Three neighbouring countries—Austria, Czechia and Hungary—noted that there was no change in the retail price of heroin or its availability, suggesting that the drug route through Turkey and the Balkans was operating as normal. While shortages of heroin were reported in Bulgaria, France, Norway and Spain, a significant number of countries reported no problems with the availability of heroin at all.[32]

In the case of cannabis, domestic production was not seen as being disrupted by Covid-19, but consumer supply appeared to be constricted by local distribution issues.[33] Interestingly, Sweden, where no local lockdown was implemented, recorded no change in price across all drug types or in the availability of drugs.

Synthetic drugs—amphetamines, MDMA and methamphetamines—were affected by declines in the nighttime economy and the closing of clubs and cancelling of music festivals. However, across Europe, they showed little fluctuation in price, although a significant proportion of countries (half of the twenty reporting) indicated shortages in availability—though this could equally have been the result of an inability of consumers to access existing supplies—at least in the early days of the pandemic and lockdown. In the case of Bulgaria, France and Spain, these shortages were reported as relatively sizeable.[34] Given that much of the synthetic drug market in Europe is served by drugs made on the continent, it appears that it was the impact of local lockdowns, rather than any disruption to transcontinental trafficking, that had an effect on local distribution and sale.

This conclusion was supported by our interviews with local dealers in several places where lockdown regulations were implemented. These dealers reported that initially the problem was not drug supply, as most had some stockpiles, but that nightclubs and bars (crucial venues for drug dealers) were shuttered. To ensure their local supplies would last, the dealers diluted the quality of their drugs and raised their prices, but this tactic was short-lived, as they soon found other ways of reaching customers.[35]

Indeed, this point seemed to apply to the state of play in drugs markets across Europe, irrespective of drug type. As the EMCDDA–Europol report argued: 'There is some clear evidence of availability issues in some places, probably linked to difficulties in intra-EU distribution rather than importation problems.'[36] While trafficking and production supply lines remained functional, it appeared that the difficulty of selling drugs in France, Norway and Spain drove prices upwards in the early days of the pandemic and during the height of lockdown, but also that in many countries, business carried on as usual.

Outside Europe, the overall situation of drugs markets likewise suggested remarkable stability. The UNODC, for example, noted that the 'situation in the Middle East and North Africa appears to be stable in terms of drug availability. The Covid-19 crisis does not seem to have disrupted domestic (retail) drug trafficking in these sub-regions.'[37] Similarly, reports from Russia have stated that there has been little or no change in the situation of the drugs market there.[38]

*Product always gets through*

Dealers responded differently in different countries. For example, reports from the United Kingdom suggested that there was a drop in the retail price of drugs when dealers tried to get rid of their stock, apparently worried that they would not be able to access it later.[39] Prices of drugs on the street then surged as many dealers ceased trading for a period because of the increased police presence. (Drugs dealers were right to be concerned: increased police activity in the UK during the lockdown resulted in a greater number of arrests for drug-related offences.)[40] Police forces in the UK were soon reporting that drug dealers had resorted to multiple disguises—dressing themselves as delivery or health workers—to make sure that their products would get through.[41]

In Cape Town, South Africa, heroin prices briefly doubled. Our own day-to-day reporting indicated an interesting twist. Gang contacts, who are deeply embedded in the local drug market, suggested that they had artificially raised the price because users were likely to expect an increase. It was a simple and short-term money-making strategy. Dealers also found innovative ways to reach their customers. In the city's gang-ridden Cape Flats, our monitors reported that drug dealers acquired the necessary permits to move around as 'essential services', often under the guise of delivering food.

Like postmen and package deliverers in the legitimate economy, drug delivery services also became acutely aware of their safety. Our reporting from several cities concluded that dealers often wore masks and gloves and insisted that clients did so too. 'No-contact drops'—already a feature of the market—were expanded. And given that local drug transactions are almost always cash-based, dealers went to great lengths to 'clean' (quite literally in this case) their cash takings, wiping down the notes with disinfectant.[42]

Many dealers in North America and Europe also shifted quickly to online drug retailing, speeding a trend that was already well under way. By March, the EMCDDA was already reporting a notable rise in activity on three popular darknet drug markets.[43] Drug distribution and sale, at least in Western cities, had in any event been shifting to WhatsApp-facilitated delivery systems, including door-to-door delivery. Dealer networks were quick to adapt and had a model in place to enable them to do so. Elsewhere, systems of face-to-face drug dealing largely remained unchanged.

Drug user patterns also shifted. Demand for party drugs—for example, cocaine and amphetamines—fell in line with the lack of social occasions. Sales of cannabis went up as people at home had more time to indulge. Sales of highly addictive drugs like heroin, meth and fentanyl also rose, as users worried that a supply crunch might be coming.[44] In some cases, the absence of drugs could be easily determined: in Punjab, India, more than 100,000 drug users registered for the first time at treatment centres providing drug replacement therapy, an increase of some 23% over the usual number treated.[45] The numbers soon declined when drugs began flowing again.

### *An undisrupted market*

Remarkably, the pandemic seems to have had very little lasting impact on the drugs trade. Production remained steady and the overall volumes of drugs moving across borders did not change significantly. There may have been temporary shocks to the market, but these were remarkably short-lived and relatively localised. Changes in the street prices of drugs may have been due to local restrictions or (as in Cape Town) dealers engaging in price gouging.

The relative lack of impact may be partly due to the fact that most successful drug-trafficking entrepreneurs, networks and organisations had already been through a Darwinian wringer in which only the fittest survive, making them well prepared for the pandemic. Reviewing past 'shocks' to the global drug economy, our colleague Jason Eligh, an expert in the area, concluded that 'actors in the illicit drug market made structural and systemic adaptations to maintain operations … The organisations that survived a crisis had become more resilient and less vulnerable to the impact of similar future crises, and the market and organisational adaptations they made became permanent.'[46] Rather than diminishing the strength of organised crime, the pandemic may in fact have increased it by forcing organisations to become even more adaptable and innovative.

But if the drug trade was not meaningfully disrupted, the pandemic did provide an opportunity for authorities and analysts to rethink the global policy approach to regulating illicit drug markets. Perhaps the most thought-provoking development in this regard during the pandemic was the precautionary release from prison of thousands of people who had been imprisoned for drug-related offences (see chapter 10). In the words of Helen Clark, the former prime minister of New Zealand and now the chair of a WHO panel to examine the lessons learned from the response to Covid 19: 'all these people were released, no harm was done—that raises the question why they were imprisoned in the first place'[47]

The South African experiment with banning alcohol—an arguably legitimate short-term response to take the pressure off the health-care system from alcohol-fuelled violence and car crashes—has proved to be a perfect demonstration (if one was needed) that declaring widely demanded commodities illegal is a perfect way to fuel the activities of criminal groups and grow their profits.

The challenge of addressing the issue of illegal drugs with a more innovative set of policy responses has become increasingly urgent. The UN's Global Strategy and Plan on Drugs—a prohibition-based drug-control strategy initiated in 1998 and renewed in 2008 and then again in 2019—has been a complete failure. Drug traffickers and markets are more powerful and influential than ever and are growing in sophistication and reach. Both production and consumption have soared. Serious questions should be asked about the global public policy response in a post-pandemic context where political openings may emerge for significant change in the regulation of drug markets, moving from law enforcement to health-oriented approaches. This is all the more urgent given that research shows that longer-term economic contractions may have important impacts on drug use, which include driving a shift towards cheaper laboratory-made drugs like amphetamines and (by pushing drug prices down) growing the number of users.

As the flow of seaborne narcotics never stopped, the Nigerian drug mules stranded by cancelled flights may in the end have been some of the biggest losers of the pandemic—but even they will no doubt be back at work when flights resume. The pandemic, and the economic contraction which could follow, may well have provided new opportunities for entrepreneurial traffickers to become more resilient and to expand their market. Might it also provide an opportunity for policy-makers to think again about how to tackle the issue of illicit drugs?

6

# CRIMINAL COMMODITIES

Before the pandemic, the global shipping community was celebrating the fact that piracy rates had dropped to a 25-year low. In the Gulf of Aden, the notorious stamping ground of Somali pirates, who had been the scourge of seaborne trade in the early 2000s, there had been no piracy attacks at all in 2019.

But, driven by the pandemic, piracy resurged in African, Asian and Latin American waters in 2020.[1] Piracy incidents doubled across Asia, with notable increases in the Singapore Strait (one of the world's busiest commercial shipping lanes) and in the South China Sea and along the coasts of the Philippines, Vietnam, Indonesia, Bangladesh and India. The types of attacks and targets involved suggested that the piracy in Asian waters was a relatively opportunistic crime carried out by fishermen and other seafarers looking to boost their incomes as the pandemic curtailed their traditional livelihoods.[2] Asian incidents mainly involved robberies at sea, where a small fishing boat carrying a few armed men robbed the crew and stole ship stores and other small things that could easily be offloaded on the black market.[3]

But in other parts of the world, the target was something bulkier: oil infrastructure. For many criminals, oil itself had been a lucrative target before the pandemic, but the collapse in demand for the commodity (and the associated fall in price, which briefly even turned negative) may have pushed pirates who had previously seized oil to shift their attention to oil infrastructure assets, kidnap-for-ransom and stealing on-board valuables. There were 132 such attacks globally in the first nine months of 2020, up from 119 for the same time period in 2019.[4]

In June 2020, the US State Department issued a security alert noting that criminal groups were targeting commercial ships, oil platforms and offshore supply vessels in the Gulf of Mexico,[5] including a floating storage hub where oil producers were anchoring their excess inventories.[6] Pirates were reported to have stripped the ships and their crew of any assets that could be sold on, such as communications gear, navigation equipment, and even the lights from helicopter landing pads. The Mexican government, already struggling with extraordinarily high levels of criminal violence onshore, was heavily criticised for barely reacting to the maritime threat.[7]

The Gulf of Guinea, off the West African coast, also saw a spike in attacks on offshore production and storage facilities and associated crew,[8] while the region accounted for the majority of kidnapping-for-ransom cases (80 out of 85 seamen taken). In July 2020, for example, eight pirates boarded a product tanker 196 miles off the Nigerian coast, held all nineteen crewmen hostage and stole the ship's documents and valuable items. They also kidnapped thirteen crew members.[9] As in Asia, the surge in the Gulf of Guinea was attributed to the sharp contraction in livelihoods for the populations onshore, who live in already poor and fragile countries.[10]

In the long term, maritime security analysts fear that a downturn in global consumer spending and a commensurate reduction in volumes of trade will reduce the profitability of shipping and transport routes, which may lessen the desire and ability of shipping firms to bear the cost of protecting ships. This threatens to reverse hard-won gains in the fight against piracy, given that it was the onboarding of relatively expensive private security services that was decisive in ending piracy off the coast of Somalia.[11]

Changes in the price of another natural resource commodity—gold—also had important implications in another illicit industry, namely the illicit mining sector, which has expanded significantly in the last number of years in several countries. The flow of illegal gold globally is enormous and enormously valuable. In Colombia and Peru, for example, the value of the illicit gold trade is comparable to that of the cocaine-trafficking economy—and the two countries are the largest cocaine producers in the world.[12] Illegal gold mining is also an important business in Brazil: in the state of Roraima, which does not have a single legal gold mine, more than 194 kg of gold was reported by authorities to have been exported to India in 2019.[13]

### *Cheap gold in the DRC*

The artisanal mining sector in the Democratic Republic of the Congo (DRC) is a vast enterprise that feeds a global supply chain running through Dubai and on to South Asia.[14] The gold sector shades into the illicit at various points along this path, from miners being subjected to criminal exploitation to gold buyers and traders engaging in gold laundering in places such as Uganda and South Sudan (where the gold acquires false certification to disguise its origins). Once this gold has been 'cleaned' and has entered the licit supply chain, it can be easily sold to consumers in countries such as the US and Switzerland.

Gold is suited to criminal exploitation for several reasons: it is nearly untraceable; it possesses high levels of liquidity; it holds its value; and, having been worked, it becomes a legitimate consumer commodity. Criminal groups often prefer it to official currencies, especially as efforts to freeze criminal assets have increased.[15] The sourcing of gold from geographically remote locations and through convoluted supply chains also makes the concealment of any illicit actors involved relatively easy. Given these features, gold is also a useful way of laundering money: gold can be bought for cash illegally and then sold 'legally' or without much oversight. For that reason, illegal mining is one of the easiest and most profitable ways to launder drugs money.

But in March 2020 the artisanal mining sector in the DRC began to feel the impact of the pandemic. By early April, the vast majority of gold-trading houses in one area of the country's gold-rich Ituri province were reported to have closed, and all the flights into the region (which brought in gold traders and took out gold) had been cancelled. Local miners—almost all young men who worked under dangerous conditions—stood around waiting or else headed home. There were no buyers and no business.[16]

But the story was very different on stock markets around the world, where gold prices began to surge as investors sought a safe asset amid the economic turmoil. By July 2020, the price of gold had risen by 28%—a record high. And it continued to rise, hitting US$2,071 per ounce by August 2020. 'One hedge in particular', said the *Financial Times* in an October 2020 review of the growing fortunes of the very wealthy during the pandemic, 'was pushed by many Swiss bankers and wealth advisors to their clients with great success this year—gold.'[17]

The rising price of gold created powerful incentives for those involved in the illicit trade of the commodity. A prominent Belgian refiner, Alain Goetz, who has been convicted of money laundering, was quoted as saying: 'for gold dealers [the pandemic represents] a once in a lifetime opportunity, but only if you can get [the gold] out of Africa and turn it into cash'.[18] While the traditional flows from the DRC had dried up, a gold dealer in Nairobi reported to researchers from IMPACT (a civil society organisation monitoring the trade) that 'he was aware of several colleagues who were personally flying into the eastern DRC and neighbouring Uganda's Entebbe [airport] to transact deals and export gold'.[19]

Other dealers were attempting to make their way directly to the mining sites.[20]

What drove the gold dealers was a widening differential in price: while the metal's price was surging on international exchanges, it was declining in the zones where illegal mining took place. In the DRC, the price of gold sold by local artisanal miners fell by about 40%, while globally it increased by about a third.[21] The illegal miners needed to make a livelihood after the initial shock of the pandemic and were willing to sell gold to whoever would buy it. There was serious money to be made—and, predictably, it was the criminals who were making it.

### *Ghosts popping up*

In South Africa, the first sign of an impending crisis for illegal miners (widely known here as *zama zamas*, meaning those who take a chance) was that they literally began 'popping out' of disused and working mines.[22] The *zama zamas* had come to the surface with no knowledge that there was a pandemic raging above them; all they knew was their supplies had run out and for some reason had not been replenished.

Before the pandemic, there were an estimated 30,000 *zama zamas*. The work they do is brutal, and scores of them are said to die underground in accidents. Deep in the mines, the *zama zamas* scrape rocks over a metal plate which is wrapped in a carpet. Gold-bearing material gets caught in the carpet and is then washed out. Mercury is then added and a nugget of perhaps 50% gold produced, which is further refined on the surface. Tonnes of gold are lost each year to illicit mining, depriving the state of urgently needed tax revenue.[23]

Working in this way, miners spend months underground, turning a ghostly greyish white from lack of sun. A complex economy of paid-off police and mine employees facilitate these lengthy sojourns in the mines. Despite pressure from legal mining companies, surrounding communities protect the illegal miners because they bolster the local economy, both legal (small butcher shops and supermarkets) and illegal (sex workers and drug dealers). But when the South African government closed the mines in March as part of the lockdown, these highly organised logistics chains weakened and then broke, and by the end of April the miners were getting hungry and desperate, and then rose to the surface.

When news of the pandemic became known, many illegal miners decided to stay underground for fear of being arrested for breaking lockdown regulations.[24] But for other illicit actors, the pandemic also represented the perfect time to 'take a chance'. Mines under lockdown were quieter and, depending on whether supplies could be brought in, the pandemic provided an opportunity to widen the areas underground where miners could work.

The pandemic also brought a brief lull in the level of violence above and below ground. But soon there were fresh reports of killings as struggles for control continued or intensified. The level of violence is particularly extreme in South Africa, where heavily armed groups of *zama zamas* battle police, mining security and each other, and firefights often take place below the surface. It is not an uncommon occurrence in South Africa to hear of multi-fatality shoot-outs, targeted assassinations or executions in areas where illicit mining occurs. A month before the nationwide South African lockdown, nine miners had been stoned to death by a rival group.[25] The weeks following the brief pandemic-induced lull saw renewed conflict; in one incident near Johannesburg in June 2020, a group of miners were professionally ambushed and pinned down by a hail of gunfire, leaving two dead and several wounded.[26]

But the illicit activity around gold in South Africa is not confined below ground. During the pandemic, another trend that had begun in South Africa in 2018 was also on display—armed attacks on gold-smelting facilities. In March 2020, as the pandemic tightened its grip on South Africa, twenty armed men stormed a Chinese-owned gold plant 140 km west of Johannesburg. They left, according to sources in the industry, with an undisclosed quantity of calcine, the gold-bearing material from which bars of bullion are processed. While the numbers of such heists in 2020 remained lower than in 2019, the high price of gold may give both *zama zamas* and gold heist syndicates a strong incentive to step up activities in the near future.[27]

### *The mining mafia*

As the South African case illustrates, illicit mining economies have become extremely violent. This is particularly the case where artisanal mining has been declared illegal, with the result that criminal groups fight for control and introduce violent forms of self-regulation similar to that in other illegal markets, such as drugs. Processes of regulating and licensing illegal miners are challenging, however. For example, in Peru the closure of an office responsible for this task in 2016 brought the licensing of illegal miners to a standstill, and has led to a surge in organised crime and assassinations; there are even rumours that Shining Path, the communist guerrilla group, is moving into mining.[28]

Territorial control of mining areas, and parts of the mines themselves, is key to the system of extraction. Territory has to be defended from other groups as well as from the state and, in some cases, legitimate private businesses that have been displaced by illegal actors. In the Amazon basin, where illegal gold mining is rampant, there are often violent conflicts between indigenous communities and miners.

From our own monitoring, it is clear that the legal and illegal mining and extractive industries—and associated criminal economies and actors—are significantly involved in mafia-style assassinations, targeted both at other mining groups and at outsiders who oppose the expansion of mining. This is particularly the case where civil society activities and environmental defenders stand in the way of resource exploitation. In 2019, Global Witness recorded the deaths of 50 environmental defenders around the world, with mining and extractives being the deadliest sector.[29] Many of these activists had been struggling against the expansion of licit and illicit mining.[30]

In Peru, seven indigenous leaders were assassinated in illegal mining and extractive areas from 2013 to February 2020. But the pace of killing has now quickened. After the state of emergency was declared in the country in early March 2020, four environmental defenders were killed in quick succession: Arbildo Meléndez Grández, Gonzalo Pío Flores and Lorenzo Wampagkit were assassinated between April and July, while in September 2020 Roberto Pacheco, son of the vice-president of the Tambopata National Reserve Committee, a local organisation fighting mining expansion, was allegedly murdered by illegal miners.[31]

Ordinary people caught in illegal mining areas controlled by criminal organisations are enormously vulnerable. Before the pandemic struck, Human Rights Watch reported that Venezuelan and Colombian armed groups involved in illegal mining in Bolívar state in Venezuela and other places were engaging in horrific abuses against local inhabitants, including amputations and torture.[32] It is said that the Venezuelan government tacitly allows these armed groups to operate in order to maintain social control by proxy.[33]

Sexual exploitation and labour exploitation are also rife in criminal-controlled mining areas. In Peru, children between 10 and 14 years of age are engaged in heavy labour in the gold mines and are exposed to multiple hazards. The US Department of Labor has also reported that children are victims of commercial sexual exploitation in and near the mining areas.[34] Our own institution's work in Peru found 'staggering' levels of sex trafficking into the mining camps, involving children as well. The Peruvian national prosecutor from Madre de Dios, a mining hotspot, has stated that almost 70% of trafficked victims are between the ages of 13 and 17, and many are recruited through deception. Sex trafficking related to illegal mining has also been reported from mining areas in Bolivia and Colombia.[35] During the pandemic, victims of labour and sexual exploitation in mining areas have been exposed to a higher probability of increased abuse and reduced chances of being identified and rescued, as a result of the decline in labour inspections and in the enforcement of laws on labour trafficking, which were already lax for victims in exploitative situations prior to the pandemic.[36]

*Illegal mining spreads under Covid*

Illegal gold mining is responsible for significant levels of deforestation, and the pandemic looks set to reverse recent gains in this area. Illegal gold mining in the rivers of the Peruvian Amazon had declined after Operation Mercury (Operación Mercurio) 2019, the largest intervention in Peruvian history against illegal gold mining. The operation drove out thousands of miners, destroyed millions of dollars' worth of wildcat mining equipment, and broke up business in La Pampa, the centre of illegal mining and other criminal activities. One result was that deforestation decreased by 92% during the first few months of the operation.

But the withdrawal of police and army forces to enforce lockdown and attend to the health crisis allowed illegal mining to return. During the state of emergency, miners were able to travel to illegal mining areas (such as La Pampa) along the Interoceanic Highway between Brazil and Peru, despite the checkpoints in place. The

Andean Amazon Monitoring Project recorded an increase in deforestation due to illegal mining in several areas, and the migration of miners from La Pampa to other gold-rich points in the Madre de Dios region.[37]

In Brazil, a long history of impunity has characterised the extraction of natural resources and environmental degradation in the Brazilian Amazon. Since his election in 2019, President Jair Bolsonaro's administration has played a significant part in driving the expansion of mining into environmentally sensitive areas, which has involved scaling back law enforcement and working to legalise illicit mining on indigenous land.[38] The rise in gold prices in the wake of Covid-19 has only accelerated this trend of expansion.[39]

Despite the concerns around the spread of the virus to vulnerable populations such as indigenous groups, illegal mines have continued to operate in the Amazon basin, notably in Brazil and Venezuela. In several cases, indigenous peoples in voluntary isolation (uncontacted people) living near mines have seen their lands more and more being invaded by illegal mining, increasing the risk of the virus spreading through their communities. In the Brazilian Amazon, indigenous leaders, local organisations and federal prosecutors have reported a growth in illegal mining, including encroachments on indigenous territory. Border closures have also led to a greater use of unofficial crossings to transport gold.[40]

In response to reports of an increase in illicit mining, the Peruvian special prosecutor's office for environmental affairs carried out more than 75 interventions against illegal mining operations in the mining hotspot of

Madre de Dios between March and early June 2020, breaking up mining sites and destroying machinery.[41] In August and September 2020, the Ministry of Environment began a series of initiatives to work out how best to combat both the pandemic and illegal economies (such as illegal mining and illegal logging) in the Amazon basin region.[42]

The Colombian media reported that cases of illegal mining had increased during Covid-19.[43] In response, a draft bill was debated in the Colombian Congress in July 2020 with the objective of imposing new sanctions and revitalising laws against illegal mining. The legislative initiative is also intended to create new crimes to cover all links in the chain and ensure the prosecution not only of those involved in extraction, but also of those who commercialise and benefit from illegally extracted minerals, in addition to penalising the use of mercury. The bill allows mining titles to expire for those who hire children in mining activities and creates penalties for mining operators who exceed the volumes established by the mining authority. In addition, the initiative obliges the government to regulate and establish mechanisms to determine the origin and traceability of minerals.[44]

### *Threats and opportunities*

The countries where there are significant levels of illicit gold mining—Peru, Brazil, Bolivia, Colombia, the DRC and South Africa—have all faced significant economic contractions in the wake of the pandemic. So too have the oil-rich nations in the Gulf and Africa. The restrictions on travel and the glut of supply will likely keep oil prices depressed in the near term, potentially driving criminals involved in the sector to engage in other, potentially more violent illicit markets. Meanwhile, the sustained period of economic volatility will most likely continue to bolster the gold price, providing powerful incentives for both criminal entrepreneurs and desperate ordinary people in those places to enter the illicit mining sector in greater numbers. Unless there is a policy rethink and effective response, these illegal miners will continue to flock to unlicensed gold-mining sites and protected indigenous lands, stripping swathes of forest bare and polluting rivers with mercury, threatening local communities and continuing to pad the pockets of criminal entrepreneurs. Associated crimes of labour exploitation and trafficking of women and children for sexual exploitation will also grow.

But as in the case of the illegal drug economy, the pandemic also provides an opportunity, not only to better regulate and manage natural resources and extractives, but also to improve the artisanal mining sector in several countries by undercutting powerful criminal interests and promoting pro-poor policies. It is an opportunity that should not be missed.

7

# WILDLIFE'S REVENGE?

Sellers in the bustling Huanan Seafood Wholesale Market in Wuhan never expected to appear on the front pages of international newspapers. But in January 2020 the market was thrust into the global spotlight, having been tagged as the alleged source of the novel coronavirus—a zoonotic disease which had jumped from animals to humans. As a 'wet' market, Huanan sold wild animals, both dead and alive. One such animal was the pangolin, which was identified as a possible carrier of the virus and potential vector for its transmission to humans.[1]

Whether this is true or not, the appearance of wet markets and the pangolin on the world stage raised the issue of wildlife trafficking more widely, and much more effectively, than costly awareness campaigns had managed to do in the past.[2] Although a link between the trade and the virus has not yet been decisively made, the seed was sown for a reckoning of attitudes towards the wildlife trade, both legal and illegal, as well as an assessment of government efforts assessment of government efforts to regulate and limit animal trafficking. Some held that the illicit wildlife trade would be eroded as traffickers and consumers saw first-hand the dangers of the trade; but others were less optimistic.

*Declining appetite for wet markets?*

Wet markets are significant places for trading both legally and illegally trafficked wildlife in Asia.[3] Chinese consumers, at home and abroad, remain the primary source of demand for many species, including big cats such as lions and tigers, as well as pangolins, bears, rhinos, elephants, and a variety of species of fish.[4] The majority of Asian consumers at the end of the illegal wildlife supply chain are well aware that the items they purchase are illegal. That said, there is a grey zone between 'legal' and 'illegal' in China, as Chinese government policies have legitimised the commercial exploitation of many threatened species.[5]

Huanan's alleged role as the place of origin of the coronavirus outbreak brought the question of whether the sale of such wildlife in wet markets should be banned into the realm of global public debate, drawing in participants far outside the pool of experts and environmentalists who usually discuss such matters. Among others, the US secretary of state, Mike Pompeo, weighed in, calling for all wet markets in China to be shut. Tedros Adhanom Ghebreyesus, director general of the WHO, argued for better regulation and the improvement of safety standards, but also for the markets to continue.[6] A plethora of specialists pointed out that wild animals were crucial sources of protein for many people around the world, and others argued that these sales points were not limited to Asia—there were, for example, village stalls in rural France that sold fish and red meat.[7]

There was also internal resistance to closing the markets. Large wet markets in Asia generate significant amounts of money, both for those that own and operate them legally and for illicit traders, which means there is considerable local economic and political pressure to keep them open. Reports from China suggest that businessmen have actively pressured officials to keep markets operating, to relax regulations, or to turn a blind eye to the sale of illegal or regulated wildlife commodities.

Away from the markets, the Chinese government has continued to allow pharmaceutical companies and hospitals to commercially produce and sell traditional Chinese medicine products containing pangolin scales.[8] And this is not an isolated incident; as Aron White of the Environmental Investigation Agency notes, 'support for commercialization of threatened wildlife is pervasive within key government institutions' in China.[9] Problematically, these are the same institutions which also have a mandate to protect wildlife. Chinese institutions, such as the National Forestry and Grasslands Administration, on the one hand pledge to preserve wildlife while they are simultaneously responsible for the 'healthy development of the rare animal medicinal industry'.[10]

Overall, the idea of closing down these sales points, which number in the hundreds across major cities around the world, may not be practical. More effective regulation of the wildlife trade, and the closing down of illegal and unregulated markets, seem more realistic goals.[11] But while these markets might not be disappearing anytime soon, the pandemic did see changes in consumer attitudes towards wildlife on sale there.

This issue became increasingly prominent as the virus spread, particularly in Asia.[12] Interviews conducted before the pandemic with potential buyers of illegal wildlife products or food from prohibited species in China suggested that consumers were much more worried about being cheated by the seller than being arrested by law enforcement officials.[13] A trust deficit is not uncommon in illicit markets, and a standard strategy, employed also in the wildlife trade, is to stick to a single known seller. Trust is of particular importance in the purchase of species such as rhino and pangolin, whose criminal supply chains stretch from Africa to Asia, and for which premium prices are paid. Since the pandemic, however, local anti-wildlife trafficking activists in China have been reporting that ordinary people are now scared to eat or use illegal wildlife products.[14] A public survey conducted in March 2020 in four Asian countries—Vietnam, Thailand, Myanmar and Hong Kong SAR—suggested that the vast majority of respondents (84%) would be unlikely or very unlikely to engage in future consumption of wildlife products.[15]

Such stats would have been almost inconceivable before the pandemic. Previous anti-wildlife campaigns in China had focused on the preservation of iconic species like the rhino, but had very limited impact. That said, it is unclear whether the recent change was driven by ethical, public health or economic considerations. 'Consumers may now well see some added stigma for some types of wildlife products,' says Steve Broad of TRAFFIC, the wildlife trade monitoring organisation, 'but they may also have less confidence in spending money now.'[16] Furthermore, it remains to be seen whether this shift represents a real and decisive shift in consumer behaviour in Asia that will outlast the pandemic or whether it is merely a knee-jerk reaction to the virus. In any case, there is very likely still a core group of users who are prepared to buy illegally traded wildlife, despite the impact of Covid-19.

*Trafficking disrupted?*

Apart from changing consumer attitudes, the pandemic and associated restrictions on movement also disrupted the logistics of wildlife trafficking (although the extent and the duration of such disruption were not uniform). Since commercial airlines have historically been an important means of trafficking wildlife products, the sudden reduction in flights had an immediate impact on the ability of criminal networks to move some, but not all, of their product. It also prevented those active in hunting and buying these sorts of desirables from getting on flights, or made it impossible for buyers to catch a flight to check the authenticity of the supplier (such buyers now had to rely on photo and video evidence from sellers).

There was some evidence to suggest that lockdowns and border closures also had a significant impact on the movement of goods in both Asia and Africa. The tiger trade, for example, was affected by land border closures between Laos and Vietnam, and traders found it more difficult to transport tigers by road from Laos farms to customers in Vietnam. The higher presence of security forces around national parks in southern Africa in the initial days of the pandemic also seems to have reduced the 'orders' filtering through to the front end of the supply chain.[17] It is worth noting here that while we often explain the core reason why criminals desist from activity as attributable to state actions, in this case the criminals themselves may have been concerned about catching the virus—in other words, the ending of poaching and buying may been self-directed.

One of the best-documented disruptions to a wildlife market in the wake of the pandemic concerned the most preyed-upon mammal: the rhino. In South Africa's Kruger National Park, rhino poaching decreased by 50% in the first six months of 2020 (see Figure 2). The numbers of poached rhinos had been declining since 2015—as a result of government actions and also the decline in the overall numbers of rhinos themselves—but a particularly sharp decline can be seen in the first two quarters of 2020. In April, for the first time in a decade, there were no reports of rhino being killed in the intensive protection zone put in place in the south of the park.[18] This was something to be celebrated in an avalanche of otherwise bad news. The South African authorities attributed the decline to the immediate disruption in the supply chain caused by travel restrictions. This included not only the decline in international air travel, but also new regulations preventing movement within South Africa itself.

But the rhino's reprieve appears to have been temporary, and poaching went on the rise as lockdown regulations were eased.[19] The evidence suggests that demand for rhino horn continued, or at least that traffickers fully expected they would be able to sell their product. There also appeared to be a displacement effect in the Kruger National Park, which witnessed an increase in elephant poaching. (Elephants are found across the park and are therefore an easier target than rhinos, which are clustered in the intensive protection zone.) While it may be too early to determine whether this activity was aimed at supplying well-established trafficking lines or just meeting immediate needs, it reinforced a growing unease that traffickers

Figure 2: Number of rhinos poached by quarter in South Africa, 2018–2020. (Source: https://www.environment.gov.za/mediarelease/rhinopoaching decreases)

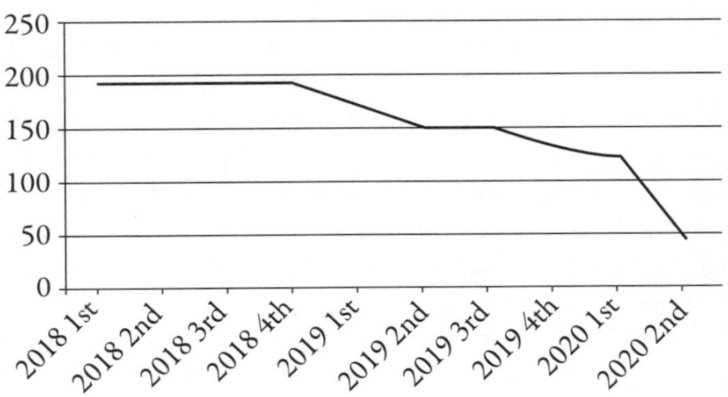

were reorganising themselves in the wake of the pandemic, readying for an upswing in their business.

And while some supply lines were disrupted, others seemed to be functioning as well as ever, facilitated by the fact that international courier services—key channels for getting trafficked wildlife, both dead and alive, to buyers around the world—continued to operate, as did sea cargo. In June, thousands of illegally smuggled songbirds were seized at an airport in Indonesia. In April and May, 26 tonnes of shark fins from Ecuador were found in two shipping containers in Hong Kong, a record haul for the city.[20] (The seizure was more than double the 12 tonnes of shark fins found in Hong Kong in all of 2019.) A month later, customs authorities in Hong Kong seized the biggest haul ever recorded of totoaba fish bladders, the species being found only off the coast of Mexico. 'The 160 kilograms of fish bladders, taken from an estimated 270 totoaba, were found after being airmailed from Los Angeles. This find was singlehandedly more than the total of all fish bladders found in Hong Kong since 2002, according to the city's customs and excise department,' reported InSight Crime.[21]

While such record-breaking seizures could be the result of greater vigilance by the Hong Kong authorities, they are nevertheless strong evidence that, for some traffickers, business continued as usual through the pandemic—and may even have increased. As the seizure of totoaba fish bladders indicated, observers saw no reduction in illegal trafficking of wildlife from Latin American nations to China during the pandemic.[22]

On 10 May, Mexican authorities found a shipment of more than 15,000 freshwater turtles at the capital's airport. There were four different species of turtles in the haul, all destined for China.[23] In the southern state of Oaxaca, observers reported an increase in the theft of wild turtles soon after the pandemic hit, a combination of a thriving turtle population owing to reduced human activity in the area after lockdown and poor vigilance by law enforcement (although that is always the case).

Even in cases where government vigilance was normally high, the pressures of the pandemic on state resources often led to gaps that criminals were quick to exploit. Reports from Kenya, the home of rich wildlife resources, suggest that backlogs on the road borders and short staffing of border posts during the pandemic resulted in much lower levels of surveillance, facilitating the movement of illegal wildlife. 'They concentrate only on flagging out illegal cross-border goods such as cigarettes, alcohol and clothes and not wildlife commodities,' a prominent conservation activist based in Kenya told us. In his opinion, wildlife flows continued, and may have risen.[24]

Criminals also showed remarkable adaptability in exploiting logistic loopholes during the pandemic, as evidenced by the case of South African abalone—a protected marine snail prized in Asia as a delicacy. We conducted detailed local interviews with the gang bosses involved on South Africa's west coast to assess the impact the pandemic had had on the trade. Orders and supply of abalone (known locally as perlemoen) came to a halt as the pandemic gained pace. One of the challenges for local gangs was that movement was severely restricted by the government at the height of the lockdown. However, as food deliveries were allowed, and with Chinese orders picking up again, gangs used fruit trucks to transport the perlemoen to ports, where they have established relationships with port officials, and so could get the produce onto ships bound for Asia. More recently, in July and August, interviews with senior figures in the local criminal economy reported that business was roaring again, 'with requests coming from China for product'.[25]

Interestingly, community members in the areas where gangs are active in smuggling reported that there was no slowdown at all during the lockdown, and that locals continued to dive on request in order to harvest perlemoen. Gangs were still eager to buy abalone at the height of the lockdown, presumably so that it could be dried, stockpiled and then dispatched.[26]

The evidence for a clear disruption to overall patterns of wildlife trafficking remains patchy. There was clearly some disruption and a decline in transcontinental movement of wildlife commodities, but also a possible increase in the movement of contraband across immediate land borders and overseas. As with other criminal sectors, where demand for illegal wildlife persisted, criminals found a way to meet it.

### *Economic need could boost wildlife crime*

Coastal communities on South Africa's west coast are deeply embedded in the local criminal economy around abalone—something that is true of many local ecosystems of poaching. This interconnectedness between crime and community may have crucial implications in a period of sustained economic crisis. As legal economic opportunities dry up, illegal booming trades may become more attractive to locals (and non-locals too).

This may already be the case in the state of Baja California, Mexico, where impoverished fishermen hunt the totoaba fish for their bladders, highly prized (as we have seen) by buyers in China. The trade is popular because of a lack of other well-paid economic opportunities in that part of the country—a situation that would only have been exacerbated by the pandemic (perhaps this in part accounts for the record seizures in Hong Kong mentioned above). That would also go part of the way to explaining the huge seizure of turtles a few months into lockdown in Mexico: turtle hunters come from extremely poor communities and are utterly reliant on the illegal trade to feed their families.

The pandemic will most likely strengthen the position of organised crime actors operating in these areas and beyond. As the lack of legal opportunities for work becomes dire, poaching networks at the front end of the trade will probably be boosted by people desperate to acquire the means to sustain themselves.[27] In some cases, a general lack of human activity could also contribute to local species emerging more than usual, such as the turtles in Oaxaca, Mexico, placing even greater temptation in front of hunters who use those populations to survive.

On top of the poaching of high-value species, wildlife parks could also face an upsurge in bushmeat poaching as poverty levels deepen and the economic crisis worsens. Indeed, this already appears to be happening. The Kenya Wildlife Service informed us that they had seized

2.8 tonnes of bushmeat between January and April 2020, a significant increase on the 1.8 tonnes they seized in the same period in 2019. In Zambia, wildlife officials found 19,232 snares in national parks between January and June 2020, having found 6,513 over the same time period in the previous year. While Zambian authorities indicated that the bushmeat was intended for local consumption, they also uncovered significant numbers of sophisticated transnational networks involving trade in bushmeat, with links to Angola and the Democratic Republic of Congo in particular.[28]

Illegal deforestation is another indicator of the extent to which communities are being pulled into environmentally damaging activities, such as chopping down trees and selling timber, in order to survive. Since the start of the pandemic, 'forest loss alerts' have increased by close to 80% compared with an average of the two years (2017–2019) before the pandemic. The largest increases in forest exploitation appear to occur in Asia. In Nepal, for example, data from 11 protected areas collected by the local authorities showed that the extraction of forest resources had grown by over 220% in the first month of the lockdown compared with the previous month. Strikingly, more environmental crimes were recorded by the authorities in that month than in the preceding 11 months combined. With law enforcement movement curtailed or diverted to other activities during the pandemic, in more isolated areas local communities have few disincentives—and very powerful incentives—to engage in illegal logging.[29]

A key question is whether localised community-driven deforestation will be drawn into wider and more organised movements of illegally sourced timber. In Latin America, a significant amount of illegal logging is carried out by networks managed by timber mafias, who depend on local muscle power (that is, residents) as well as their own ranks to cut down and process wood illegally. In Mexico, there is also an overlap in some parts of the country between drug trafficking and illegal logging, and residents—more often than not from the low socio-economic strata of society—can get caught between brutally violent organised crime groups and a lack of other economic opportunities.[30] As life become increasingly desperate for residents, for example, in the state of Chihuahua, who are surrounded by abundant pine forests, alternatives like illegal logging become more attractive and a means for them to feed their families, especially when there already exists an entire criminal ecosystem into which they can easily be absorbed. Illegal logging groups in Chihuahua have a production chain that extends from the cutting down of trees and transportation through to sawmills that are paid (often under coercion) to process illegally logged wood and then filter it into the legal system, so that its illegal origin becomes undetectable.[31]

Such deforestation will obviously have broader consequences. As well as reducing the habitat of many protected species, any destruction of global forests will have huge consequences for climate change, as such forests are absorbers of carbon dioxide. While many have claimed the lockdown period will have been environmentally beneficial—for example, by reducing the amount of carbon dioxide produced by air travel—a major academic study published in the journal *Nature Ecology and Evolution* concluded that 'the net conservation impacts of Covid-19 will be strongly negative'.[32]

The marine environment has also been heavily affected during the pandemic, in part owing to a decline in law enforcement activities and patrols. There have been multiple accounts of illegal, unreported and unregulated (or 'IUU') fishing across the world. In Argentina, Indonesia, Brazil and the Philippines, for example, there have been reports of heightened illegal fishing activity by foreign vessels as government efforts shifted to pandemic control.[33] Satellite data from the Philippines indicate a surge in illegal fishing activities in coastal waters, with reports of commercial fishing vessels entering prohibited coastal waters almost doubling (from 3,602 cases in February 2020 to 5,950 in March, when the lockdown was implemented).[34] In one of the most dramatic reported cases, a huge fishing fleet of mostly Chinese-flagged vessels was located on the edge of the protected zone around the Galapagos marine reserve. While the Chinese fleet has visited several times before, the size of the fleet and the timing of its arrival suggest an assumption that the guard of the local naval vessels tasked with protecting the reserve would be down.

Law enforcement apart, many African and Asian countries which host wildlife reserves are likely to shift their focus because of pandemic pressures. Conservation and wildlife budgets may be slashed or reprioritised. Generally, environment and wildlife departments are not influential politically and get short shrift from governments at the best of times. The high-end hunting and tourism industries that provide vital income for conservation (and, in South Africa, for private game farms) had all but collapsed by late 2020 as restrictions on who could come into the country continued to apply. Economic survival and social issues may well take precedence over wildlife trafficking issues, as they usually do.[35]

*The spectre of the next pandemic*

Before the pandemic, the illegal wildlife trade had not been a global policy priority. Despite rhetoric about protecting the world's natural heritage, the resources that states dedicated to battling the illegal wildlife trade were paltry compared with those pledged in the fight against drug trafficking.[36]

But the status of the illegal wildlife trade changed almost overnight in January 2020. Given the possible connection between wet markets where trafficked wildlife was sold and the coronavirus outbreak, there was hope that 2020 might be decisive in ending the trade. Indeed, both government actions and general public opinion appear to have been galvanised by the pandemic, creating a new front in the push against wildlife trafficking. Even deforestation appeared on the agenda, in view of the fact that it displaces wildlife and introduces other animals into new areas, therefore increasing the chances of a virulent virus, bacterium or fungus jumping to humans.[37]

This new focus on the (human) public health dimension of the wildlife trade was exemplified in the discussion around CITES (the Convention on International

Trade in Endangered Species of Wild Fauna and Flora)—the only global legal instrument (entered into force in 1975) dedicated entirely to regulating the illegal wildlife trade. The former head of CITES, John Scanlon, said that while CITES had been 'quite effective' in avoiding the over-exploitation of listed species, 'the same cannot be said when the Convention is viewed through the lens of public health'.[38] That the two were now being discussed in the same breath potentially marked a breakthrough in how global governance would respond to wildlife issues in the future. There was hope that while governments might act not out of respect for wildlife, they would do so for human health concerns.

However, while the possible cause of the virus led to a shift in consumer attitudes and habits, markets for illegally trafficked wildlife remained resilient. A review of the available data for rhino and abalone, for example, shows there were jolts to supply and demand, but in both cases the volume of the rhino horn and abalone being sourced and transported is once again ticking up. In the case of shark fin and totoaba fish bladders, record seizures were made during the pandemic itself, either a result of increased surveillance or an indication of a booming trade. The pandemic also broadened the already established use of the internet as a platform for the sale of wildlife commodities.

One thing therefore is already certain: Covid will not mean the end of the illegal wildlife trade—even if the pangolin is eventually identified as the likely source of transmission of the virus. Both the residual power of the criminal networks involved and the resilience of a small but important group of consumers guarantee that. On a broader policy scale, wildlife crime remains a sideshow in the larger fight against organised crime: during the pandemic, the idea of adding a new protocol on wildlife trade to the UN Convention Against Transnational Organized Crime (which had been floated before but had found little support) was raised again, but it gained little traction. Temporary disruption seems the most likely conclusion in respect of most illicit wildlife markets, including that of the rhino.

For global governance of the trade, the pandemic may be a critical opportunity that has already been missed. Despite all the early enthusiasm about tackling the problem, economic considerations have now leapt to the front of the policy queue and governments are unlikely to prioritise money for wildlife over voters. But this decision, while understandable in the short term, may have disastrous long-term consequences. As many scientists have suggested, if the wildlife trade is not curtailed, this may not be the last pandemic—or the most serious.

# 8

# IT'S VIRTUAL

'It's not real sex, because no one touches. It's not real crime, because no one gets hurt.' This is what the families of the children used for online sexual exploitation tell us, tell the police, tell even themselves to justify why they can ask their children—sometimes younger than five years old—to strip, touch themselves, mouth sex toys, and talk dirty to unblinking cameras in the backrooms of their houses.[1]

Before the pandemic began, it was estimated that there were 750,000 individuals actively looking to connect with children for sexual purposes at any moment in time. The Philippines is the primary source of exploitative sexual material containing children, and in particular the streaming of live sex acts on demand.[2] A remote client, usually male and based in Europe, directs a child over webcam to act out his perverted desires, in a criminal industry that has become known as 'webcam child sex tourism'.[3] It supplemented the pre-existing child sex tourism for those unable to travel to the exotic

Asian localities where young girls and boys could be easily procured for patrons paying in dollars. A 2015 study found that in 75% of cases, it was a family member, guardian or close family friend who facilitated children's online abuse, because they needed the money and because they saw online offences as less harmful than the physical alternative.[4]

Livestreaming is a low-cost and low-risk alternative for paedophiles as well. It is harder for law enforcement and internet service providers to detect abuses during livestreams, and children can be revictimised when the recorded videos and photos are shared in private groups online. When Covid-19 struck, it provided an outlet for those no longer able to travel. And the boredom and isolation of lockdown gave too much opportunity for those who previously had maybe only thought of child sexual abuse, to act upon their latent desires.

Prior to the pandemic, there were 46 million unique images or videos of child sex abuse material (CSAM) in Europol's repository, and 80% of internet traffic on the dark web was generated by visits to websites that offer CSAM, with 2.88 million accounts registered globally to the ten most harmful CSAM sites.[5] During lockdown, the CSAM community grew and the rate of material produced and in circulation increased dramatically.[6] A 200% spike in posts on known child sex abuse forums was recorded between February and March. At the same time, there was a drop of almost 90% in the amount of CSAM material being removed from the internet as investigators and watchdogs struggled to keep up after their own staff numbers and capacity were reduced by lockdowns.[7] The Internet Watch Foundation reported almost nine million blocked attempts to access child pornography during just one month of coronavirus lockdown in the United Kingdom alone, from just three internet service providers.[8]

Neither were these child sex predators content with just recirculating the material already available—they took advantage of the growing population of children online during lockdown to approach new targets. Before the pandemic, there were more than 800 million children actively using social media. That number only grew during lockdown as more children were given access to social media, and those already there spent longer online trying to replicate the connections no longer available physically, and to share their anxieties about the situation.[9] Others began playing online games which allow players to connect together and communicate. Both these channels have been used by perpetrators to make casual contact with children online, gain their trust, and then progressively coax or coerce kids into sharing explicit images or videos of themselves.

In parallel, surveillance over children's behaviour was reduced. Not only were busy parents less able to monitor what their children were doing as they themselves tried to grapple with the implications of working from home, losing their jobs, or generally just being preoccupied with other concerns for the interminable hours of lockdown, but the mechanisms to remove dangerous material or to police chat forums were also cut back. Facebook, for example, placed their entire team of 15,000 content moderators on furlough and delegated the responsibility for identifying and removing illegal and exploitative content to algorithms.[10]

In the months of lockdown, the FBI, INTERPOL and Europol all reported an increase in the recruiting and grooming of victims online.[11] The scale of the numbers at play can sometimes seem so overwhelming—the millions of pictures available, the hundreds of thousands of sexual predators stalking children online every second—that it numbs us to the real atrocity of the crime. It can be hard to remember that each photo is a moment of lived agony for a real child in a nightmare situation. And while criminal groups often prey on the most vulnerable children in the system—migrants, the poor, kids who are living in institutional homes or in detention[12]—as the pandemic and its aftermath extend in time, more and more children will find themselves falling into the category of vulnerable.

### *Open season*

While perhaps the gravest and most troubling, child sexual exploitation was by no means the only online vulnerability and victimisation that occurred and increased as a result of Covid-19. Arguably, cybercrime was the criminal market that profited the most from the pandemic, and organised crime networks of all kinds saw a booming opportunity for their illicit operations. It was a veritable open season for organised crime online.

Cybercrime typically divides into two schools, 'cyber-dependent' crime, and 'cyber-enabled' crime. Cyber-dependent crimes are those which can only be committed through the use of a computer and in which the computer is typically the object of the crime, whereas cyber-enabled crimes are those whose efficacy, scale or reach is enhanced by the use of computers, the internet or other communication technology, as with child pornography.[13] One study in 2018 found that cybercrime costs the world roughly US$600 billion globally—equivalent to 0.8% of global GDP. It affects nearly two-thirds of people who use online services, and it is rapidly increasing thanks to new technology and the growth of cybercrime service centres that help to proliferate the number of people able to perpetrate thefts and scams.[14]

And so, when the pandemic began, even before lockdowns started, this army of fraudsters went straight to work. Internet service providers and online security firms recorded an eye-watering 30,000% increase in coronavirus-themed attacks from January to March 2020, including phishing, malicious websites, and mal-

Figure 3: Domain names registered, January–April 2020. (Source: https://globalinitiative.net/cybercrime-covid-19/)

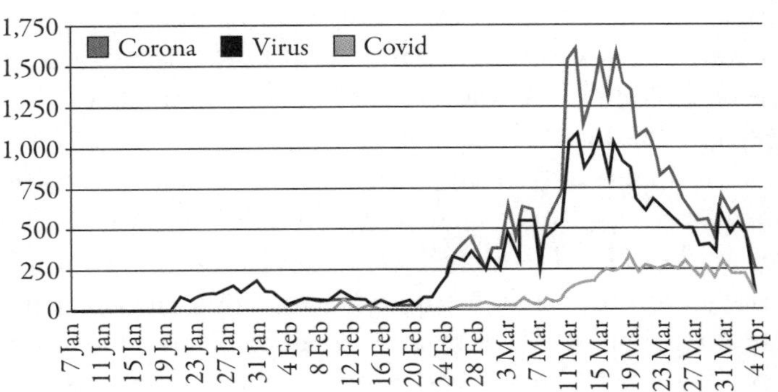

ware targeting remote users.[15] In April, Microsoft reported blocking 60,000 coronavirus-themed malicious email attachments and URLs per day.[16] Most of these attempts capitalised on the fear, anxiety and desperate desire for information that people were feeling as the pandemic spread.

Beginning in February, as the WHO warnings about the scale of the pandemic were escalating, there was an immediate and massive increase in the number of cybercriminals registering domain names containing keywords such as 'coronavirus' or 'Covid'—the majority of these classified by the industry as suspicious or potentially malicious sites (see Figure 3).[17] These fraudulent websites underpin a wide variety of pernicious activities, including phishing sites, which target people's personal information, which can then be sold online or used for a variety of other crimes; and straight-up frauds, where goods are promised and paid for but never delivered. The websites are amplified very effectively on social media sites—one civil society watchdog found that health misinformation websites were viewed 460 million times on Facebook in April 2020 alone, and that misinformation sites were receiving almost four times as many views as legitimate sources like government health services or the WHO.[18]

Criminal groups found other means to deliver ransomware and sophisticated bots into people's computers and networks. The Trickbot Trojan campaign, for example, used fake emails that appeared to come from the US Department of Labor, sharing guidelines on how to apply for the family and medical leave policy during

Covid-19. If the recipient clicked, a Trojan software was activated that allowed attackers to gain complete control of the computer, resulting in bank account takeovers, high-value wire fraud and ransomware attacks.[19] In Costa Rica, a ransomware app called CovidLock became popular in March, purportedly claiming to prevent contagion by providing interactive maps of the virus's spread. Instead, it hijacked victims' devices and demanded a ransom in Bitcoin.[20] Phishing scams in Puerto Rico, Mexico and Guatemala used emails promising government stimulus money or free Covid-19 tests in order to solicit personal information and introduce malware. Some criminal networks disguised malware within apps to check body temperature or monitor other health functions.[21] A massive 98% of all 'Internet of Things' devices—the internet-connected devices used in the home and in workplaces—are unencrypted, making it possible for those who can secure access to listen, observe and record people going about their daily business, giving them opportunities to collect personal or confidential information.[22] With more people working from home, the vulnerability presented by this lax security approach created new criminal opportunities. People who used streaming sites to access pirated movies (a practice that doubled during the virus) also found themselves victims of cybercrime delivered alongside their entertainment. Ironically, Microsoft found the movie *Contagion* was particularly targeted, coming laced with a malware code.[23]

Contact-tracing apps provided a raft of other vulnerabilities. More than fifty countries employ digital applications to support contact-tracing efforts to clamp down quickly on viral transmission. These apps use the GPS functions of mobile phones to alert users when they have been in close proximity to someone who has tested positive for Covid-19. The health emergency and the urgency to develop and disseminate these apps meant that privacy and data security was often pushed aside. Approximately 15% of the apps in circulation did not have a privacy policy in place, meaning there was no indication of how personal data would be stored, or who owned it.[24] Similarly, the offline equivalent in some countries that required restaurants, hotels and airlines to record data for customers and visitors in case they were needed for contact tracing also increased the volume of data held insecurely and potentially available for access either through cybercrime or by fraudulent calls from those claiming to be responsible for identifying and tracing outbreaks.[25]

The result of all these attacks was a series of massive data breaches. In April, 7.4 billion personal information records of current and former subscribers of *Le Figaro*, a leading newspaper in France, were exposed.[26] Elsewhere, the details of 11 million credit cards linked to the state bank of Costa Rica were stolen,[27] half-a-million Zoom accounts were compromised,[28] and 115 million Pakistani phone subscriber records were made available for sale on the dark web for US$2.1 million in bitcoins in April.[29] Numerous smaller breaches also took place, creating a treasure trove of personal data for cybercriminals to exploit, just as the army of criminals was itself also growing.

As the last economic downturn showed, when the economy is bad, more people turn to online crime.[30]

Cybercrime is a surprisingly and disturbingly easy business to break into, thanks to the 'cybercrime as a service' ecosystem that has developed. Identification lists are available online quite cheaply, as are malware and ransomware codes, with video tutorials and toolkits that teach you how to use them. Security experts have documented how cybercrime service providers offer customer support helplines and ancillary services to disguise provenance and launder bitcoins.[31] With such low barriers to entry, no direct contact with the victims—no violence, no bloodshed—and often many micro-transactions characterising the entry-level cybercrimes, it is an industry that for many seems more virtual than a real criminal enterprise. But cybercrime's impacts are very real.

*The second wave*

In an interesting flash of ethical behaviour, in the early days when Covid-19 felt like a shared global scourge, ransomware gangs demonstrated a brief flash of moral behaviour. In March, some ransomware groups pledged not to target health and medical organisations during the pandemic, and even offered a free decryptor to any hospital, orphanage, nursing home or charitable foundation that was attacked during the pandemic.[32] Unsurprisingly, relying on the moral compass of cybercriminals was quickly proven to be a short-lived and far from foolproof defence.

By the end of April 2020, every country in the world had seen at least one major coronavirus-themed cyberattack.[33] As the weeks went by, the nature of the crimes began to evolve. In the early days of the pandemic, it was mainly small scams aimed at soft targets—individuals and small businesses—but the focus then shifted to major corporations, governments and critical infrastructure, including health infrastructure.[34] This second wave was a strategic scale-up—instead of trying to access one individual's personal data, the goal was to get behind corporate firewalls to access whole corporate databanks, to infiltrate supply chains or to hit strategic assets in order to steal corporate secrets with a value on the black market, or to hold a corporation hostage for larger ransoms. In some cases, either state or corporate espionage was considered.

The WHO reported that it experienced a five-fold increase in the number of cyberattacks since the outbreak of the coronavirus: email addresses and passwords of thousands of staff working directly on the virus response were leaked online.[35] A known Iranian criminal group, Charming Kitten, was believed to be behind the attacks.[36] Microsoft's detection team also reported an increase in the volume of ransomware impacting on health-care and other critical services.[37] On the night of 12 March 2020, Brno University Hospital in the Czech Republic was hit by a ransomware attack which held patient files hostage. In April, there were failed cyberattacks against hospital systems in France,[38] and a successful one at a medical centre in Colorado.[39] In early May, a contractor building two emergency facilities to treat coronavirus patients in the UK was targeted,[40] and Fresnius, Europe's largest private hospital operator, was reported to have been hit by ransomware, forcing it to limit its services.[41] In September, a critically ill German woman died after a ransomware attack against a German hospital led to her being transferred to another facility some 32 km away, resulting in a fatal delay of treatment—the first known death caused by ransomware.[42] Later that month, a large American hospital chain with more than 400 locations fell prey to a similar ransomware attack.[43]

As the race for a vaccine for Covid-19 began to heat up, there was a clear spike in cyberattacks against medical research institutes and biopharmaceutical companies, in Canada, the UK, Japan, Korea and elsewhere.[44] As Figure 4 shows, the education sector was one of the most heavily targeted for cybercrime activity, and in some cases there appeared to be a clear link between the

Figure 4: Reported enterprise malware encounters in April 2020 (Source: www.microsoft.com/en-us/wdsi/threats)

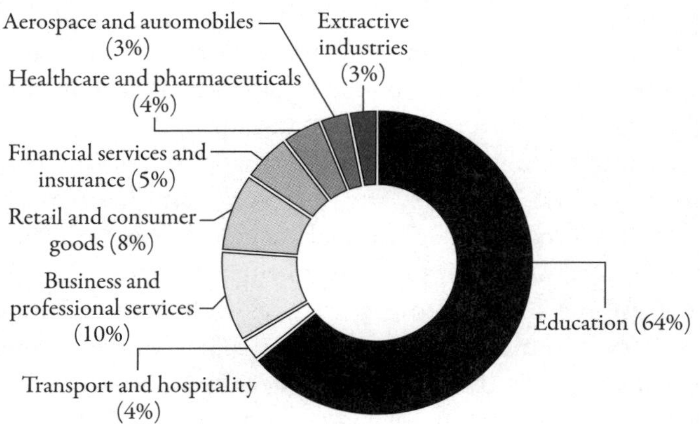

research, research funding and the timing of the attack. York University in Toronto was attacked in May 2020, just after the announcement of a major funding award for Covid-19 research at the institute.[45] As soon as Germany announced the first successful vaccine, there was a cyber-attack on the European Medicines Agency, Europe's medicines regulator,[46] as well as vaccine distribution operations.[47]

Cybercrime and cyber-enabled crimes offer criminal groups of all sizes and scales the possibility of replacing income lost from their traditional criminal enterprises, which have been constrained by the virus control conditions. A recent article also suggested that this might extend as far as cash-strapped states under sanctions, whose national economies rely on transnational crime and illicit financial flows to underpin their economies and evade controls. North Korea and Iran, both illicit economy hubs and active agents in the global criminal economy, are reportedly looking for solutions to alleviate economic hardship, and may therefore ramp up their cybercrime activity as an alternative source of income.[48]

The UK and the US issued a joint warning that state-sponsored cyber-espionage was targeting the health sector, though they did not specify suspected countries.[49] Shortly after, however, the US government formally accused China of trying to steal vaccine research through 'cyber actors'.[50] The Chinese in turn reported that the government of Wuhan province, as well as the Chinese ministry for emergency management, had been targeted by cyberattacks that had originated in Vietnam.[51] This perception led to some bizarre conspiracy theories developing online, including most notably the claim that the virus was a form of Chinese biowarfare spread by 5G towers.[52] This resulted in people in the Netherlands physically attacking and defacing 5G towers.[53] In the UK, 77 mobile phone towers were burned.[54]

Attacks also targeted global supply chains by going after the leading logistics and transport companies. The Swiss-owned Mediterranean Shipping Company experienced a network outage in April, forcing it to shut down its servers at HQ, after a suspected malware attack.[55] The Australian logistics company Toll Group, which is a crucial distributor of basic and consumer goods across the Asia–Pacific region with operations in fifty countries, experienced a complete systems shutdown in May 2020 after being infected by ransomware.[56]

*Stimulus payments targeted*

The urge to inject liquidity back into the economy in the face of unprecedented levels of layoffs made governments susceptible to fraud and predation. Millions of people filing for benefits, huge amounts of money being distributed via accelerated payments, and limited due diligence all created the perfect conditions for cybercriminals to thrive. In May, the US Secret Service announced that hundreds of millions of dollars had been scammed from the US government's emergency unemployment stimulus payments.[57] They attributed it to 'a well-organised Nigerian fraud ring' known by security analysts as 'Scattered Canary'.[58] The group apparently used existing lists of personal identification information and submitted unemployment applications on behalf of workers who were in fact still gainfully employed, and siphoned off their US$600 unemployment benefits.[59]

As with other markets, the Scattered Canary scam allowed an agile criminal group a strategic opportunity to exploit existing weaknesses in data protection and oversight capacity. Identity theft and business enterprise crime (BEC) have been on the rise for the past decade. Pulling off the Scattered Canary unemployment insurance fraud would have required only the sort of personal information—names, social security numbers, birth dates and addresses—that is readily available for sale on the dark web, having been mined through massive data breaches such as the 2017 hack of credit agency Equifax, which revealed the data of more than 145 million individuals,[60] as well as the new breaches that were reported during the early days of the pandemic.

The German government, which prioritised ensuring that economic assistance would swiftly reach the accounts of those who needed it over bureaucratic safeguards, found itself quickly exploited by scammers. The states of Hamburg, Berlin, Saxony, Bremen and North Rhine–Westphalia (NRW) all reported cases of fraud with their state aid websites. Here the fraudsters created clones of the states' official websites in order to intercept prospective applicants, who subsequently entered their personal information into the fake site unwittingly. Having now created registers of the relevant applicants' data through their clone site, the scammers were then able to use that data to apply on the real website, but substituting their own bank details. The scale of lost funds has not been estimated, but the NRW website was closed down completely for more than a week, halting stimulus payments to vulnerable individuals when they needed it the most.[61]

*Cyberspace unsecured*

The legal and enforcement architecture governing the internet has always been weak. Its networked foundation and the cross-jurisdictional nature of online activity have made policing the internet an enormous challenge. In most cases, the perpetrator of a cybercrime resides in one country, the victim in a second, and the profits earned from that criminal behaviour will move swiftly through several banking jurisdictions—or, increasingly, through undetectable cryptocurrencies—before ending up hidden in a tax haven or secrecy jurisdiction where the criminal's fortunes can remain anonymous.

This multi-jurisdictional nature of cybercrime means that national responses cannot be effective singly, and while there have been a number of regional treaties and norms of behaviour adopted, the reality is that achieving the kind of multinational cooperation needed to take down complex criminal operations is the occasional exception rather than the rule.[62] National police agencies struggle to attract or develop the kinds of specialised technology skills required to keep pace with the burgeoning criminal enterprises, which evolve more rapidly than they can be discovered. Owing to limited capacity, the police have also long reported needing to triage in law enforcement action—addressing counterfeit goods or other forms of illicit trade online is typically a far lower priority than the response to terrorism or CSAM.[63]

The Covid-19 pandemic crippled the law enforcement response still further. As the UNODC reported, in many countries the specialist counter-cybercrime law enforcement units were furloughed, fell sick or were diverted into other forms of policing as required by the pandemic. In other countries, whole criminal justice systems were frozen in stasis during lockdown.[64]

For counter-cybercrime law enforcement to be effective, there needs to be the involvement of the major internet platforms. The giants of tech carry enormous weight and financial resources to control the narrative on a range of sensitive topics and to protect the most vulnerable online. As a result of the pandemic, huge pressure has been put on social media platforms and internet service providers to provide better policing of the websites that are registered on their servers or the websites shared on their channels. In March, the most prominent tech companies released a joint statement committing themselves to fighting coronavirus-related fraud and misinformation, but there was little outcome in practical terms,[65] and subsequent efforts by governments to hold them to account led to only very vague assurances.[66] More importantly, key parts of the tech ecosystem remained absent—the domain name registration system most notably,[67] but also the financial centres and 'virtual value sector' that regulate the use of cryptocurrencies and serve as the interface between digital and real money.[68]

Tech leaders were also put under pressure during the pandemic for anti-trust reasons, hauled onto the Congressional carpet to answer the accusation that their outsize monopolies were too big to be allowed to continue.[69] But a more fragmented market does not mean a better-regulated one, and the fractured international consensus shows little promise in achieving the rigorous legal framework and architecture that would provide a safer online space.

Thus, for the most part, the internet appears set to remain a virtual Wild West, without a global governance framework and with far too few tools to regulate behaviour. What exists is often generated and owned by the private sector, either by the increasing number of internet security providers or by the platforms themselves. The complexity of the challenge may prove overwhelming, and the role of internet companies, law enforcement and even national governments is only one part of the complex reality that is regulating online behaviour. Celebrities, prominent public figures and social media influencers have proved a powerful vector in the spread of disinformation online—while they may not produce the content, they supercharge the ability of false rumours to spread. A study by the University of Oxford found that the posts of public figures accounted for 69% of social media engagement around false claims about the coronavirus.[70] Consumers and the general public need to educate themselves more effectively to protect themselves online. Children should be taught the dangers of running around the internet unsupervised, just as they are taught to cross a road safely. And companies, as they muse on the potential post-pandemic work dynamic and institutions, will need to factor cybersecurity into those calculations. If action is not forthcoming, the number of victims of virtual crimes will only grow, and the harm being done will become ever more apparent and real.

9

# THE FISH ROTS FROM THE HEAD

On 11 March 2020, the WHO director general, Dr Tedros Adhanom Ghebreyesus, officially declared the coronavirus a pandemic and urged countries to take action. 'We cannot say this loudly enough, or clearly enough, or often enough,' he said, 'that all countries can still change the course of this pandemic if they detect, test, treat, isolate, trace and mobilize their people in the response.' But, he ominously concluded, 'the challenge for many countries who are now dealing with large clusters or community transmissions is not whether they *can* do the same—it's whether they will.'[1]

Even in those early days, there were adequate grounds for concern about how the global response would shape up. By the time of Dr Tedros's announcement, the world was awash with stories about fake PPE, fake tests and bogus cures, and assailed by a storm of false claims and misinformation surrounding the virus and potential cures, pushed not only by illicit actors, but also at times by the highest levels of governments. In many places such narratives found a receptive audience among those who were all too ready to cast doubt on institutions, objective science, expertise and information. And this provided the perfect opening for criminals.

*The parallel pandemic*

China is the world's leading manufacturer of surgical masks, accounting for more than half of global capacity in 2019, and it quickly ramped up production in response to the pandemic. Between March and May, China exported more than 70.6 billion masks, as well as other PPE, testing kits and medical supplies, to meet the ten-fold explosion of demand for emergency medical equipment.[2] It supplied 83% of global requirements for the four major types of PPE that medical staff need to prevent infections. This market grew worldwide from US$900 million in January 2020 to US$9.2 billion by May.[3] At the height of the first wave of infections, at a time when their own domestic production was lagging, the rest of the world was absolutely dependent on Chinese exports to save lives.

But before the pandemic, Chinese exports had been far less popular. There has been a long-standing global complaint that China is—by a considerable stretch—the largest source of counterfeit and pirated products in the world, in terms of both value and volume. Global estimates suggested that some 67% of counterfeit and pirated goods by value originate in China.[4] Illicit trade, counterfeiting and pirating are hugely lucrative for criminal groups: a 2019 Organisation for

Economic Cooperation and Development (OECD) report estimated the worth of counterfeit and pirated goods at US$509 billion per year, representing up to 3.3% of total world trade.[5]

Of this total, the production of counterfeit medicines—including antibiotics, analgesics, lifestyle drugs like Viagra, and even treatments for serious diseases—is estimated to be worth some US$4.4 billion a year. These too originate mainly in China and in India and are shipped all over the world, with bulk shipments physically concealed in licit trade flows. They are then bought by consumers on dubious websites and sent by hard-to-track small parcel post, or else obtained from rogue pharmacies.[6] In Mexico, the Jalisco New Generation Cartel uses its control of small and medium-sized pharmacies to insert its counterfeit products into the supply chain.[7]

This existing infrastructure was perfectly suited to the pandemic. At this time countries were expediting supplies of essential goods through borders; customs and enforcement capacities were reduced; and people were actively seeking information and medical equipment online—and ordering everything from the internet. An illicit industry that was almost impossible to regulate effectively in normal times[8] became completely impossible during the pandemic.

Particularly culpable for the failure of the global economy to regulate illicit trade has been the proliferation of 'special economic zones': parts of countries, typically ports, that are designated to attract new business, facilitate production and promote trade under special rules—typically financial or tax incentives, infrastructure support, or limited and streamlined regulation and oversight. There are more than 5,400 of such zones distributed across 147 countries in the world.[9] A portion of these are designated free manufacturing zones, which employ millions of workers in secondary and tertiary production. The reduced oversight in these zones facilitates criminality.[10] A recent OECD publication reported that the packaging and labelling of fake drugs often take place within these free manufacturing zones.[11]

While the opaque, long and complex supply chains associated with the pharmaceutical industry provide multiple entry points for illicit interests, it is, typically, lack of consumer awareness, vigilance or purchasing power that creates the real vulnerability of people to counterfeit medicines. Cheap, authentic-looking products appeal to consumers who may not be aware of the dangers of counterfeit medicines. Informing consumers about how to identify the hallmarks of fake products is a huge component of the response that needs to be taken to counterfeit goods and medicines in particular. This is why the disinformation trends that were sent into overdrive by the pandemic are an even more troubling development.

### *Medical misinformation*

Touting miracle cures for deadly afflictions is a governance strategy as old as civilisation itself, because it is very hard for governments to ensure the compliance of their citizens when they are dying in large numbers.[12] There is evidence of rulers, even before the time of Nero, proffering miracle cures to deadly diseases.[13] In this regard, then, contemporary governments continue to echo their ancient forebears.

In Africa, the Tanzanian president, John Magufuli, drew criticism for claiming that inhaling steam could be a potential cure, and Nairobi governor Mike Sonko claimed that alcohol (as a drink, rather than as a sanitising product) could protect the public from the virus.[14] Madagascar's president, Andry Rajoelina, promoted an unproven herbal cure called 'Covid-Organics' and began exports of that drug to other countries in the region.[15] In Belarus, President Alexander Lukashenko called Covid-19 a 'psychosis' that could be treated with vodka, ice hockey and saunas.[16] The Chinese government included a special chapter on traditional Chinese medicine (TCM) in its coronavirus guidelines and released a White Paper in June which claimed that 92% of the country's Covid-19 patients were being treated with TCM in some form.[17] One of the products promoted by the Chinese National Health Commission included injections containing bear bile from the protected moon bear species.

Most potent and most damaging were the efforts of the US president, Donald Trump, and his coterie, who promoted a variety of drug interventions as preventions, therapies and cures. Each was a dog whistle to the counterfeiting community across the globe. In March, for example, Trump began aggressively promoting the anti-malarial drug hydroxychloroquine as a preventive measure and game-changing miracle cure, despite the absence of reliable studies and against the recommendation of his own medical experts.[18] Shortages and overdoses quickly ensued, but so too did counterfeiting. The WHO issued an alert that nine different falsified chloroquine products had been reported in Cameroon, the DRC and Niger.[19] A BBC investigation discovered that bottles of chloroquine—a commonly found anti-malarial that is normally sold for about US$40 for 1,000 tablets—had skyrocketed in price to as high as US$250. The medicine the BBC found on the market was sold with a label of the manufacturer, 'Brown and Burk Pharmaceutical Limited'. However, when consulted, Brown and Burk, a pharmaceutical company registered in the UK and based in Belgium, said, 'We don't manufacture this drug, it's fake.'[20]

The problem is particularly bad in Latin America, where limited access to legitimate health care makes populations particularly susceptible to snake-oil salesmen, whether they come in the form of elected officials or criminal groups (or the two working hand in hand).[21] In Brazil, President Jair Bolsonaro followed Trump's lead in promoting hydroxychloroquine's preventive benefits, despite the fact that he subsequently caught Covid-19 himself.[22] The Bolivian Senate passed a bill legalising the use of chlorine dioxide, a bleach solution used to disinfect swimming pools, as a Covid-19 treatment.[23] The Peruvian government bought ivermectin, a drug used to treat intestinal worms, to fight the pandemic, even though there was no indication whatsoever that it offered any medicinal benefit. Nonetheless, it prompted a surge in demand for the drug that created a new black market for the veterinary equivalent, prompting the US Food and Drug Administration to issue a warning for citizens not to use drugs intended for farm animals.[24]

*Something's rotten in the health sector*

But it is not just in the information space or just in times of emergency that politics, business and crime have collaborated together at the cost of public health systems. In fact, chronic underinvestment in public health is common in most countries in the world. So, too, is the for-profit privatisation of national health assets; and the means by which these public contracts and tenders have been handled have often proved suspicious. This has contributed to an erosion of citizens' trust in the belief that governments act in their interest in the area where it arguably matters most: in ensuring their health and well-being. An article published just before the pandemic in the respected medical journal *The Lancet*, written by a former minister of health in Peru, referred to corruption in global health as 'the open secret'.[25]

For a number of reasons, the health sector is the prize bull of national enterprises, which makes it extremely attractive for exploitation by criminal groups. It is very resource-intensive and expensive. The scale and range of procurement required to cater for the diverse medical needs of a population is vast, extending from massively expensive medical equipment like scanners and specific drugs to mundane food, laundry, cleaning and maintenance needs. It is a sector characterised by acute information asymmetry—the medical and pharmaceutical professions know an enormous amount more than their clients—and the structure of the industry and its supply chains are complex and fragmented, allowing for a multiplicity of actors to be involved. The privatisation of health-care assets often takes place in a system of vested interests, revolving door lobbyists and consultants, and involves an outsize role for private sector venture capital.[26]

In many countries, these features are coupled with low state capacity in relevant institutions and diminished budgets. In such cases, corruption and impunity manifest from top to bottom: while elites rob the system at the point of procurement, front-line workers extract their tributes directly from those seeking services. Surveys by Transparency International and other civil society groups have shown how widespread the practice is of paying bribes for health care; in some places, up to 80% of respondents report making additional informal payments for health services.[27]

Globally, it is estimated that US$500 billion of health-care spending is lost to corruption every year.[28] A study published in the *Journal of the American Medical Association*, for example, estimated that US$98 billion was lost to failures in oversight leading to fraud in Medicare and Medicaid in 2011.[29] While such corruption is systemic, it typically sees a surge around an emergency. During the Ebola epidemic in 2014, for example, systemic corruption in the affected West African countries clearly undermined the global response. An audit report of the response in Sierra Leone suggested that as much as a third of funding could not be properly accounted for.[30]

In 2019, prosecutors in Guatemala opened an investigation into a scheme within the public health ministry involving millions of dollars in contracts to refurbish public hospitals after a 2012 earthquake. The scheme involved not only procurement, but also the creation of 'ghost payrolls', whereby corrupt officials and crime groups collected salaries without ever doing any work.[31]

Several cases in southern Italy over the past twenty years have highlighted the extent to which the Italian mafia has extensively penetrated Italy's hospitals and health sector; income from this source is now estimated to represent up to 5% of mafia financing.[32] In 2015, for example, Operation Black Cross (so named to contrast with the Red Cross) revealed that the Camorra were the de facto managers of a network of hospitals. For more than a decade, the mafia group had been manipulating the tender process for public contracts, inflating contracts for everything from vending machines and medical procurement, to elevator construction in order to maximise the profit margins, and were using their control over admissions and access to hospital beds to placate or punish local populations who resisted their control.[33]

As well as making billions of euros in profits from capturing public health contracts, the Italian mafia also installs clan members into key positions in government and local authorities in order to ensure their continued control. They expand their infiltration in every direction—not only geographically, but also along the industry value chain, using threats of violence and price gouging to establish monopolies on everything from elderly care homes to medical waste and ambulance services—all at the expense of the Italian taxpayer. They have even captured funeral homes, so that as the pandemic fatalities spiralled, the mafia were well placed to profit. One investigation reported:

> The men from the funeral company somehow knew which patients had passed away even before their own families did. Through intimidation they had gained access to the hospital's central medical records, allowing them to screen for those sickest and most likely to die. If relatives considered picking a different funeral company to take away their loved one, then the men would intimidate their relations into changing their mind.[34]

The problem was so widespread and acute that it became a point of contention in the EU negotiations around the coronavirus response and the distribution of aid. A German journalist wrote an open letter to the German chancellor, Angela Merkel, to resist approving the so-called corona bonds from the EU, because Germans feared that giving money to Italy was equivalent to feeding the mafia directly.[35]

### *Between the buttocks*

Political classes were also quick to capitalise on the urgency that the pandemic posed to suddenly liberate and allocate billions or even trillions in new funding. The speed at which contracts needed to be put out to tender in order to meet extraordinary needs meant that many countries suspended their usual rules of funding accountability and public procurement—in many cases, with terrible results.

With great fanfare, in March 2020 the Indian Prime Minister, Narendra Modi, announced the establishment of the Prime Minister's Citizen Assistance and Relief in Emergency Situations Fund—or the 'PM Cares Fund' for short. The irony is that a day after the announcement, Modi appealed to all Indians to donate their money to support his caring. The fund received more than 100 billion rupees (US$1 billion) in contributions from businesses, celebrities and ordinary individuals, all keen to strengthen the country's fight against Covid. However, while money donated to the PM Cares Fund has been celebrated and publicised by the Fund and its donors alike, there has been far less information about the money that has gone out. No information has been shared on the government-hosted website for the Fund on how it was set up, how it will be managed, how much in total has been received and how it will be spent. The prime minister's office has been tight-lipped and reticent in providing any clarification, when questioned by journalists or through right-to-information petitions, on how his caring with other people's money was proceeding. In fact, the reply offered by his office was that the PM Cares Fund is not actually a public authority, since it includes no government financing (notwithstanding the mandatory 'donation' of 10 million rupees from the budgets of each ruling party member of parliament) and is thus not accountable to public oversight or government auditors. A spokesman for the ruling party openly asked, 'What is this urgent need for public accountability at a time when everyone is busy battling a pandemic?'[36]

President Jair Bolsonaro of Brazil, despite being a coronavirus sceptic of the highest order, nonetheless authorised the government to lift controls over public procurement in order to allow local administrations to respond to the crisis as quickly as possible and purchase medicine and equipment and hire staff.[37] In a nation plagued by corruption, this quickly spiralled into a spending free-for-all with little transparency or control. Investigations into the misappropriation of funds have been opened in all 27 Brazilian states, and the list of egregious cases is long. In Rio, public tenders were rigged, and contracts to buy urgently needed ventilators for hospitals packed with Covid patients were never fulfilled, and the equipment never arrived.[38] In Amazonas state, ventilators were mysteriously ordered, at well over market prices, from a wine retailer.[39] In July, tender fraud led to the arrest of Rio's health secretary, Edmar Santos, and in August, allegations of corruption linked to the misuse of the state's coronavirus budget led to the suspension of Rio de Janeiro's governor, Wilson Witzel. But the rot was widespread. In September, a Brazilian senator from the northern state of Roraima was raided as part of an investigation into the misappropriation of around US$4 million in pandemic funding. The police found much of the money stashed in his house, including some US$5,000 down his trousers, wedged between his buttocks.[40]

Honduras is one of the poorest and most violent countries in the world, and public health access is highly limited, with less than one hospital bed available per thousand people. In an effort to increase capacity and respond to the escalating Covid crisis, the government sought to build a number of field hospitals. But the award, worth US$47 million, was made to an unknown company, Elmed Medical Systems, found on the internet and registered to a UPS store in a mall in Florida, without a contract ever being signed. A media investigation accessing confidential documents showed that Elmed was run by a middleman, Axel G. Lopez, a self-confessed 'pragmatist' in the use of corruption to ease business transactions. Lopez promptly took a US$16 million facilitation fee upfront, but proved far less effective in filling the order, as he cast frantically around, eventually subcontracting to a Turkish firm. Only four of the five hospitals arrived, after a six-month delay, in poor condition, apparently largely second-hand, lacking ventilators and necessary facilities for intensive care. It later transpired that the questionable middleman had ties to the family of the executive director in charge of procurement.[41]

This scale of corruption was by no means just a southern hemisphere problem. The Organized Crime and Corruption Reporting Project (OCCRP) collected information on 37,000 European Covid-related tenders and contracts, collectively worth more than €20.8 billion (US$24.5 billion) and all issued within a six-month period between February and October 2020. These were contracts to acquire key medical equipment, including ventilators, PPE, medication and testing kits. The OCCRP found that the largest contracts and tenders, ranging from €1 million to €15 billion, were awarded mostly to single companies with no competitive tender.[42]

According to the OCCRP data, the UK's decision to negotiate independently of the rest of Europe made it one of the largest procurers but left it negotiating at a disadvantage, resulting in the UK paying higher per unit costs than other members of the EU bloc. There have been fierce criticisms of the UK's procurement decisions, including accusations of insider dealing, nepotism and pay-for-play favours (where political contributions come in apparent exchange for tenders).[43] As is often the case with weak and potentially corrupt procurement, these awards came with poor results—underperforming contracts, which, in the case of the health sector, cost lives. The UK contracts for tracing systems—both the custom-made application, for which a £108 million contract was awarded to a cherry-picked supplier,[44] and the £12 billion contract for a nationwide contact-tracing capacity—have been riddled with errors, inefficiencies and abuses.[45] Millions of respirators went missing after a £45 million contract signed with a supplier registered in the British Virgin Islands (a tax haven) to supply 3M masks was subcontracted to a South Korean company dubiously known as Win Billion Investment Group. Win BIG took their first 35% payment and then promptly began procrastinating while reeling off a string of excuses that meant the products could never be delivered. This was apparently one of more than 7,700 cases of fraud involving fake 3M-brand PPE.[46]

A number of the EU's Covid-related procurement contracts have benefited people with histories of corruption or ties to, if not outright involvement in, companies operated by criminal groups. In March, Romania ordered

PPE from a company with Turkish connections, whose majority shareholder had links both with the Romanian prime minister and with organised crime, having been arrested for recruiting a criminal gang to threaten a taxi service in a bid to capture control of its route. The order arrived with masks that were substandard and body protection that was marked up at over 100% of cost.[47]

*Rights on the line*

Enshrined within the constitution of the WHO is the declaration that access to health care is a human right. Seen through that lens, corruption that erodes or denies people access to good-quality health care is arguably a denial of fundamental human rights.[48] Accordingly, there is a clear interconnection between the agendas of business, human rights and anti-corruption, especially as numerous studies have shown a strong correlation between the presence of corruption and human rights violations—and that it is typically the poor and the marginalised who suffer the most.[49]

There is also little doubt that, in the name of responding to 'the emergency', human rights have been compromised in multiple ways. The think tank Freedom House's annual index saw 80 countries decline in terms of indicators for quality of democracy and respect for human rights since the pandemic began. It observed that governments have abused power, silenced their critics, weakened institutions of service delivery, and kneecapped systems of accountability and transparency—all under the justification of public health and security.[50]

The suppression or control of independent oversight is key for those seeking to spread misinformation or distract attention from their corrupt practices.[51] Thus, eroding, undermining or outright attacking the free press has become a distinct feature of the pandemic response. The watchdog Reporters Without Borders reported to the UN Human Rights Commission that a violation of media rights had occurred in 90 countries in connection with coverage of the coronavirus.[52] In addition to being actively attacked, journalists were de-funded, furloughed or denied timely access to information. In March, for example, the FBI announced that it would be severely limiting freedom-of-information requests,[53] while the OCCRP investigation noted that the governments of Belgium, the Netherlands and Denmark rejected data requests outright from journalists on their procurement actions.[54]

Access to reliable, timely and quality information is essential to promoting an effective response to the pandemic and preventing consumers from being gulled into buying fake medicines. Having an independent and objective media is also essential to countering misinformation, fighting organised crime, preventing corruption, and holding systems of governance to account.[55] All of the cases, examples and horror stories presented in this chapter have been brought to light by investigative journalists and an active civil society. These are critical functions to be protected, not suspended, during the pandemic, at a time when the amounts of money and the levels of anxiety and fear in respect of the system are at their highest and the potential for abuse is greatest.

But these journalists and civil society face an increasingly normalised system of kleptocracy, which journalist and author Sarah Chayes characterises as a self-dealing network that utilises and co-opts state institutions, political office, the private sector, criminal actors and even civil society in order to enrich its members at the cost of ordinary people. These actors disable the mechanisms intended to prevent their corrupt actions and are progressively 'rewriting the rules of the political and economic game to favour the networks and their ongoing dominance: to turn what ordinary people consider corruption into "business as usual".'[56]

As Dr Tedros suggested as early as March 2020, the narrative of the Covid-19 pandemic would too often be a story of leaders choosing not to take the necessary steps to protect their populations. Such failures of governance, together with the sense that state actors have operated with impunity at a time of crisis, are extremely disenfranchising and erode the overall quality of democracy, public discourse and the rule of law, all of which expands the space for criminal governance. The year 2020 appears to have done massive damage in this regard, handing a bounty of opportunities for the corrupt and the criminal to aggregate money and power, while ordinary people have borne the two-fold brunt of a public health crisis and a critically flawed state response, at the cost of countless lives.

10

# COVID AND PUNISHMENT

Government health systems were clearly at the forefront of the fight against the pandemic as it swept across the world. But the criminal justice system—the police, courts and prisons—was next in line.

As lockdowns were announced and regulations for ensuring social distancing came into effect, the job of implementation fell to the police. That reduced personnel and resources available for specialist law-enforcement functions, not least tackling organised crime. It also put police in the viral firing line—like their counterparts in the health sector, many police officers around the world became infected with the coronavirus.

One of the most directly measurable impacts of both the advance of the virus and the retreat of the police was the closing of police stations. In South Africa, there were regular reports of police stations being closed during the pandemic as staff and officers fell ill; in July 2020 alone, 16 stations were closed over just two days.[1] There were reports of shut or quarantined police facilities in multiple countries, including Austria, Brazil, Colombia, France, Honduras, India, Kenya, Mexico, Namibia, Northern Ireland, Pakistan, Puerto Rico, Russia and Uganda. Many others went unreported.

Senior police officers grumbled to us about how unprepared law enforcement was for the pandemic. While health systems may at least have had some plans in place, police institutions seemed to have precious few. That applied to ordinary front-end policing as well as parts of the security forces focused on offences such as cybercrime, which, as we have seen, grew significantly during the pandemic.

For ordinary policemen and women, there were shortages of masks and other PPE. All over the world, police officers were forced to improvise, often using their own resources. Confusion around what regulations allowed and did not allow—and how these were presented and interpreted by politicians—made day-to-day policing challenging.[2]

### *'We are all getting ill'*

The front-end role of the police in enforcing the lockdowns—which required contact with large numbers of the public—made police officers very vulnerable to being infected with the virus. In most policing jurisdictions, officers work in difficult and cramped conditions—in police stations, locker rooms, police cars and other forms of transport like vans or trucks. Given this close proximity, once a few officers had been infected, the virus spread rapidly. Most operational police were relatively young and could weather the virus well, but there were numerous fatalities involving older police officers who had underlying conditions.

Police agencies in Latin America seemed particularly affected. A senior Brazilian police officer suggested in a seminar that some police agencies in Brazil may have had infection rates of up to 70%.[3] In Peru, the chief of police reported that as a result of high infection rates among personnel, the police had been forced to bring back retired officers to reinforce their flagging numbers, while students at the police school were graduated early in order to assist.[4] The New York Police Department indicated that at the height of the pandemic in the city, around 15% of the force's personnel were sick and unable to serve.[5] In Belgium, badly affected by the virus, 2,368 police officers tested positive for Covid-19 in October 2020 alone (there are an estimated 33,000 police in the country); in the province surrounding the city of Liège, the police union reported that around 50% of officers were not at work.[6]

All of this had important impacts on the operational effectiveness of the police as the pandemic spread. With fewer officers available to respond to calls, many police departments (and individual officers) began filtering what they should respond to—and what they should not. Reports from the Cape Flats in Cape Town said that the police were much less responsive to gang violence, burdened as they were with overseeing Covid regulations, but police officers also said that they did not want to stand among the crowds that always accumulated around the corpses of gang victims.[7] Traffic stops were curtailed in some places, but many crimes still demanded a response. Reports of vandalism and in particular domestic violence increased, putting pressure on limited resources.[8] Domestic violence often required officers to enter people's homes to deal up close with both victims and offenders, who at home were generally maskless, thereby putting officers at risk of infection. Cheekily, in Zimbabwe, police officers demanded a 'risk allowance' from the public at roadblocks—a form of daily bribery adapted for Covid times.[9]

A study of more than 200 local US police departments in Illinois in June 2020 concluded that 'Covid-19 has significantly affected both [their] internal and external operations'. Significantly, an overwhelming proportion of the state's local police agencies (83%) restricted public access to their facilities. A similar proportion of departments reduced their activities related to community policing, in order to reduce contact between the police and members of the public.[10]

Covid-19 also introduced new occupational stressors into already very stressful environments. This included having to implement new policies on social distancing among an often sceptical public, particularly as lockdowns dragged on. One study noted: 'As the agents of new and unpopular restrictions, officers may have experienced additional anxiety and disapproval from the citizenry.'[11] This was particularly the case in countries such as the US, where the application of the restrictions themselves took on a political or racial dimension.

### *Pared-down policing against organised crime*

Little information has emerged on the impact of Covid-19 on specialist investigators working on organised crime cases, but many investigators must also have fallen sick. Investigative capacity was further compromised by the fact that face-to-face interviewing was restricted and specialist police officers were drafted into new roles, particularly that of public order. In some cases, specialist investigations were simply put on ice. The chief of the Argentine police reported that most investigations had been paused or dropped during Covid-19 as a result of the changing role of law enforcement agencies and the requirement to have additional personnel for public order duties.[12] These included investigations into serious and organised crime.

Customs agents at the front end of the effort to interdict illicit goods also faced challenges. More than fifty countries changed their port protocols: most closed minor ports completely and concentrated or redirected what remained of maritime traffic through their major ports, while lockdowns and health protocols reduced the availability of labour to unload ships, perform inspections and control customs. Staff worked shifts to avoid the risk of contamination, and fewer people on the ground meant that a smaller proportion of the containers moving through ports were examined to verify that their contents were indeed what was stated on the waybills.

In some countries, physical inspections by port officials were suspended completely so as to limit movement and contacts. Customs and border control staff working in headquarters and regional offices, who typically file the goods declarations and also carry out the higher-level intelligence analysis of shipping and trade patterns to identify suspicious vessels, all began working from home.[13]

The net result was that the overall effectiveness of policing efforts against organised crime weakened during the pandemic. This makes the seizures that did occur, particularly of drugs, all the more remarkable. Intelligence gathering, seizures and arrests were the results of Herculean efforts by the police agencies involved. But some agencies may also have been keeping their powder dry. With courts either shut down or processing fewer cases during the pandemic, police reckoned that if a big arrest was to be made, in some cases it seemed better to wait things out.

### *Virtual justice*

Court systems were significantly affected by the pandemic, as staff were sent home and physical facilities shut down. South Korea—widely praised for its response to the virus—was one of the first countries to act. At the end of February 2020, the government closed down both parliament and the courts.[14] In March 2020, following the example of South Korea, the Indonesian Supreme Court made the decision to suspend most trials across the nation owing to the Covid-19 pandemic, effectively shutting down the nation's extensive system of justice.[15] There was predictably a murkier side to shuttered courts: in Kenya, some police arrested gang members and extorted money from them for their release, threatening them with indefinite detention if they did not pay. (In normal circumstances gang members can post bail within 24 hours, but with the courts closed, they were in legal limbo.)[16]

Mirroring the response of business, courts systems across the world began to make the sometimes bumpy transition to online operations. By late March, the Indonesian Supreme Court's decision had been reversed and a shift to virtual hearings had begun. Between 23 March and 17 April, around 25,000 criminal cases had been tried online. There were numerous issues to contend with, including patchy video and audio quality and poor internet connections, which hampered the examination of witnesses and defendants.[17]

Despite these hiccups, the shift to online justice took place at unprecedented speed, signalling potentially a wider shift in how justice may be delivered in future (removing, for example, the need to bring suspects to court, which often slows or halts court proceedings in many developing countries). In the UK, the number of cases heard each day with the use of audio and video technology increased from less than 1,000 in the last week of March to more than 3,000 by mid-April. The judiciary and lawyers were reported to be 'largely positive' about the move towards using video and audio channels.[18]

But while it appeared that run-of-the-mill cases could be easily shifted online, there were more challenges with complex cases related to organised crime, in which public interest was higher. The trial hearings for the murder of Slovakian journalist Ján Kuciak and his fiancée by individuals linked to organised crime—a case our own organisation followed closely—was postponed in March 2020 as a result of measures implemented to curb the coronavirus outbreak.[19] Several other cases globally which we were monitoring suffered the same fate, as justice slowed.

In March, the Swiss Federal Criminal Court postponed the long-awaited war crimes trial of former Liberian rebel leader Alieu Kosiah because of the rapid spread of the coronavirus. The judges concluded that the decision taken by the court was appropriate to 'safeguard the health of all the trial participants, including the victims who reside abroad', since Liberian witnesses were being called to testify at the trial. The trial was due to be held in the last weeks of April and was initially postponed to June and July. It was subsequently rescheduled for the end of 2020.[20]

In the trial for the murder of Kuciak in Slovakia, the verdict was delivered in April, convicting the contract killer. A parallel trial, however, which had also been postponed, found a politically connected businessman and his associate not guilty of ordering the killing.[21] Whatever one's views on the outcome, Slovak courts had moved with commendable speed on two cases that had significant public interest.

In other cases involving organised crime, questions of transparency were raised when reporters were restricted from attending trials or prevented from following the proceedings online. The Indonesian courts were criticised for failing to livestream cases which in normal times would be accessible to the general public. A government spokesperson defended the decision by arguing that the anonymity of witnesses, judges and prosecutors was of paramount importance in cases related to 'drug-related crimes, terrorism and graft … that often involve criminal organisations'.[22]

As the legislative branches of governments ground to a halt and attention became, at least for a few months, focused exclusively on reacting to the pandemic, the passing of legislation that promised to have some impact on organised crime and criminal markets was also frozen. That was the case, for example, in Mexico, where the pandemic was one of the factors setting back the enactment of a marijuana legalisation bill.[23]

### *Prison: A hotbed for Covid-19*

Some of the biggest impacts of the virus on the criminal justice system were felt in jails and prisons. Given rates of overcrowding and the poor conditions under which prisoners, both convicted and those waiting trial, are held around the world, prisons were identified as potent places for the spread of the virus.[24]

Brazil's large and overcrowded prison system—the country's National Penitentiary Department counted 773,151 inmates in 2019[25]—looked particularly vulnerable, and so it proved to be. By September 2020, the Brazilian National Council of Justice reported that 38,021 people within prison had tested positive; of these, 28,233 were prisoners.[26] The incidence of Covid-19 cases in Brazil was calculated to be 70% higher in prisons than in the wider population.[27] In mid-2020, Brazilian authorities reported that there had been a remarkable 800% increase in prison inmate contamination rates from May to June.[28] On 23 June 2020, more than 200 Brazilian organisations filed a complaint with the UN and the Inter-American Commission on Human Rights against the Brazilian state for its failure to manage the prison system effectively, especially during the pandemic.[29]

Many of the issues raised by the Brazilian complaint were echoed in other countries, where questions were raised about how social-distancing measures could be enforced in cramped and often unsanitary prisons without violations of human rights. People in detention often have 'generally poorer health than the rest of the population, often with underlying health conditions', making them particularly vulnerable to Covid-19, noted Penal Reform International, a prominent civil society organisation which monitors prison conditions.[30] In many countries a growing number of older and longer-term prisoners, including those convicted of offences related to organised crime, provided the worrying possibility that deaths rates within the correctional system might reach serious levels.

Prison administrators everywhere appealed to governments to halt prison visits by outsiders and to release inmates. As early as March 2020, the Irish Prison Service announced contingency measures, among them the temporary release for prisoners regarded as not posing a risk. The Netherlands announced that those about to serve short sentences would not be called upon to do so. In some places the courts stepped in. In March 2020, judges, prosecutors and the sheriff in Cuyahoga county in Ohio began holding mass plea hearings in order to be able to release those held in pre-trial detention in the county's jails. Similar initiatives occurred in many jurisdictions.[31]

In recognition of the growing threat, on 17 March 2020 the Brazilian National Council of Justice officially recommended the release of prisoners to avoid the spread of the virus.[32] The Council encouraged magistrates to review the pre-trial detention and sentencing of people from at-risk groups and those at the end of serving periods. These prisoners should not have committed violent crimes, such as murder or rape. Significantly, those who belonged to criminal organisations were also excluded. New restrictions were later added in September 2020, clarifying that persons accused of corruption, money laundering, grave crimes and domestic violence could not benefit from a review of the pre-trial detention or sentencing regime because of Covid-19 considerations.[33]

After being criticised for not disclosing the numbers of released inmates, the Brazilian Council of Justice reported that from March to June 2020 more than 32,500 prisoners had been released. These are significant numbers, although they are themselves an undercount: the Brazilian authorities conceded their record-keeping in those days was poor, and hasty decisions were made to release prisoners whose were nearing the end of their sentence.[34]

For its part, Europe moved quickly to release people from prison. A report by the Council of Europe suggested that Europe had avoided devastating outbreaks in its prisons through the release of about 128,000 prisoners. By mid-April 2020, 20 of the 43 members of the Council of Europe had released prisoners to prevent outbreaks.[35] Turkey (which was included in the Council of Europe count) released by far the most prisoners. Remarkably, by emptying its prisons of 102,944 detainees,

Turkey freed about a third of its prison population (this tally excludes prisoners awaiting trial).[36]

Within the European Union, Cyprus, Slovenia, Portugal, Norway, Ireland and Italy released the most prisoners (as a proportion of total inmates).[37] Italy set free 5,739 prisoners, or about 9% of its prison population. Nearly 2,000 inmates were allowed to serve the remainder of their sentences under house detention, and 420 other inmates were granted semi-liberty. France released 10,188 prisoners, or about 14.4% of its prison population. In Spain, 4,356 prisoners were released, or about 6% of its total prison population. (Catalonia was far above the national average, with 17% of its prison population being set free.)[38]

Even where there were no mass releases, as in the United Kingdom, prison populations still declined. As of August 2020, the prison population in the UK stood at 79,600, a reduction of more than 4,400 since March 2020. This drop is largely the result of pandemic-driven delays in the criminal justice system which have prevented new inmates from entering prison, while prisoners completing their sentences were released as normal.[39]

Outside Europe, the numbers were also impressive. Iran, badly affected by the virus, released 85,000 people from custody, while Afghanistan freed some 10,000.[40] India and Indonesia—which both have large prison populations—released 50,000 prisoners each. In Colombia, 7,000 inmates were set free as a mitigation measure, although the country's prison system remained 40% overpopulated.[41] South Africa released 7,000 prisoners on special parole in a bid to protect inmates from the virus by decongesting its overcrowded correctional centres. A total of 19,000 offenders considered as low-risk are scheduled to be pardoned under the country's Correctional Services Covid-19 Disaster Management Response Strategy, which aims to achieve a 12% reduction in prison overcrowding.[42]

In places where prison conditions were regarded as extremely poor and medical options limited, some fortunate inmates were set free (see table).[43]

| *Country* | *Prisoners released* |
|---|---|
| DRC | 12,000 |
| Chad | 3,200 |
| Egypt | 4,000 |
| Haiti | 322 |
| Libya | 466 |
| Malawi | 1,392 |
| Mali | 1,200 |
| South Sudan | 1,485 |

Given the constraints of life under lockdown, some experts have suggested that releasing prisoners during the pandemic may make integration into society much more difficult. Where such services existed, parole officers were reported as being overstretched and monitoring much larger numbers of released prisoners. But this seemed a small price to pay for preventing the spread of the disease in prisons and getting minor offenders, including those convicted for low-level drug offences, back outside.

By May 2020, Human Rights Watch calculated that some 580,000 prisoners in eighty countries had been released.[44] It seemed a decisive win for prison reform, but in most countries the number of inmates released was comparatively small compared with the total incarcerated. Those released were often convicted prisoners serving short sentences. In many places, pre-trail detainees, despite not having been convicted of any offence, continued to be held.[45]

In authoritarian states, political prisoners and human rights activists were seldom among those released. Turkey's law specifically prohibited the release of people unjustly convicted under terror laws, including journalists, lawyers and human rights defenders, regardless of whether they were suffering from serious medical issues. Some political prisoners paid the price. In July 2020, Egyptian journalist Mohamed Monir died after contracting Covid-19 in pre-trial detention following his arrest on 15 June on charges of joining a terrorist group, spreading false news and misusing social media.[46]

### *Freeing mafiosi*

The largest controversy over prison releases occurred in Italy with regard to prisoners convicted of mafia-related offences. In March 2020, a memo from the Italian penitentiary administration department asked prison directors to disclose the names of all detainees with precarious health conditions. This was done in order to assess the measures that would have to be taken should the prison service not be able to provide the necessary health care in the event that the virus spread through the prison system.

The problem was that several aged prisoners in Italy are prominent members of the mafia. There was an immediate public outcry, and the Ministry of Justice had to clarify that it had not made any provision for the release of 'high-security prisoners'.

But lawyers for incarcerated senior organised-crime figures quickly spotted a gap in the regulations that allowed them to submit release requests for their clients, especially those above the age of seventy.[47] Of the prisoners granted their freedom, some 376 were thought to have high-level links with organised crime. Important Cosa Nostra, Camorra and 'Ndrangheta affiliates such as Antonino Sacco, Francesco Ventrici and Fabio Costantino were among this number. Some of the released inmates were serving their sentences, while others were still awaiting trial.[48]

In April 2020, three prominent mafiosi bosses, serving their sentence in isolation under the so-called 41-bis regime, were released.[49] First out was Rocco Santo Filippone, who was on trial for ordering the bombings that killed two carabinieri in 1994. Sick and elderly, the 'Ndrangheta boss was placed under house arrest without so much as an electronic tag. He was followed a few days later by Francesco Bonura, a Cosa Nostra member who had been due for release eleven months later but who had applied for early release on the grounds of serious ill health. Near the end of the month, Pasquale Zagaria, the economic brains of the Casalesi clan of the Camorra, was also set free. Zagaria was ill with cancer and there was no hospital capable of treating him, as all hospital beds were being set aside for Italy's acute Covid-19 emergency. He was sent to serve the rest of his sentence under house arrest in Pontevico, Lombardy.[50]

By May 2020, a fresh public outcry in Italy had forced an about-face. The government approved a new decree by the Ministry of Justice which aimed at re-imprisoning the 376 inmates convicted of offences linked to organised crime. The decree made provision for judges to assess the health conditions of the released prisoners every fifteen days, ordering them to be returned to prison if their health risks declined.[51] As of September 2020, just under a third (112 of the 376) of the Cosa Nostra, Camorra and 'Ndrangheta affiliates are still out of prison on health or Covid-related grounds.[52]

### *Implications*

It almost seems unfair to make a judgement call about police responses to organised crime in a period when law enforcement systems were rushing to adapt to a pandemic. It is clear that there was seldom any contingency planning, and none that involved responding to criminal organisations. Police resources became focused primarily on issues of public order, although some of these activities (as we have reported earlier) also impact upon organised crime. Police agencies, particularly in the developing world, had few resources to deal with the boom in online crime.

In retrospect, the greatest immediate challenge for the worst-affected police agencies was that their members themselves became sick. Police and security planners will undoubtedly draw lessons from this as they plan for a potential new pandemic, identifying some of the lessons that have been learnt about the growth and resilience of organised crime.

Further along the justice chain, court systems adapted quickly—although not without teething problems. The delivery of virtual justice, even if it was not applied in more serious cases involving organised-crime figures, is likely to bring a shift to the 'online courtroom'. One of the biggest consequences here may be to reduce the requirement for stringent physical security around high-profile cases. Issues over access and transparency for the public can and should be resolved.

The release of 5% of the world's prison population, even if it included some ageing and ill mafiosi, did not seem to impact on crime levels. Or, more accurately, it was difficult to determine whether increases in crime, where they occurred, were due to released prisoners, but it seems doubtful, given that most releases had specifically excluded dangerous offenders. When prison releases were linked to increases in crime, media reporting often carried the smell of stories planted by the police with an axe to grind about the release of suspects who had taken an effort to put behind bars.[53] Violent crime trends—while difficult to interpret at the best of times and very dependent on data quality—did plummet as lockdowns were instituted, but then increased as regulations were eased. This U-shaped curve was particularly noticeable in reports from several US cities. But homicides, often used as a proxy for violent crime, stayed higher than the 2016–2019 average and in some cases (Chicago, New York, Philadelphia) actually increased, although no one is sure why[54]—a topic likely to be the subject of many criminology PhDs in future.

Prison releases during the coronavirus pandemic do not appear to have resulted in any longer-term impetus to question the efficacy of incarceration, particularly for low-level offences. Perhaps the releases were too small in number (about 5% of the huge global prison population, which is estimated at 11 million people) to drive this point home in any meaningful way. Ultimately, the pandemic did little to erode the logic of a system in which enormous numbers of people are held in crowded prisons or for long periods awaiting trial, often for minor offences such as drug possession.

# 11

# GANGLAND RULES

The press reports in April 2020, just as South Africa had just gone into lockdown, were almost breathless with excitement. In Cape Town, one of the country's most violent areas, gangs had declared an 'unprecedented peace'. Even the BBC got in on the act, reporting 'how coronavirus had inspired a gangland truce in South Africa'.[1] The *Daily Telegraph* said that the truce was being 'hailed as a miracle'.[2]

On the face of it, it was certainly something worth reporting. With an estimated membership of 100,000 in Cape Town alone, gangs are major contributors to the levels of violence in the city. The city's murder rate had spiralled upwards since 2012, reaching some sixty homicides per 100,000 by 2018, with some areas passing the 100 homicides per 100,000 mark—an astonishing level of violence and a rate exceeded by only a handful of cities in the world.[3] By 2019, the military had been deployed in the gang-dominated Cape Flats to curb a series of gang 'wars'. Was there an upside to the coronavirus, after all?

With some probing, the story quickly crumbled. Senior gang bosses denied knowledge or intent. A mid-level gang member almost immediately told one of our fieldworkers: 'When you say a truce, what do you mean? No, my brother, there's no such thing. Think for yourself. That's a load of shit … where the fuck will you get these gangsters making a truce for the government?'[4]

Where indeed? It turned out that a small number of low-level gang members had manufactured the peace; none of the city's top gang bosses—a criminal elite of about twenty people—were involved. It is not entirely clear why they did so. One theory, provided by gang members themselves, was that the truce was a bluff—as indeed had been the case on a previous occasion a few years before—manufactured so the gangs could 'reorientate their operations' in preparation for a long lockdown. The truce, it was said, allowed not only the distribution of food to communities, but also the movement of drugs away from the unsuspecting eyes of law enforcement officers, who, thinking a peace deal was in place, would take their focus elsewhere.[5]

Although the truce may have been fake, the global media circus that developed around it was an indication of how prominent criminal gangs have become in the local governance and politics of a city like Cape Town. Much of the enthusiastic reporting about the truce focused on gangs taking on 'government functions' in their communities, such as providing food or supporting destitute families with payouts—but such reporting often masked as much as it explained. How did the gangs come to hold such sway in these communities? Had they in fact 'replaced' the government, and, if so, what were their motives?

*When gangs take charge*

Criminal gangs wield real influence in many urban areas of the world.[6] That idea might conjure images of drug dealers lurking on street corners and midnight shootouts, but the reality is in fact far more complex—and insidiously destructive. Many gangs are closely woven into the social and political fabric of their areas of operation, so much so that criminal bosses have become the bloody arbiters in the lives (and deaths) of those who live under their diktat.

At the heart of gang influence is the concept of territory. Territory can be understood as the area where the gang not only controls the local criminal economy—such as illicit drugs or extortion—but also where it comes into contact with (and challenges) the various mechanisms of the state (including service provision and law enforcement), as well as encountering (and coercing) the wider community.

Gangs maintain their control of territory most obviously through violence, against other gangs and also ordinary people, with such violence often reaching appalling levels. Where the gang economy exists in cities in Latin America and Africa, for example, rates of murder are among the highest on the planet, often well above 50 per 100,000 residents. Ordinary people who live in such places experience enormous suffering. Such violence is often directed at the most vulnerable, including children, who are targeted both as potential clients for drug sales and as new recruits for gangs.

But gangs know that fear alone is not enough; the 'host' community must also perceive the gangs as the 'real' authority in their area. Building this legitimacy, which on the face of it is the opposite of the practice of violence, is key to a gang's longer-term survival and recruitment. To achieve this, gangs have long resorted to providing handouts and services to people in marginalised communities when the going gets tough—and the going is almost always tough. Cash, water, food, school fees, transport, security from an attack by a threatening spouse or father, even electricity and cable TV—the list of basic needs is long. In this sense, the gangs provide state-like services, or at least they exist on a continuum with it, as many analysts pointed out during the pandemic.[7] And this provision in turn erodes the role and influence of the state within a gang's territory, helping establish the gang as the de facto authority.

Communities under the sway of gangs therefore often have (at least to outsiders) a strange Janus-faced relationship with their gang overlords. On the one hand, they fear them for their violence, disruption and unpredictability. On the other hand, they rely on them for resources and the (paradoxical) security they provide. This is all part of the plan as far as gangs are concerned, but for communities it is a lose-lose situation. In turning to the gangs, ordinary people become entangled in a web of obligations from which they can't escape; if they dare challenge them, they risk violent, sometimes fatal, retribution.

These are the unwritten rules of what we call 'criminal governance', in which gang bosses preside over communities through a combination of kindness and killing. Both are carried out with great symbolism—in Mexico, for instance, social media coverage of food handouts goes alongside the public display of splayed and mutilated corpses. In some places like Japan, China, Italy and Russia, criminal groups are much older and more sophisticated and levels of violence are lower, in part because organised crime has reached an understanding with the state to keep levels of violence dialled back (at least in comparison with the hyper-violence of Rio or Cape Town) and to confine operations to a limited number of criminal markets. But the principles of organisation are broadly the same.

But while in many cases gangs exploit shortfalls in central governance to establish their own forms of criminal governance, for the most part mafia operations depend upon protection from the state or politicians; few criminal groups strike out on their own as an independent political force. Safety—or at least survival—is to be found in cooperation with corrupt state actors.[8] One of the crucial measures of this in a gang-controlled community is the rate of impunity—essentially, how often criminals are brought to justice for their deeds. In Latin America, where several notorious gangs have corrupted local police forces, the rate of conviction is staggeringly low. Regionally, only twenty murders out of every 100 lead to a conviction, less than half the global average, although the rate is much lower in certain countries and cities (Brazil, for example, saw only eight convictions per 100 murders).[9]

But it is a balancing act: if gangs get too close to the state, they risk losing their unique criminal identity; on the other hand, should they flaunt their activities too much, they risk bringing the wrath of the state upon themselves. As such, mafia-style groups are constantly struggling with a dilemma of public perception. In the words of a leading analyst, Maurizio Catino: 'Illegal as they are, mafias must try to keep their activities and their membership secret, but at the same time, in terms of reputation, they must in some ways make themselves visible.'[10]

The pandemic saw many criminal groups choose the latter option, having spotted that government attention was distracted elsewhere. The South African truce was one example of this criminal brand-building: gang members knew full well that it would attract media attention and communicate the gangs' core message: 'we are in control and can end the violence when we want to'.

There were similarly symbolic and actual demonstrations of power by gangs in Latin America. Some of the most prominent of these came in the shape of gangs and criminal groups imposing lockdowns of their own.

### *'The message has been given'*

In March 2020, when the first case of the coronavirus was recorded in a sprawling complex of slums called City of God, in Rio de Janeiro, it was the gangsters and not the Brazilian government that imposed a curfew. According to local media reports, gangsters drove around the City of God playing a recorded message to residents.[11] 'We're imposing a curfew because nobody is taking this seriously. Whoever is in the street screwing around or going for a walk will receive a corrective and serve as an example. Better to stay home doing nothing. The message has been given.'[12]

In gang-ridden El Salvador, where state governance has long been conducted alongside the nation's formidable street gangs, President Nayib Bukele moved before all other countries in the region to institute one of Latin America's most stringent lockdowns. But the leaders of MS-13, who have long governed from the shadows, alongside and, sometimes, in competition with the state, also instituted their own curfew, and government regulation of social distancing would not have been possible without the cooperation of the gangs. 'It was a rare overlap between the gang and the government,' noted an article in the *Washington Post*.[13]

In Brazil, El Salvador and elsewhere in Latin America, social media and other 'outreach' from gangs spread the message about the need for social distancing and for wearing masks. As many commentators pointed out, given that states had limited access or little legitimacy in gang-dominated areas, the gangs were in fact performing a vital social function. 'Their reputations for using violence and their detailed knowledge of those neighbourhoods make them powerful enforcers,' concluded a researcher with years of experience in gang areas.[14]

And it seemed to be effective too. A study in Brazil found that neighbourhoods with a strong presence of drug gangs had 43% fewer cases of severe acute respiratory infections than neighbourhoods where the government exercised de facto control. The study also suggested that neighbourhoods controlled by militia groups—whose business model is dependent on extortion—had 29% more deaths in comparison with areas under government control. The researchers concluded that the difference in infection rates was a result of how these different groups 'relate to local communities and enforce their territorial control'.[15] Gangs seemed to do it better.

Indeed, the Brazilian state took a strikingly pragmatic approach to the situation. The then Brazilian minister of health, Luiz Henrique Mandetta, told local officials in April 2020 that they needed to talk with gang leaders and drug lords about how to encourage measures in communities to reduce the spread of the disease. Mandetta said that officials needed to 'understand that these are areas where the state is often absent and the ones in charge are the drug traffickers'.[16]

A gang–government 'overlap' was evident in several other places. In Indonesia, this occurred at the invitation of the state. In major Indonesian cities where local gangs provide security in communities (including for guarding cars in exchange for a 'protection fee'), the police reached out for assistance. It was reported that the deputy national police chief argued that the assistance of gang leaders was 'needed as part of efforts to discipline the public amid the ongoing pandemic, especially regarding mask-wearing and physical-distancing measures'.[17] Such a request—sure to be accepted by local criminal bosses—inevitably confers legitimacy on the gangs, although unsurprisingly, not everyone agreed with it. The police plan was immediately rejected by the Indonesian Market Traders Association, who noted that their members had lost considerable revenue during the lockdown: 'They are recovering now. They will be intimidated by the presence of gang members watching their activities,' their chairman said.[18]

But while the gang-imposed lockdowns may have had public health benefits, criminal motivations are rarely altruistic. Curfews, for example, helped gangs to retain their strength among their own membership—the rapid spread of the virus threatened to be potentially debilitating, especially as access to medical care for gangs remained problematic. (Gang members everywhere are suspicious that the public health system discriminates against members who are often tattooed or clearly identifiable as belonging to gangs.)[19] And this strategic response to the pandemic was perhaps most visible in how the gangs responded to the economic crisis caused by the pandemic.

### *Gangsters bearing gifts*

The arrival of the coronavirus immediately placed communities in marginalised and gang-controlled parts of urban areas under great stress. Schools were closed and children roamed the streets or were confined in small dwellings, challenging their parents' control. Jobs disappeared and cash was chronically short. For those families who relied on a sole breadwinner and lived from hand to mouth, the situation quickly became desperate.

It was the perfect opportunity for the gangs, who mobilised rapidly to provide community support, often in the form of food supplies but in some cases cash handouts. While such actions may in certain places have been motivated by genuine concern for the community (ordinary gang members are deeply embedded in their areas and usually have extensive family ties), they were also a potent piece of gang propaganda: 'when things get really tough, you can count on us'.

The gangs made sure the message was broadcast far and wide. Gang handouts were widely covered in the media; gangs even organised some of that coverage, particularly in local media outlets. The Brazilian mainstream media did not name organised crime groups (so as not to give importance to the groups and their activities),[20] but there were other ways to get the message across, among them the use of social media, WhatsApp groups, and locally publicised handovers of provisions.

Food distribution was often a form of theatre. Alejandrina Guzmán—the daughter of the notorious drug lord Joaquín 'El Chapo' Guzmán—was filmed handing out food parcels to people in need in Mexico. Ms Guzmán was shown in the video, which was posted on Facebook and subsequently made the global news, filling a box with food, cooking oil and toilet paper. The marketing was not subtle: on the box was stencilled an image of her father, while the video's narrator described the supplies as 'Chapo's provisions'. (Ms Guzmán said that the provisions were funded by the profits of her own company, Chapo 701, which sells clothes and other El Chapo-branded items.)[21] The company's language was not that of a criminal group, despite the association with the notorious drug trafficker.[22] 'A great pleasure to visit your homes and give you these Chapo handouts,' said a friendly post on Chapo 701's home page. (The post was later removed.)

The handing out of food parcels seems to have been widespread in Mexico, as different cartels proved eager to be seen as supporting the poor, as Robert Bunker and John Sullivan have shown.[23] Photos revealed armed cartel foot soldiers lugging sacks of donated rice and flour for little old ladies. The Jalisco New Generation Cartel, the Gulf Cartel, Los Durango and Los Viagras were among the Mexican criminal groups reported to have handed out food parcels. There appeared to be a degree of copycatting, and different criminal groups jostled to demonstrate that they were as kind-hearted as their rivals. Indeed, the distribution of goods by the cartels was so widespread, or at least so widely reported, that the Mexican president, Andrés Manuel López Obrador, openly condemned it, saying: 'These criminal organisations that have been seen distributing packages, this isn't helpful. What helps is them stopping their bad deeds.'[24]

But it did help the criminals, in Mexico and elsewhere. Distributing money and food parcels is a strategy that criminal organisations have long used to win over communities—they know it is an investment that pays off. In the future, police inquiries, even into brutal murders, will be met by a wall of silence, not only out of fear, but also because gangs have community support. Community members who accept gifts from gangs can expect to have a visit at some point in the future, from gang members asking locals to store guns, drugs or other items that the gang needs to stash—and they will likely comply. 'Even old ladies hide stuff for them. They appreciate the support they get when times are tough. It is very hard to say to people then that the gangs are illegitimate,' a Cape Town community worker told us early in 2020 as numerous accounts of gangs running soup kitchens and handing out cash were reported.[25]

*Violent expansion*

There is sometimes a tendency—as shown by the stories of the South African gang truce and those of food distribution in Mexico—to romanticise social welfare and gang governance and to attribute a 'Robin Hood' quality to it, a 'bad guys making good' narrative. It may have seemed that, in imposing local lockdowns, gangs were more mindful of people's health than the government, but, as always, violence was never far away. There were multiple reports and images from several cities of gangs administering beatings to residents who had broken lockdown 'regulations' or had failed to wear masks or exercise appropriate social distancing.

Violence was not only confined to lockdown enforcement. For criminal entrepreneurs running a gang, the pandemic presented dangers and opportunities which necessitated the use of violence. After a period of reduced conflict at the start of the pandemic, many places witnessed a ratcheting up of incidents of violence. These increases in violence were uneven and often due to individual gangs looking to expand their turf or market.

Some gangs who normally relied in part on the income from extortion payments lifted the requirement of businesses to pay their monthly protection fee, once these businesses were forced to close because of the pandemic. In other cases, the fee was retained, increased, or reinstituted at a higher level, as gangs themselves became hungry for cash.[26] Spare muscle also meant that extortion economies had incentives to grow. Central Cape Town, whose night-time economy of bars and clubs has long been characterised by a system of criminal protection, saw the extortion threats spread to day-time businesses.[27] Post-lockdown, there was also extensive reporting of acts of extortion aimed at many small businesses in the city's former African townships.

Militia groups in Rio, who practise extortion and not drug trafficking (which provides an income stream largely independent of legitimate business), could not sustain the imposition of curfews for such a long period of time, as they needed businesses to operate so that protection money would flow again. It was reported that right after the curfew was implemented, the militia put pressure on businessmen to reopen establishments in areas dominated by them.[28] (This also perhaps explains the comparatively high level of infection in militia-controlled zones described in the study cited above.)

In Kenya, our interviews suggested that gang violence had increased in the west of the country, primarily in the city of Nakuru. With government attention directed elsewhere, several gangs attempted to use the period of the lockdown to expand their territory, bringing them into conflict with their rivals. Gang members also used the confusion of the lockdown period to engage in looting and robberies. As a study of tension in the area concludes: 'As the control over territory also equates to control over looting and robberies within a given area (and income derived from that), territorial conflicts have become more fiercely contested.'[29]

Gang members in Dar es Salaam, Tanzania, were also involved in a rise in the number of street robberies and armed robberies of businesses, homes and vehicles during the lockdown.[30] This clearly was opportunistic, but it was significant enough to suggest that it was based on a strategy to accumulate economic advantage while the state's focus was concentrated elsewhere.

After a period of comparative calm in Cape Town when the lockdown was first imposed, there were numerous reports from our gang monitoring system of shootouts between gangs as they tried to consolidate drug turf and moved to subvert state controls. 'For gangs, too, the sheer economic drive to make money through drug sales overrode any impetus to observe the lockdown,' concluded our review of the period.[31] There is also evidence that gangs upped their recruitment strategies, targeting in particular young people who were not attending school.

Along the northern drug routes in Brazil, which run through Amazonas state, the pandemic saw a spasm of violence linked to instability in the control of the regional drug trade. The drug route is known as Rota Solimões, after the river along which drugs are transported from Colombia and Peru on their way to the north-eastern ports, where they are prepared for shipment to Europe. The route used to be controlled by the Northern Family (Familia do Norte, or FDN). Following the collapse of the group's alliance with Rio's Red Command (Comando Vermelho, also known by its

Portuguese initials, CV), the local CV outlet (in Amazonas as well as in the neighbouring Acre state) waged a violent campaign against FDN members, killing many and inscribing the CV logo on walls in several urban peripheries.[32] In August 2020, after a large seizure of cocaine paste, the Brazilian federal police began an operation against criminal groups in the region.[33]

### *Digging deeper*

Gangs have used the opportunity of the pandemic to extend their legitimacy within communities, establishing themselves as the go-to providers of aid and assistance, while at the same time reinforcing the impression that they are in charge. In places where the state response has been slow or lacking, gangs have been able to portray the state as unresponsive or even uncaring, while painting themselves as community allies through their distribution of food parcels and cash.

In parallel, gangs have sought to expand their criminal economies through violence or by taking over markets where the opportunity arose. Perhaps the clearest case was South Africa, where gangs expanded their existing role in the illegal alcohol and cigarette markets in response to the government's ban on these. (And here criminal ingenuity was on full display: gangs bought alcohol from cruise ships in Cape Town harbour for resale, and colluded with liquor store owners to rob their shops for a fee so that they could then claim insurance.)[34]

But, as mentioned above, the very visibility of these efforts may bring dangers for gangs. Sustained coverage of gang-led community support is bound to irritate political elites (as it did the Mexican president), even if in some cases they need criminal muscle (and votes) at election time. When gangs are judged to have gone too far, the instruments of the state—both rhetorically and from a security perspective—will be deployed against them. To strike out on their own brings dangers. Indeed, it is noticeable that some gangs seem to be making efforts to slip back into the shadows: pictures of gang members distributing food parcels were soon deleted from Facebook pages and other forms of social media in several places. Their utility was time-limited, and could even backfire if preserved as a goading reminder of state inaction.

The displays of gang largesse and lockdowns should then be seen for what they are—fanfare to build legitimacy—rather than attempts by gangs to displace the state. In that sense, the more visible humanitarian actions of gangs and similar criminal formations described in this chapter should be distinguished from their largely under-the-table entrepreneurial efforts, which include buying up businesses and providing loans at exorbitant rates of repayment (see chapter 12). Humanitarian actions are immediate and often symbolic, and are designed to build reputation and consolidate community support. Other economic forms of support are about consolidating criminal enterprise.

In any event, the burst of media coverage of the gangs' social kindness and their role in the lockdown has now passed. Sensible gang leaders prefer it that way. Gangs like to have influence and like to compare themselves to the state, but prudent gangs are wary of overstepping the agreed mark. That does not mean that organised crime does not erode the state—it clearly does—only that, like the virus, its survival also depends on a host.

On the other side of the coin, the fact remains that gangs cannot be easily supplanted in the areas they control without major state interventions and community support. Some hoped that the pandemic might provide a window of opportunity for this to happen, even in a country like Mexico where US intelligence assessments conclude that drug-trafficking groups have gained control of about 20% of the country's territory.[35] Mexican commentator Alejandro Hope argued that the pandemic was a chance to 'create state presence where it has never existed',[36] but in most places this seemed unlikely. Gangs are deeply embedded in their communities, leveraging both violence and benevolence to fuse parasitically with the local society. Covid-19 ultimately reinforced the toxic success of this approach.

# 12

# WHO'S GOING TO PAY?

Four hundred million flowers were destroyed in the Netherlands in March 2020, including 140 million of the country's signature tulips. They were thrown into machines that crushed their multi-coloured beauty, shredded and pulped them, until they came out on the other side as mulch. Along with the flowers went a huge chunk of the industry's income. The Dutch flower industry typically earns €7 billion in the months between March and May—its peak season.[1]

The Netherlands was not alone in seeing its flower industry take a huge hit. Cut flowers are also a major money-maker in Kenya, forming its second-largest export, after tea. The country is Europe's biggest supplier and ships around £815 million worth of flowers each year,[2] but flower producers lost some 80% of their 2020 spring crop.[3] A continent away, flowers are Ecuador's fourth-largest export and earn the country US$400 million a year, but the social distancing requirements cost the industry 10,000 jobs and US$130 million in losses.[4]

These producers are just one part of a complex global supply chain of farmers, workers, wholesalers, shippers and couriers, florists, and distributors (from supermarkets to flower shops) who were affected by the pandemic. Theirs were the blossoms that should have gone into lavish displays in hotel lobbies, convention centres and cruise ships around the world, onto dining tables in restaurants, into decorations for Mother's Day, birthdays, anniversaries, quinceañeras and bar mitzvahs. They should have been held in the hands of hopeful brides in their bouquets on their wedding day.

But all of these events were abruptly cancelled or postponed indefinitely, firstly by government-mandated shutdowns, then by social-distancing protocols preventing large gatherings or full occupancy, and subsequently by consumers' reluctance or reduced income that prevented them from spending in the ways they used to. And as those events were cancelled, those businesses were left with no way to pay back-end suppliers, florists, performers, artists, caterers and staff.

Ironically, the business of selling cut flowers is not dissimilar to a number of labour-intensive criminal enterprises, such as gold and narcotics. Flowers, gold and narcotics involve a large number of artisanal workers at the point of production and are driven by the need to keep transnational commodity flows in motion. However, unlike the illicit industries, demand for flowers fell when the pandemic began, and there were few incentives to keep it alive. While illicit supply chains seem to have remained for the most part intact, adapting to changing conditions and continuing to move contraband goods and illicit money, legitimate industries crumbled.

The destruction of those beautiful blooms is symbolic of the horrible damage that has been done to almost every sector of the global economy, to people's livelihoods and to the hopes many had for a bright future. The IMF estimated in October that cumulative global output will fall short of pre-pandemic expectations by US$11 trillion between 2020 and 2021, and by US$28 trillion by 2025.[5] Unemployment rates across the world have risen by between 2.4% and 12.7%, with further rises expected when government support comes to an end.[6] According to estimates made by the World Bank in June 2020, national lockdowns and the ensuing economic shutdown will push between 71 million and 100 million people into extreme poverty; as a result, not only will they have to live on less than US$1.90 per day, but the majority of their most basic needs will not be met. The UN estimates that 490 million people in 70 countries will fall under the US$1.90 per day threshold into poverty, reversing almost a decade of gains made in pursuit of sustainable development goals.[7]

Some of the earliest economic impacts of the shutdowns in various places were cushioned by government stimulus payments, unemployment benefits and furlough schemes, bailouts, the introduction of tax deferments, rent and mortgage freezes, or bankruptcy moratoriums. But even in the most generous and wealthy of countries, these were always only ever going to be short-term fixes. As the pandemic continued to spread in autumn and into the winter of 2020, triggering second and third waves of infection at rates even higher than the initial peak of spring 2020, the true scope of the economic contraction was being felt and was reinforcing itself in multiple ways.

### *Speculating on the stimulus*

When the pandemic began, a number of world leaders moved quickly to deploy emergency financial measures and aggressive stimulus packages and bailouts in an effort to avoid the economic collapse precipitated by lockdowns and border closures. These injections were to the tune of trillions of dollars. Most of this money was delivered into the right hands and temporarily staved off the most acute financial impact of the pandemic. At the same time, these stimulus efforts presented a treasure trove of opportunities for the criminal and the unethical to enrich themselves at taxpayers' expense.

In addition to the phishing scams we saw in the chapter on cybercrime, in which individuals procured or created fake identities to apply for government benefits during the pandemic, there have been massive amounts of financial fraud related to the stimulus payments. In Brazil, the public sector watchdog identified some 620,000 cases of emergency aid being defrauded, amounting to more than BRL 1 billion (US$200 million).[8]

The individual stories themselves can be quite remarkable. German authorities arrested a man with links to a militant Islamic movement who had taken €18,000 in financial assistance from Berlin's development bank, the IBB.[9] A former American footballer submitted a mass of false paperwork to access the US$2.2 trillion Paycheck Protection Program (PPP), a US grant programme intended for small businesses, and used it to buy jewellery, clothes and a US$63,000 party weekend at the Florida Hard Rock Hotel. Another small business owner took his PPP money and bought a yacht.[10] One enterprising Virginia business owner and his wife managed to create four shell companies in just a few days, and then applied for 18 separate PPP loans, securing US$6.6 million in subsidies.[11]

At the corporate level, a significant number of workers have been asked to commit 'furlough fraud'. More than a third of employees surveyed in the UK—where a widespread furlough system put the workforce on paid leave during the lockdown—reported that their employers asked them to continue to work as normal so they could remain in business.[12] Larger companies, in decent financial shape, found ways to access funding meant for the small and the struggling to pay workforces and stave off bankruptcies, and used it for payouts to executives and shareholders.[13] In one particularly galling example, a California-based aviation company shared its PPP loan with its jet-owning uber-wealthy clients.[14] In total, the US Federal Trade Commission estimates that more than US$77 million has been lost to fraud on the bailouts, although it acknowledged that even this figure was likely to be an underestimate.[15]

### *Mafia capital*

The Covid-19 crisis and the lockdowns put many small businesses at risk of bankruptcy, particularly in the hospitality and service industries, such as hotels, leisure and retail. This had knock-on effects up and down supply chains, as well as on transportation and logistics sectors. With income hugely restricted, businesses—particularly cash-intensive ones—floundered and failed. And more are likely to follow suit as the economic impact of the pandemic plays out. As a bankruptcy lawyer explained to *Forbes*, 'Bankruptcy has a long tail. The timeline is going to be long. We're not talking months but probably two or three years.'[16]

Small and medium enterprises have been particularly hard hit, as they tend to get caught in a capital trap. Where government funding was available, it came with conditionalities or complex filing processes that made it difficult for owners to access, or else the funding fell well short of need.[17] Banks are often reluctant to lend to small businesses as they generally do not have the capital and liquidity to pay back this type of long-term loan, especially when the need comes from an economic downturn rather than a planned business expansion. Big businesses, like airlines, might be too big to fail, but in the current financial system a neighbourhood café, bar or restaurant seems always far more replaceable.

If banks will not offer a lifeline to struggling businesses, and businesses cannot access public money, then their owners must turn to more shadowy operations—and organised crime is usually a good source of plentiful, albeit dirty, money.[18] Loan-sharking, or usury, is a well-established organised crime enterprise. It offers criminals an easy and lucrative way of laundering the profits from other illegal activities, such as drug trafficking, by lending money to other businesses at usurious rates—those that far exceed the interest rates set by the legitimate legal or financial sector.[19] Loan-sharking is a core business for the Yakuza in Japan, the Chinese Triads and the Mexican gangs.

According to Amedeo Scaramella, of the San Giuseppe Foundation Moscato organisation, which fights against such loans, the Italian mafia traps borrowers by offering seemingly reasonable rates and then, once the loan is accepted, raising the interest by up to 300%. And whereas a normal lender is able to guarantee the safety of their loan by providing collateral, as Italian mafia public prosecutor Nicola Gratteri explained, in organised crime the costs of default can be far more terrifying: 'The 'Ndrangheta lenders don't need to take collateral. The 'Ndrangheta know that their collateral is the borrower's life.'[20] If businesses fail to repay, they can be taken or bought out by the mafia and, in the process, are legalised and placed at mafia disposal. In the seven weeks of lockdown in Italy, 2,500 businesses changed hands in the city of Milan alone, and it is far from inconceivable that many of them passed into the hands of organised crime.[21] Analysts even reported that agents of the mafia waited outside the banks in Milan, ready to solicit business owners as their financing applications were turned down.[22]

As well as handing the mafia plenty of suffering businesses, the pandemic also raised demand in sectors in which the mafia has long invested, such as cleaning companies, the food industry and funeral homes—thus giving the criminals even more financial resources to infiltrate other sectors weakened by the downturn.[23]

This strategy to profit from a crisis and a weak economy is an established part of the mafia playbook. In Italy, a national assessment of the impact of the 2007 subprime financial crisis and recession on new enterprises clearly showed a far higher turnover of businesses in regions with a high presence of organised crime. Analysts made a confident link that the new businesses being registered represented mafia investments in the legal economy.[24] Now, as the entire global economy contracts because of Covid-19, organised crime will be one of the few actors capable of bailing out businesses and investing in new markets. The Italian mafia already has footholds in Germany, Spain, the Netherlands and the US, but the pandemic will provide new openings. According to Robert Saviano, mafia analyst and author, 'Who might possibly buy up the tourist resorts on the Côte d'Azur or the Costa del Sol that have been destroyed by the 2020 tourism crisis?'[25]

### *Debt load*

But it is not only the small enterprises that have become vulnerable to criminal or questionable investment because of the pandemic. The entire global economy has softened, and new entry points for organised crime are opening up. World trade is projected to fall by 13.4% in 2020,[26] its steepest drop in at least sixty years, kicking volumes back to 2014 levels. Foreign direct investment in emerging markets—financing the new bridges, roads, factories and ports that bring the developing world the chance of prosperity—is expected to plunge by about

20% to levels not seen since 2006. Moreover, foreign direct investment as a share of GDP is expected to fall to the lowest level since the early 1990s.[27] Without new injections of funding, many infrastructure projects may never be realised or, at least, not without additional sources of funds.

National economies are shrinking in both the developed and the developing world, causing strains for indebted governments in meeting their financial commitments. Oil prices, which briefly hit negative values in the US markets, have stayed low owing to vanishing demand.[28] Governments typically borrow heavily against oil revenue, calculated on the expected price per barrel they should get on the global market. Nigeria, for example, based its budget on a per barrel oil price 50% higher than what oil has sold for throughout 2020, leaving the country in a massive funding crunch.[29]

Africa's debt load is enormous, and a sizeable share of it consists of resource-backed loans from China. Angola, another massive oil producer, has in excess of US$21 billion in resource-backed loans.[30] As of 2019, half of African low-income countries were in debt distress, or at high risk of being so, and debt repayments for these countries are so large that they are squeezing out development investments in education and health.[31] Globally, there are 64 countries in the world that are paying more on external debt repayments than they spend on public health care. There have been calls for debt cancellation to be extended to the lowest-income countries for 2020 to prevent them from being pushed into critical, life-endangering budget choices, seeking urgent cash injections from other sources or striking even more burdensome financing deals.[32]

In 2009, the executive director of the UNODC, Antonio Maria Costa, claimed that drug money had provided liquidity and had underpinned the international banking system after the banking crisis and recession of 2008.[33] In the present crisis caused by the coronavirus, it is likely that Chinese state or parastatal loans will provide the bailouts, given that the Chinese economy has rebounded far faster than others from Covid's impact.[34] The question is, with what risk?

Chinese financing has often come with strings that put nations at risk of losing control of their resources or assets that have been underwritten with Chinese money. In 2015, Sri Lanka was required to hand over control of its major deep-water port along one of the world's busiest shipping lanes for 99 years as a penalty for defaulting on a Chinese loan.[35]

Such loans may also come with an associated risk of increased criminality. The Chinese Belt and Road Initiative—a global infrastructure project funded by huge Beijing-backed loans—has introduced some 113 different forms of free-trade agreements, including export processing zones, free ports and free trade zones (FTZs) placed across the world, which are a clear soft spot for the entry and storage of illicit commodities.[36] As we mentioned in chapter 12, FTZs have emerged as one of the greatest challenges to the enforcement of illicit trade. FTZs are more lenient regarding financing, ownership, taxes, transparency requirements and other regulatory measures. In some cases, particularly in developing economies in Asia and the Middle East, FTZs also include manufacturing hubs that employ millions of workers. But this reduction in oversight also enables criminality.[37] An OECD study found that each additional FTZ within an economy results in an associated 5.9% increase in illicit trade, counterfeits and substandard goods.[38]

At this point, foreign investment has the potential to become both a crime and a security risk—risks likely to be borne by contracting economies, as states need capital more than ever, although some have already put up their guard. Italy, for example, has long scrutinised foreign investments in its security, defence, transportation and telecommunication sectors. But with the pandemic pushing the country into recession, in April the government passed an emergency decree that vastly expanded the government's authority to veto meaningful foreign investment in any firm working in electricity, water, health, media, data collection, aerospace, elections systems, banks, insurance, robotics or biotechnology. This is in part an effort to prevent predatory and hostile investment into parts of the economy which might one day be strategic to the health sector, or even vaccine development. The pandemic has actually changed the definition of a critical national asset.[39]

The problem in the current context of the global financial system, however, is that sometimes the source of funding for investment, both private and public, cannot be easily discerned. One of the greatest challenges in dealing with illicit financial flows is that it has become easier to hide the true ownership and provenance of funds as they wend their way through the international financial system.

*The great leveller*

In the early days, some commentators—including the UK government—referred to the coronavirus as the 'great leveller' because it would hit rich and poor equally; presidents, prime ministers and paupers were at risk.[40] But rather quickly it became clear that the experiences of rich and poor during the pandemic were not going to be even slightly comparable.

The rich were able to cushion themselves from the greatest pains of the pandemic—the public health risks, the economic downturn and the uncomfortable confines of lockdowns. While ordinary people worried about paying the rent and avoiding eviction, others were throwing down tens of thousands a month to get access to six-bedroom houses, pools and tennis courts for the summer.[41] Billionaires chartered superyachts for months at a time, to ride out the pandemic in splendid isolation, at a cost of between US$100,000 and US$500,000 per week, with onboard tutors to school their children.[42]

The growing gulf between the super-rich and the rest of us is not a unique feature of the pandemic, but a trend that had come with millennial globalisation. It was just that somehow, in the pandemic, the gulf became all the more apparent and galling. A report by the US Institute for Policy Studies found that the wealth of many billionaires rose during the pandemic while most people's fortunes stuttered and millions lost their jobs.[43]

Most notable among all this was the case of Jeff Bezos. Already the world's richest man, Bezos saw his fortune increase by an estimated US$74 billion between January and September 2020, a wealth surge three times the GDP of gang-riddled Honduras.[44] Some have suggested that to fully comprehend the scale of his wealth accrual, you need to be tracking it at a rate of dollars per second, not an annual estimate—because on a good day, Bezos's net worth (driven mostly by Amazon shares) is rising at a rate of US$150,000 per second.[45] E-commerce sales skyrocketed in the pandemic—in the US they almost doubled in the month of May alone[46]—as most people bought everything from basic necessities to entertainment goods online. A huge portion of those sales were made on Amazon, which has an impressive 38% share of the e-commerce market, and an outsized, controversial influence on online sales.[47] While Amazon took some positive steps during the pandemic, such as cracking down on pandemic speculators who were stockpiling health-related goods to sell at a premium,[48] and pledged to invest more than US$4 billion in workplace safety equipment, testing, and raising wages of essential staff at risk to ensure a Covid-free supply chain,[49] at the same time the company, which earned US$13 billion in 2019, pays little to nothing in taxes.[50]

Aggressive tax avoidance is another feature of the millennial landscape that has become commonplace among international corporations and the very wealthy. The exploitation of tax-code loopholes, creating multiple subsidiary branches to move profits and liabilities in order to benefit from the most preferential tax regimes, and the strategic use of tax havens are all now key tenets of corporate management. A study that estimated the scale of profit shifting by international businesses globally suggests that around US$420 billion in corporate profits are moved annually into tax havens, meaning a loss of tax revenue for the countries in which those profits are earned of around US$125 billion a year.[51] The total sitting in tax havens (also known as secrecy jurisdictions) is estimated to be in the region of US$36 trillion.[52]

Tax havens have long been a means by which both individuals and corporations can hide their money from the taxman, the police and the regulators. The funds of the rich, powerful and criminal commingle in these secrecy jurisdictions, available to be diverted and directed at their will. This is potential tax revenue that should be used for state investments in infrastructure, public education and health, safety and security, or emergency response. Instead, it allows those with great wealth the opportunity to influence political, corporate, legal and social priorities and policies across the world.[53] Increasingly, governments find themselves having to look for private investment to achieve the basic functions of governance, including the funding of infrastructure and the building of hospitals and schools.

Thus, during the pandemic, at a time when governments are digging deep into their budgets to fund the public health response, corporate profit maximisation glaringly undermines the ability of states to protect the lives and livelihoods of citizens. Regardless of how much private philanthropy the wealthy may support, or the urgent emergency appeals that they may respond to with impressive-sounding million-dollar pledges, this is hardly the equivalent of paying consistently into the national treasury for public spending and the funding of social safety nets. A 2013 World Bank report entitled 'Pandemic risk' suggested that a mere US$3.4 billion a year would have allowed developing countries to build up a robust capacity to prevent and respond to a pandemic.[54] But the funds for such investment were unavailable or unprioritised, and the cost of that failure is now being counted in the trillions of dollars and in millions of lives.

In May 2020, a number of countries, including France, Belgium, Denmark, Poland and Argentina, introduced legislation that would prevent any pandemic relief funding going to companies with a presence in tax havens. But for many people, the number of countries prepared to take this step was far too few; and even in those that did, the bar was arguably set too low. In the UK, for example, where some 25% of corporate tax revenues are estimated to be lost to aggressive tax avoidance practices,[55] only Scotland and Wales voted to restrict Covid-related subsidies to those that were tax compliant. England refused to do so, and among the companies on the Bank of England's bailout list, 14 of 52 receiving grants had links to tax havens, including, for example, a German chemical firm that received £1 billion (US$1.25 billion).[56]

With taxes paid by honest individuals being poured into companies that elect not to pay tax themselves, it does not feel like a coincidence that it was at the height of the pandemic's second wave that the FinCEN leak occurred. The leak of the FinCEN files, as they have become known, involved the release to journalists of more than 2,600 Suspicious Activity Reports (SARs) that are filed with the US Treasury's Financial Crimes Enforcement Network (FinCEN), the US body with the mandate to investigate financial crime. Covering the years from 1997 to 2017 and more than US$2 trillion worth of transactions, the FinCEN leak provided proof of billions of dollars' worth of dirty money transactions, including the money of drug traffickers and criminals, oligarchs diverting state money, and politicians evading sanctions.[57] It also showed that, despite being fined for similar misconduct in the past, prominent banks like JP Morgan Chase, HSBC, Standard Chartered and Deutsche Bank all continued to process transactions for criminals and the corrupt, cleaning it in the process or hiding it in tax havens. They did so with relative confidence that the global financial regulatory bodies would not have the capacity to monitor or respond to what they were doing.[58]

The same banks that refuse credit and loans to a multitude of owner-operated small businesses harmed by the pandemic have enriched themselves by hiding the money of criminal, corrupt and corporate elites. The problem with this system, as the pandemic has highlighted, is its fundamental injustice as well as the failure of those in positions of power to provide oversight or marshal the political will needed to change the financial framework, mostly because they stand to benefit personally. It is, to quote Alex Cobham, chief executive of the advocacy body the Tax Justice Network, 'the grave cost of an international tax system programmed to prioritize the interest of corporate giants over the needs of people'.[59] Designed for the wealthy and the privileged, tax havens, secrecy jurisdictions and lax requirements for corporate registration have also served criminal interests and enabled illicit financial flows. That money—the dirty and the unethical commingled—then goes to warp the priorities of government policy, investment and philanthropy yet further to their own ends, leaving hard-working and honest people, as well as the vulnerable and impoverished, to get sucked further underwater.

# 13

# PREVENTION, TREATMENT AND CURE

During the pandemic, many world leaders used the metaphor of war to describe the fight against the virus. 'We are at war,' declared the French President, Emmanuel Macron, in March 2020.[1] The head of the African Union's centre for disease control said that coronavirus is an 'existential war for the continent'.[2] The UK Prime Minister, Boris Johnson, argued that his government 'must act like any wartime government and do whatever it takes',[3] and the Australian Prime Minister, Scott Morrison, urged his country's citizens to summon the spirit 'of those who won the great peace of World War II and defended Australia'.

In a press briefing on the coronavirus, also in March, President Donald Trump used the analogy of war to justify everything from economic stimulus to emergency procurement—and pompously declared himself a wartime president. 'A number of people have said it, but—and I feel it, actually: I'm a wartime president. This is a war. This is a war. A different kind of war than we've ever had.'[4] Health workers around the world have routinely been described as the 'front line' and as 'heroes' in the war against the disease.

In general terms, beyond a call to rally round the flag, the metaphor of war is justification to suspend the usual rules of the game, to demand unprecedented sacrifices including the loss of life, and to normalise the centralisation of power along with reduced accountability. Ultimately, war is (by definition) antagonistic—it requires establishing an enemy and mobilising all of your forces and fervour against it—but it is difficult to do this in the case of an invisible virus. In many countries, as the initial solidarity of the emergency faded, that bellicose sentiment has been directed at the virus's proxies: people who might be seen to be carrying it—whether they are marginalised groups, political opponents or irregular migrants—or those that hoard necessary goods, from toilet paper at the supermarket to speculators on the internet. Unwarranted and sometimes lethal violence has also been used against ordinary people by authorities enforcing lockdowns, as if those not falling in line with the state's response were valid enemy combatants.

Yet in this scramble to cast the bad guys of the pandemic, organised crime rarely, if ever, came to the fore. This is odd, because the extent to which criminals have profited from Covid-19 has been so widespread and so obvious. We have documented them throughout the book: the pandemic profiteers, the cybercriminals, the counterfeiters and the traffickers of drugs, humans and more. So, it is interesting that this oversight did not muster much outrage in a time when passions were running high.

This may have been because during the pandemic, unlike in normal times, there was just no political profit to be had in targeting organised crime. Firstly, throwing up a new issue might have left politicians open to the accusation that they were getting sidetracked by a secondary, 'less important' issue; secondly, because victories against organised crime are always limited and rather hard won; and, finally, because for some in leadership, targeting organised crime might have meant cutting a bit too close to the bone. But another potential reason is that there are too many similarities between organised crime and the pandemic. Organised crime is the underworld: omnipresent, a dark, parasitic cancer on legitimate society, good governance and the economy. And maybe it is exactly its similarity to the pandemic that made it a poor foil for leaders looking for a straw man to rail at during the struggle against the disease. The lines between licit and illicit, legitimate and criminal, are too ill-defined: like the pandemic itself, crime is also an invisible enemy.

But whatever the rationale for this reticence, it suited criminals down to the ground. No longer public enemy number one, they could focus on adapting their businesses to the changing conditions. Indeed, the sense of fear and emergency and the loosening of oversight measures created new opportunities that broadly served to strengthen crime groups and offered them opportunities for long-term gain. For, as recent history has shown time and time again, criminals love a crisis.

### *Organised crime: war or disease?*

Like the coronavirus, criminal actors are no stranger to the metaphor of war. It has been in parlance for fifty years, ever since President Richard Nixon declared a 'war on drugs' in 1971 through the use of militarised anti-drug programmes and a hardline, zero-tolerance criminal justice approach that remains one of the most dominant forms of anti-narcotics policy globally.[5] In the last ten years, wars have been declared on rhino poachers in southern Africa, on gangs in Kenya, human smugglers in the Mediterranean, and pirates in the Gulf of Aden. The war on crime has been a clarion call sounded by many leaders in times of domestic strife, and embattled politicians have used heavily armed troops, helicopters and warships to project strength.[6] But the results have been deeply divisive and, in many cases, only led to rising levels of violence and suffering. Thousands and thousands of lives have been lost in the war on drugs; 'victory' is an ever-receding illusion.

The pandemic has shown us that the language of contagion and disease may be far more apt to describe the phenomenon of organised crime. Such language has, of course, been regularly applied in the past. From the 1990s and through the first two decades of the new millennium, the language of disease was often employed to describe the spread of organised crime and illicit markets. Criminal groups and networks, and the violence that they generated, were variously described as a 'virus', an 'epidemic' or a 'cancer' that 'mutated' or underwent 'metastasis', undermining the body politic and political institutions. As we mentioned in chapter 1, the UNODC head, Antonio Maria Costa, was a regular user of such terminology.[7]

The coronavirus has highlighted these similarities in the most visceral way. Like the virus, crime spreads quickly and violently, doing damage along the way. It infects communities and takes advantages of vulnerabilities to embed itself and to degrade the organs of the state and society. It exploits the very mechanisms that bind us together in this globalised, interconnected world, to reach into our private lives and exploits us.

The diagnostic we have made throughout this book suggests that the criminal contagion is metastasising and damaging its hosts—potentially fatally in some cases. And if action is not taken now, that damage may become irreversible: by the time we emerge from the pandemic and come to grips with the scale of the growth and penetration of the illicit economy, it may well be too late. By that point, entire communities could be tied into mafia ownership or indebtedness at a scale that will compromise legitimate governance, even in countries that never considered themselves at risk of organised crime before.[8]

But while the idea of crime as an invasive 'disease' may be compelling, we must also remember that in many places crime has been able to gain such a foothold because society itself was already sick. As we have shown, crime thrives because of the existing and acute vulnerabilities in the infrastructure of the global economy and governance that have been created—often purposely for the goal of self-enrichment and wealth protection by elites—over the past few decades. Systemic poverty, entrenched inequality, political oppression: crime did not create these, but it knows how to exploit them. Opportunistic politicians looking to cast crime as the viral 'enemy' from without should heed the old proverb: physician, heal thyself.

*Prevention, treatment and cure*

If organised crime is a disease, what is the treatment plan? As with all effective medical responses, any plan will need to be holistic, addressing prevention, treatment and cure. But for organised crime, what does that really mean?

On the prevention side, it means shoring up and protecting those who are most exposed and vulnerable. Some of the things needed are basic economic and social policy—creating safety nets, including unemployment benefits and access to credit, and ensuring they are equally accessible to men and women, majorities and minorities in society. Access to credit prevents people from having to resort to criminal groups—usury for businesses; prostitution, drug muling and collecting extortion payments for women; drug dealing, security and 'protection' for men; errand running, lookouts and sometimes killing for the kids.

Prevention also means providing a spectrum of social and education interventions for all children, beginning in the earliest years with health and well-being education for parents, and extending through primary and secondary education, including after-school programmes, summer camps and work apprenticeship schemes. All of these have been proven to reduce the exposure of youths at risk of criminal recruitment and build stronger societies that are more resilient to threats from organised crime.[9] They can be targeted at the most vulnerable communities but should be universally available. As the *New York Times* has noted, the pandemic reduced the efficacy of many of the most successful violence prevention programmes by taking violence interrupters off the street, shuttering social outreach programmes, and closing public spaces.[10] After the pandemic, these need to be built back better, with a long-term commitment and with resources.

Efforts also need to be made to reach vulnerable groups and potential victims. Hotlines for domestic abuse sufferers or initiatives to identify and report victims of trafficking are crucial in providing an exit for people caught in vulnerable situations and provide a lifeline when people are trapped. Raising awareness and building a better understanding of criminal threats are also important. Some of the most effective prevention programmes work with at-risk populations and consumers to help them to identify risk factors and avoid them. This means, for example, helping communities to distinguish fake medical products from real ones, or helping workers to recognise the false promises in a contract that will trap them into labour exploitation.

In the context of organised crime, 'treatment' is often interpreted as strengthening law enforcement capacity to investigate criminal groups and interdict illicit commodities. This is, unquestionably, one part of the solution, and there is already a considerable amount invested in building law enforcement capacity to counter organised crime. Global annual expenditure on law enforcement for drug control alone has been estimated to exceed US$100 billion a year.[11] Continued investment is required, particularly in the countries of source and transit for illicit supply chains, since these are often much weaker in capacity.

The legal framework—the way it criminalises and penalises certain crimes—is what defines the boundaries of the illicit economy. The challenges and the risks in operating within a particular jurisdiction are what determine the price that criminals can charge for their goods and services. It is for this reason that legalisation—or, at least, decriminalisation—of certain acts which are widespread is a credible expedient to take some of the profits out of the illicit economy, to destigmatise certain practices, and to allow law enforcement to focus on issues and criminal figures of higher concern. This has become an increasingly accepted position in regard to the use of narcotic drugs, but the approach also applies in other sectors, such as the response to artisanal mining, where it is felt a regulatory approach would be more beneficial than an enforcement one. Equally, promoting legal alternatives for irregular migrants is by far the more humane solution than pushing them into the arms of smugglers and traffickers who may potentially exploit them. In all cases, there is a benefit to states in legalisation, as it allows them to engage openly in reforming and improving their responses to those previously criminal sectors and addressing the harm that they can cause by using policy tools that do not make matters worse.

Law enforcement and criminal justice responses alone cannot be the whole answer to the problem of illicit markets, particularly in the very many places in the world where the quality of governance, the rule of law and economic systems are weak. In this study, we have seen many cases where political leaders and state officials at all levels have worked to undermine the pandemic response to protect their own power and interests. Corruption is potent and powerful and does extraordinary damage in bending state institutions away from the interests of the citizenry and towards those with power and influence. In these contexts, law enforcement can be bent into an instrument that enables crime rather than prevents it. And in places where people depend on the illicit economy for a living, a hard crackdown on crime may prove more divisive and damaging than beneficial. The pandemic and the challenges some nations have faced in policing the lockdowns have put into circulation a new set of dialogues.[12] So, strengthening law enforcement must mean building up systems of government and law so that they develop integrity, behave with respect for human rights, and retain the trust of the populations they are meant to serve.[13] Tackling corruption is crucial to achieving this.

Treatment will also require an effort to strengthen local resilience in the face of organised crime and make communities a partner in building safe spaces where people can grow up, live and work. This is a call to policy-makers, urban planners, architects, social innovators, tech geniuses and entrepreneurs to develop a role for themselves in community safety and security, to find ways to invest in innovations that will erect barriers to the transmission of criminal interests into everyday society.[14] It requires an investment in the growth and protection of civil society actors of all kinds—including NGO service providers, youth centres, religious groups, media houses and journalists, academic researchers, think tanks, data observatories, environmental lobbies and human rights advocacy groups—to bring back the public perspective into political and economic discourse. Civil society is at present being targeted by organised crime, often with a terrifying degree of impunity at national and international levels, and this cannot be allowed to continue.

And as for the cure? It seems unlikely that there will ever be a full cure for organised crime. Organised crime is too innovative, and there are always advantages to breaking the rules rather than following them. There are no easy solutions—only the urgency to improve our methods of response. Organised crime is a disease we have to learn to manage, to reduce the harm it can do to society, and to keep the lives it takes to a minimum. But we are a long way from that point, and arguably we have been moving in the wrong direction for some time.

Before the pandemic struck, the global instrument for responding to organised crime—the UN Convention Against Transnational Organized Crime, which had been negotiated in the wake of Giovanni Falcone's death and then agreed to by a record number of states—seemed to be faltering. While the Convention does create scope for the preventive actions and social interventions that are required, at its heart it is primarily a legalistic instrument, which has not lent itself to ensuring the range of social and economic interventions and innovations needed to respond to the many facets of the illicit economy. It is therefore imperative not only to build and reinforce this global blueprint, but also to expand its reach.

If we are going to achieve a cure for our rapidly spreading criminal contagion, and to prevent this pandemic (and any other future shock to the global system) from further strengthening criminal groups at the expense of citizens from all walks of life, then we need to take urgent steps to reorient financial systems; close down the tax havens and secrecy jurisdictions; restore as a matter of course measures for transparency, accountability, and independent oversight over politics, governance, procurement and trade; close down the free trade and manufacturing zones and strengthen regulation of trade and commerce; and take the steps to provide better governance and accountability in cyberspace—the world's most powerful means of communication should not sit in the hands of a few tech CEOs.

Such steps are not easy to achieve and will take unprecedented political will. Currently, we have handed the keys of the castle to the wealthy and unscrupulous—and ordinary people are paying the cost. Almost all other efforts are merely playing at the margins if we cannot address the means by which criminals and the corrupt launder and hide their profits, use them to subvert elections, undermine democracies, lobby governments, and distort competition. This, more than anything else, has chronically weakened our global immune system to the criminal contagion, and has allowed organised crime to reap long-term, potentially irreversible benefit from the pandemic.

It is time to end the war talk, all the bellicose, blustery rhetoric—both against the pandemic and against organised crime. It creates fear when we need unity, and brings violence and emergency powers to the table when what we need is solidarity, care for the most vulnerable, and a shared set of global solutions for the common good.

# NOTES

## 1. INTRODUCTION

1. Lily Kuo, 'China confirms human-to-human transmission of coronavirus', *The Guardian*, 21 January 2020, https://www.theguardian.com/world/2020/jan/20/coronavirus-spreads-to-beijing-as-china-confirms-new-cases.
2. Sarah Boseley, 'WHO declares coronavirus pandemic', *The Guardian*, 11 March 2020, https://www.theguardian.com/world/2020/mar/11/who-declares-coronavirus-pandemic.
3. Alan Rappeport, 'IMF predicts deeper global downturn even as economies reopen', *New York Times*, 24 June 2020, https://www.nytimes.com/2020/06/24/business/imf-world-economic-outlook.html.
4. Mara Mordecai and Shannon Schumacher, 'In many countries, people are more negative about the economy amid Covid-19 than during Great Recession', Pew Research Centre, 14 September 2020, https://www.pewresearch.org/fact-tank/2020/09/14/in-many-countries-people-are-more-negative-about-the-economy-amid-covid-19-than-during-great-recession/.
5. Speech to the 50th Session of the UN Commission on Narcotic Drugs (CND), Vienna, 12 March 2007. The phrase is from a presentation of UNODC's report on opium poppy cultivation in Afghanistan in 2007.

6. See Jennifer C. Finnegan and Anthony J. Masys, 'An epidemiological framework for investigating organised crime and terrorism', *Science Informed Policing* 19, p.37.
7. Ivan Krastev, *Is It Tomorrow Yet? Paradoxes of the Pandemic*, London: Allen Lane, 2020, p. 7.
8. Barbara Tuchman, *Distant Mirror: The calamitous 14th century*, New York: Penguin, 2017, p. 617.

## 2. DISRUPTION

1. 'Coronavirus: Italy extends emergency measures nationwide', BBC, 10 March 2020, https://www.bbc.com/news/world-europe-51810673.
2. Statement by President Cyril Ramaphosa on measures to combat Covid-19 epidemic, 15 March 2020, http://www.thepresidency.gov.za/press-statements/statement-president-cyril-ramaphosa-measures-combat-covid-19-epidemic.
3. Christie Aschwanden, 'How "superspreading" events drive most Covid-19 spread', *Scientific American*, 23 June 2020, https://www.scientificamerican.com/article/how-superspreading-events-drive-most-covid-19-spread1/.
4. Tom Phillips, 'Brazil's Jair Bolsonaro says coronavirus crisis is a media trick', *The Guardian*, 23 March 2020, https://www.theguardian.com/world/2020/mar/23/brazils-jair-bolsonaro-says-coronavirus-crisis-is-a-media-trick.
5. Jake Horton, 'Coronavirus: what are the numbers out of Latin America?', BBC, 23 September 2020, https://www.bbc.com/news/world-latin-america-52711458.
6. Ian Petchenik, 'Charting the decline in air traffic caused by Covid-19', Flightradar24, 29 March 2020, https://www.flightradar24.com/blog/charting-the-decline-in-air-traffic-caused-by-covid-19/.
7. Phillip Connor, 'More than nine-in-ten people worldwide live

in countries with travel restrictions amid Covid-19', Pew Research Center, 1 April 2020, https://www.pewresearch.org/fact-tank/2020/04/01/more-than-nine-in-ten-people-worldwide-live-in-countries-with-travel-restrictions-amid-covid-19/.

8. '25 million jobs at risk with airline shutdown', IATA, 7 April 2020, https://www.iata.org/en/pressroom/pr/2020-04-07-02/.
9. Bryce Baschuk, 'A trade collapse that is heading into the history books', Bloomberg, 26 March 2020, https://www.bloomberg.com/news/articles/2020-03-26/supply-chain-latest-a-trade-plunge-worthy-of-the-history-books.
10. 'US oil prices turn negative as demand dries up', BBC, 20 April 2020, https://www.bbc.com/news/business-52350082.
11. Anatoly Kurmanaev, 'Latin America is facing a "decline of democracy" under the pandemic', *New York Times*, 29 July 2020, https://www.nytimes.com/2020/07/29/world/americas/latin-america-democracy-pandemic.html.
12. Sally Hayden, '"I realized my body was burning": police brutality in Uganda lockdown', *The Guardian*, 28 May 2020, https://www.theguardian.com/global-development/2020/may/28/i-realised-my-body-was-burning-police-brutality-in-uganda-lockdown?utm_term=Autofeed&CMP=twt_gu&utm_medium&utm_source=Twitter#Echobox=1590648735.
13. 'Coronavirus: security forces kill more Nigerians than Covid-19', BBC, 16 April 2020, https://www.bbc.com/news/world-africa-52317196.
14. Eimhin O'Reilly, 'In Honduras, coronavirus lockdown is enforced at gunpoint', InSight Crime, 7 May 2020, https://www.insightcrime.org/news/analysis/honduras-coronavirus-lockdown-gunpoint/.
15. Natalie Huet and Anelise Borges, 'Amnesty slams alleged

police brutality in French lockdown enforcement', Euronews, 7 May 2020, https://www.euronews.com/2020/05/07/amnesty-slams-alleged-police-brutality-in-french-lockdown-enforcement.

16. Darren Taylor, 'Report clearing soldiers in South African man's death sparks anger', Voice of America, 29 May 2020, https://www.voanews.com/africa/report-clearing-soldiers-south-african-mans-death-sparks-anger.
17. 'Crime and contagion: the impact of a pandemic on organised crime', Global Initiative Against Transnational Organized Crime, March 2020, https://globalinitiative.net/wp-content/uploads/2020/03/GI-TOC-Crime-and-Contagion-The-impact-of-a-pandemic-on-organized-crime-1.pdf.
18. Hank Tucker, 'Coronavirus bankruptcy tracker: these major companies are failing amid the shutdown', *Forbes*, 3 May 2020, https://www.forbes.com/sites/hanktucker/2020/05/03/coronavirus-bankruptcy-tracker-these-major-companies-are-failing-amid-the-shutdown/; and Timothy Rooks, 'Bankruptcy: going out of business during the Covid-19 pandemic', Deutsche Welle, 17 June 2020, https://www.dw.com/en/bankruptcy-going-out-of-business-during-the-covid-19-pandemic/g-53823620.
19. 'The impact of Covid-19 on organised crime', UNODC, 2020, https://www.unodc.org/documents/data-and-analysis/covid/RB_COVID_organized_crime_july13_web.pdf.
20. Richard Behar, 'Organised crime in the time of corona', *Forbes*, 27 March 2020, https://www.forbes.com/sites/richardbehar/2020/03/27/organized-crime-in-the-time-of-corona/#26d2a979150d.
21. Alessia Cerantola, 'Japanese gangs vie for power amid pandemic', OCCRP, 22 April 2020, https://www.occrp.org/

en/coronavirus/japanese-gangs-vie-for-power-amid-pandemic.

22. Nicholas Wells, 'Crime and quarantine: how the pandemic is squeezing Italian crime groups', OCCRP, 24 March 2020, https://www.occrp.org/en/blog/11905-cocaine-corona-how-the-pandemic-is-squeezing-italian-crime-groups.
23. Alexandra Harney, 'China's coronavirus-induced supply chain woes fan concerns of possible drug shortages', Reuters, 11 March 2020, https://www.reuters.com/article/us-health-coronavirus-pharmaceuticals-ap/chinas-coronavirus-induced-supply-chain-woes-fan-concerns-of-possible-drug-shortages-idUSKBN20Y1C7.
24. '"We can't produce anything": how the coronavirus epidemic is affecting the counterfeits industry in China', *World Trademark Review*, 25 February 2020, https://www.worldtrademarkreview.com/anti-counterfeiting/we-cant-produce-anything-how-the-coronavirus-epidemic-affecting-the.
25. Lucia Bird, 'Smuggling in the time of Covid-19: the impact of the pandemic on human-smuggling dynamics and migrant-protection risks', Global Initiative Against Transnational Organized Crime, April 2020, https://globalinitiative.net/wp-content/uploads/2020/04/GIATOC-Policy-Brief-003-Smuggling-COVID-28Apr0930-proof-4.pdf.
26. Fatemeh Aman, 'Afghan migrants: unwanted in Iran and at home', Atlantic Council, 15 May 2020, https://www.atlanticcouncil.org/blogs/iransource/afghan-migrants-unwanted-in-iran-and-at-home/.
27. 'Impact of the Covid crisis on migrant smuggling', UNODC, 10 September 2020, https://www.unodc.org/unodc/frontpage/2020/September/impact-of-the-covid-crisis-on-the-crime-of-migrant-smuggling.html.
28. Sam Morgan, 'Keep on trucking: EU deploys "green lanes" to unclog freight', Euractiv, 23 March 2020, https://www.

euractiv.com/section/transport/news/keep-on-trucking-eu-deploys-green-lanes-to-unclog-freight/.

29. 'Coronavirus: cocaine haul in boxes of face masks seized', BBC, 15 April 2020, https://www.bbc.com/news/uk-england-52300095.
30. Mireri Junior, 'Kenya Red Cross warns Kenyans against fake coronavirus masks', *The Standard*, 21 March 2020, https://www.standardmedia.co.ke/health/article/2001365072/kenya-red-cross-warns-kenyans-against-fake-coronavirus-masks.
31. Brian Otieno, 'Ten people arrested as police raid clinic over fake coronavirus test kits', *The Standard*, 17 March 2020, https://www.standardmedia.co.ke/article/2001364467/ten-people-arrested-over-fake-coronavirus-testing-kits.
32. 'Global operation sees a rise in fake medical products related to Covid-19', INTERPOL, 19 March 2020, https://www.interpol.int/News-and-Events/News/2020/Global-operation-sees-a-rise-in-fake-medical-products-related-to-Covid-19.
33. 'Pandemic profiteering: how criminals exploit the Covid-19 crisis', Europol, March 2020, https://www.europol.europa.eu/publications-documents/pandemic-profiteering-how-criminals-exploit-covid-19-crisis.
34. Riaan Grobler, 'Reserve Bank warns against scammers "recalling cash contaminated with coronavirus"', News24, 17 March 2020, https://www.news24.com/news24/southafrica/news/reserve-bank-warns-against-scammers-recalling-cash-contaminated-with-coronavirus-20200317.
35. Jane Bradley, 'Scammers returning to "traditional" methods post lockdown', *The Scotsman*, 7 September 2020, https://www.scotsman.com/business/consumer/scammers-returning-traditional-methods-post-lockdown-2963624.
36. AR Winstock, EL Davies, G Gilchrist, A Zhuparris, JA Ferris,

LJ Maier and MJ Barratt, *Global Drug Survey: Special edition on Covid-19*, 2 June 2020, https://www.globaldrugsurvey.com/wp-content/themes/globaldrugsurvey/assets/GDS_COVID-19-GLOBAL_Interim_Report-2020.pdf.

37. Tammy Ayres and Craig Ancrum, 'PPE and contactless delivery: drug dealers reveal how they are adapting to coronavirus', *The Conversation*, 21 May 2020, https://theconversation.com/ppe-and-contactless-delivery-drug-dealers-reveal-how-they-are-adapting-to-coronavirus-138952.
38. Max Daly, 'Drug dealers are dressing up as delivery drivers, joggers and nurses to sell heroin during lockdown', Vice, 7 April 2020, https://www.vice.com/en_uk/article/n7jgyg/drug-dealers-crack-heroin-coronavirus-lockdown.
39. 'Covid-19 and drugs: drug supply via darknet markets', EMCDDA, May 2020, https://www.emcdda.europa.eu/system/files/publications/13042/EMCDDA-report_COVID19-darknet-final.pdf.
40. Jason Burke, 'South Africa's alcohol ban has given "massive boost" to criminal gangs', *The Guardian*, 31 May 2020, https://www.theguardian.com/world/2020/may/31/south-africas-alcohol-ban-has-given-massive-boost-to-criminal-gangs.
41. 'Government bans sale of hot pies, roast chicken', *Business Insider South Africa*, 20 April 2020, https://www.businessinsider.co.za/lockdown-hot-food-2020–4.
42. Lynsey Chutel, 'Taking on Covid-19, South Africa goes after cigarettes and booze, too', *New York Times*, 17 May 2020, https://www.nytimes.com/2020/05/08/world/africa/coronavirus-south-africa-tobacco-alcohol-ban.html.
43. Lester Kiewit, 'Gangs profit though guns are silent', *Mail & Guardian*, 23 April 2020, https://mg.co.za/article/2020-04-23-gangs-profit-though-guns-are-silent/.
44. 'The illegal industry booming under lockdown in South Africa', CNN, 9 June 2020, https://edition.cnn.com/vid-

eos/world/2020/06/09/south-africa-coronavirus-covid-19-pandemic-cigarette-ban-smuggling-mckenzie-pkg-intl-ldn-vpx.cnn.

45. Emanuele Ottolenghi, 'Covid-19 in Latin America: organised crime gains and states weaken', Foundation for Defense of Democracies, 22 May 2020, https://www.fdd.org/analysis/2020/05/22/covid-19-in-latin-america%3A-organized-crime-gains-and-states-weaken/.
46. Ricardo Moraes, Debora Moreira and Rodrigo Viga Gaier, 'Gangs call curfews as coronavirus hits Rio favelas', Reuters, 24 March 2020, https://www.reuters.com/article/us-health-coronavirus-brazil-favelas-fea/gangs-call-curfews-as-coronavirus-hits-rio-favelas-idUSKBN21B3EV.
47. Rukshana Parker, Michael McLaggan and Kim Thomas, 'Cape gangs in lockdown: saints or sinners in the shadow of Covid-19', Global Initiative Against Transnational Organized Crime, 22 April 2020, https://globalinitiative.net/gangs-in-lockdown-manenberg/.
48. Bismee Taskin, 'Daughter of drug lord El Chapo distributes Covid aid packages for cash-strapped Mexicans', *ThePrint*, 17 April 2020, https://theprint.in/world/daughter-of-drug-lord-el-chapo-distributes-covid-aid-packages-for-cash-strapped-mexicans/403924/.
49. 'State of the network: updates on Covid-19, as of 21 September 2020', TeleGeography, https://www2.telegeography.com/network-impact.
50. Ella Koeze and Nathaniel Popper, 'The virus changed the way we internet', *New York Times*, 7 April 2020, https://www.nytimes.com/interactive/2020/04/07/technology/coronavirus-internet-use.html.
51. Louis Columbus, 'How Covid-19 is transforming e-commerce', *Forbes*, 28 April 2020, https://www.forbes.com/sites/louiscolumbus/2020/04/28/how-covid-19-is-transforming-e-commerce/#12f08d6d3544.

52. 'How coronavirus is boosting e-commerce across Africa', Africanews, 16 May 2020, https://www.africanews.com/2020/05/16/virus-restrictions-boosts-e-commerce-across-africa/.
53. 'Internet anti-virus protection', Self, accessed 8 September 2020, https://www.self.inc/info/coronavirus-scams/.
54. Tonya Riley, 'Internet domain names are ripe for scam during coronavirus crisis', *Washington Post*, 8 September 2020, https://www.washingtonpost.com/politics/2020/09/08/cybersecurity-202-internet-domain-names-are-ripe-scam-during-coronavirus-crisis/.
55. 'BEC attacks surge as fraudsters eye pandemic opportunity', PYMNTS, 6 July 2020, https://www.pymnts.com/news/b2b-payments/2020/data-corporate-fraud-pandemic-bec/.
56. Alexis Kleinman, 'Porn sites get more visitors each month than Netflix, Amazon and Twitter combined', HuffPost, 7 December 2017, https://www.huffpost.com/entry/internet-porn-stats_n_3187682#:~:text=According%20to%20this%20infographic%20by,across%20the%20Internet%20is%20porn.
57. Julie Baumgardner, 'What you need to know about the coronavirus pandemic and porn', *Times Free Press*, 15 August 2020, https://www.timesfreepress.com/news/life/entertainment/story/2020/aug/15/what-you-need-know-about-pandemic-porn/529791/.
58. Harriet Grant, 'World's biggest porn site under fire over rape and abuse videos', *The Guardian*, 9 March 2020, https://www.theguardian.com/global-development/2020/mar/09/worlds-biggest-porn-site-under-fire-over-videos-pornhub.
59. 'Pandemic profiteering: how criminals exploit the Covid-19 crisis', Europol, March 2020.
60. Nanchanok Wongsamuth, 'Online child sex abuse in Thailand nears record high with coronavirus', Reuters, 18 June 2020, https://www.reuters.com/article/us-thailand-

sexcrimes-internet-trfn/online-child-sex-abuse-in-thailand-nears-record-high-with-coronavirus-idUSKBN23P33K.

## 3. BETWEEN COLD WAR AND COVID

1. Brunon Holyst, 'Organised crime in Eastern Europe and its implications for security of the Western world', in Stanley Einstein and Menachem Amir (eds.), *Organised Crime: Uncertainties and dilemmas*, Chicago: Office of International Criminal Justice, University of Illinois, 1999, p. 87.
2. Moisés Naím, *Illicit: How smugglers, traffickers and copycats are hijacking the global economy*, New York: Doubleday, 2005; Misha Glenny, *McMafia: A journey through the global criminal underworld*, New York: Vintage Books, 2009; Nils Gilman, Jesse Goldhammer and Steve Weber, *Deviant Globalisation: Black market economy in the 21st century*, New York: Continuum, 2011.
3. 'The globalisation of crime: a transnational organised crime threat assessment', UNODC, 2010, https://www.unodc.org/toc/en/crimes/migrant-smuggling.html.
4. Branko Milanovic, *Global Inequality: A new approach for the age of globalization*, Cambridge, Mass.: The Belknap Press, 2016, pp. 19–22.
5. 'Brave new world? Container transport in 2043', McKinsey, July 2018, https://www.mckinsey.com/~/media/mckinsey/industries/travel%20transport%20and%20logistics/our%20insights/brave%20new%20world%20container%20transport%20in%202043/brave-new-world-container-transport-in-2043.pdf.
6. International Civil Aviation Organisation (ICAO), Annual Report 2018, Presentation of 2018 Air Transport Statistical Results, https://www.icao.int/annual-report-2018/Pages/the-world-of-air-transport-in-2018-statistical-results.aspx.

7. 'Measuring digital development: facts and figures', International Telecommunication Union, 2019, https://www.itu.int/en/ITU-D/Statistics/Documents/facts/FactsFigures2019.pdf.
8. 'A criminal culture: extortion in Central America', InSight Crime and Global Initiative Against Transnational Organized Crime, May 2019, https://globalinitiative.net/wp-content/uploads/2019/05/Central-American-Extortion-Report-English-03May1400-WEB.pdf.
9. Guilhem Fabre, *Criminal Prosperity: Drug trafficking, money laundering and the financial crises after the Cold War*, London: Routledge, 2003, p. 71.
10. Intelligence and Security Committee of UK Parliament, *Russia*, HC 632, 21 July 2020, p. 16.
11. See https://wdr.unodc.org/wdr2020/.
12. Julia Black, Kate Dearden, Ann Singleton and Frank Laczko, *Fatal Journeys*, vol. 2, part I, Geneva: IOM, 2016, p. 1.
13. https://www.savetherhino.org/rhino-info/poaching-stats/.
14. 'How Somalia's charcoal trade is fuelling the acacia's demise', UNEP, 21 March 2018, https://www.unenvironment.org/news-and-stories/story/how-somalias-charcoal-trade-fuelling-acacias-demise.
15. See https://globalinitiative.net/toc-unsc/.
16. Phil Williams, 'Transnational criminal organizations: strategic alliances', *Washington Quarterly*, 18, 1, 1995, p. 57.
17. Lorenzo, Vienna, July 2020.
18. UNHCR, *Global Trends Report 2018*, https://www.unhcr.org/globaltrends2018/.

## 4. NO ESCAPE, NO WAY HOME

1. 'Annual growth in global air traffic passenger demand from 2006–21', Statistica, 2020, https://www.statista.com/statistics/

193533/growth-of-global-air-traffic-passenger-demand/, last accessed 24 September 2020.

2. 'Charting the decline in air traffic caused by Covid-19', Flightradar24, 29 March 2020, https://www.flightradar24.com/blog/charting-the-decline-in-air-traffic-caused-by-covid-19/.
3. Michael Gross, 'A planet with two billion cars', *Current Biology*, 26, 8, 25 April 2016, https://www.sciencedirect.com/science/article/pii/S0960982216303414.
4. United Nations, *Key Global Migration Figures, 2017–19*, Updated 30 September 2019, https://migrationdataportal.org/sites/default/files/2019–10/key-global-migration-figures.pdf.
5. UNHCR, *Figures at a Glance*, 18 June 2020, https://www.unhcr.org/ph/figures-at-a-glance.
6. 'The globalisation of crime: a transnational organised crime threat assessment', UNODC, 2010, https://www.unodc.org/toc/en/crimes/migrant-smuggling.html.
7. 'Migrant smuggling networks', Europol and INTERPOL, May 2016, https://www.europol.europa.eu/newsroom/news/europol-and-interpol-issue-comprehensive-review-of-migrant-smuggling-networks.
8. 'Secretary-General denounces "tsunami" of xenophobia unleashed amid Covid-19 calling for all-out effort against hate speech', UN, 8 May 2020, https://www.un.org/press/en/2020/sgsm20076.doc.htm.
9. Daniel Strauss and Oliver Laughland, 'Trump calls coronavirus criticism Democrats' "new hoax" and links it to immigration', *The Guardian*, 29 February 2020, https://www.theguardian.com/us-news/2020/feb/28/trump-calls-coronavirus-outbreak-a-hoax-and-links-it-to-immigration-at-rally.
10. Mimi Dwyer, 'US has expelled 8800 migrant children under coronavirus rules', Reuters, 12 September 2020, https://www.reuters.com/article/us-usa-immigration-children-idUSKBN26301L.

11. Benjamin Dodman, 'Doors slam shut across borderless Europe as coronavirus spreads', France24, 14 March 2020, https://www.france24.com/en/20200314-doors-slam-shut-across-borderless-europe-as-coronavirus-spreads.
12. 'Doors slamming shut in Hungary for asylum seekers', France24, 30 August 2020, https://www.france24.com/en/20200830-doors-slamming-shut-in-hungary-for-asylum-seekers.
13. Ian Austen, 'In shift, Trudeau says Canada will return asylum seekers to U.S.', *New York Times*, 20 March 2020, https://www.nytimes.com/2020/03/20/world/canada/trudeau-asylum-seekers-coronavirus.html.
14. 'The impact of Covid-19 related measures on human rights of migrants and refugees in the EU', International Commission of Jurists, 26 June 2020, https://www.icj.org/wp-content/uploads/2020/06/Covid19-impact-migrans-Europe-Brief-2020-ENG.pdf.
15. European Union Agency for Fundamental Rights, 'Migration: Key fundamental rights concerns', *Quarterly Bulletin*, 1.1.2020–31.03.2020, https://fra.europa.eu/sites/default/files/fra_uploads/fra-2020-migration-bulletin-2_en.pdf.
16. 'Syrian refugees in Cyprus pushed back to Turkey', Euromed Rights, 19 May 2020, https://euromedrights.org/publication/syrian-refugees-in-cyprus-pushed-back-to-turkey/.
17. Loreno Tondo, '"We give you 30 minutes": Malta turns migrant boat away with directions to Italy', *The Guardian*, 20 May 2020, https://www.theguardian.com/global-development/2020/may/20/we-give-you-30-minutes-malta-turns-migrant-boat-away-with-directions-to-italy.
18. 'Covid-19 puts asylum seekers at a higher risk as conditions in camps deteriorate and asylum procedures are suspended', European Union Agency for Fundamental Rights, 27 May 2020, https://fra.europa.eu/en/news/2020/covid-19-puts-

asylum-seekers-higher-risk-conditions-camps-deteriorate-and-asylum.

19. 'Meeting of heads of state or government with Turkey: EU–Turkey statement', Council of the European Union, 29 November 2015, http://www.consilium.europa.eu/en/press/press-releases/2015/11/29-eu-turkey-meeting-statement/.
20. 'How to defuse tensions in the Eastern Mediterranean', Crisis Group, 22 September 2020, https://www.crisisgroup.org/europe-central-asia/western-europemediterranean/how-defuse-tensions-eastern-mediterranean.
21. Harun al-Aswad, 'Rule of the ribers: inside one of Turkey's largest people-smuggling rings', Middle East Eye, 19 April 2020, https://www.middleeasteye.net/news/turkey-syrian-refugees-smuggling-fraud-extortion-addiction-run-show.
22. Patrick Kingsley and Karam Shoumali, 'Taking hard line, Greece turns back migrants by abandoning them at sea', *New York Times*, 14 August 2020, https://www.nytimes.com/2020/08/14/world/europe/greece-migrants-abandoning-sea.html.
23. Edward McAllister, 'Locked out by Covid refugees' lives on hold', Swissinfo, 31 August 2020, https://www.swissinfo.ch/eng/locked-out-by-covid-refugees-lives-on-hold/4600 1966.
24. Lucia Bird, 'Smuggling in the time of Covid: the impact of the pandemic on human-smuggling dynamics and migrant-protection risks', Global Initiative Against Transnational Organized Crime, April 2020, https://globalinitiative.net/analysis/smuggling-covid-19/.
25. Mélissa Godin, 'Covid-19 outbreaks are now emerging in refugee camps. Why did it take so long for the virus to reach them?', *Time*, 9 October 2020, https://time.com/5893135/covid-19-refugee-camps/.
26. 'Three asylum seekers at camp near US border test positive

for coronavirus', Reuters, 30 June 2020, https://www.theguardian.com/us-news/2020/jun/30/us-asylum-seekers-covid-19-mexico-matamoros.

27. Martin Chulov, 'Aid agencies warn of Covid-19 crisis in refugee camps as winter approaches', *The Guardian*, 23 September 2020, https://www.theguardian.com/global-development/2020/sep/23/aid-agencies-warn-of-covid-19-crisis-in-refugee-camps-as-winter-approaches.
28. Benedettta Zocchi, 'What coronavirus looks like at the Bosnian–Croatian frontier for Europe's unwanted migrants', *The Conversation*, 30 April 2020, https://theconversation.com/what-coronavirus-looks-like-at-the-bosnian-croatian-frontier-for-europes-unwanted-migrants-137226.
29. Tuesday Reitano and Lucia Bird, 'Understanding contemporary human smuggling as a vector in migration', Global Initiative Against Transnational Organized Crime, May 2018, https://globalinitiative.net/understanding_human_smuggling/.
30. 'Impact of Covid-19 on migrant smuggling', Mixed Migration Centre, 1 September 2020, https://reliefweb.int/sites/reliefweb.int/files/resources/126_Covid_Snapshot_Global_smuggling.pdf.
31. Local contact and journalist working in the region, reporting to the Global Initiative Against Transnational Organized Crime, March 2020.
32. 'Covid-19 impact on migrant smuggling and human trafficking', INTERPOL, 11 June 2020, https://www.interpol.int/en/News-and-Events/News/2020/Covid-19-impact-on-migrant-smuggling-and-human-trafficking.
33. Diane Taylor, 'Refugees tell of brutality as people-smuggling across Channel booms', *The Guardian*, 7 August 2020, https://www.theguardian.com/uk-news/2020/aug/06/refugees-tell-of-brutality-as-people-smuggling-across-channel-booms.

34. 'Rohingya crisis: nearly 300 refugees land in Indonesia after months at sea', BBC, 7 September 2020, https://www.bbc.com/news/world-asia-54034014.
35. Swaminathan Natarajan and Moazzem Hossain, 'Rohingya refugee crisis: "The bodies were thrown out of the boat"', BBC, 29 May 2020, https://www.bbc.com/news/world-asia-52832841.
36. Arun Gupta and Michelle Fawcett, 'Refugees in the time of Covid-19', *The Nation*, 21 April 2020, https://www.thenation.com/article/society/refugees-asylum-coronavirus-mexico/.
37. 'Global estimates of modern slavery: forced labour and forced marriage', ILO, September 2017, https://www.ilo.org/wcmsp5/groups/public/---dgreports/---dcomm/documents/publication/wcms_575479.pdf.
38. 'Labour migration in the Arab States', ILO, https://www.ilo.org/beirut/areasofwork/labour-migration/WCMS_514910/lang--en/index.htm.
39. Sameer Hashmi, 'Coronavirus leaves Gulf migrant workers stranded', BBC, 15 May 2020, https://www.bbc.com/news/world-middle-east-52655131.
40. Rezaul H. Laskar, 'Almost 200,000 Indians register to be repatriated from UAE', *Hindustan Times*, 5 May 2020, https://www.hindustantimes.com/india-news/almost-200-000-indians-register-to-be-repatriated-from-uae/story-40Qw66k1TJVwKqocLY5EsM.html.
41. Hannah Ellis-Petersen, 'NHS rubber gloves made in Malaysian factories linked with forced labour', *The Guardian*, 9 December 2018, https://www.theguardian.com/global-development/2018/dec/09/nhs-rubber-gloves-made-in-malaysian-factories-accused-of-forced-labour.
42. Jane Feinmann, 'The scandal of modern slavery in the trade of masks and gloves', *BMJ*, 1 May 2020, https://www.bmj.com/content/369/bmj.m1676.

43. 'Impact of the Covid-19 pandemic on trafficking in persons', UNODC, https://www.un.org/ruleoflaw/wp-content/uploads/2020/05/Thematic-Brief-on-COVID-19-EN-ver.21.pdf.
44. Mélissa Godin, 'As cities around the world go on lockdown, victims of domestic violence look for a way out', *Time*, 18 March 2020, https://time.com/5803887/coronavirus-domestic-violence-victims/.
45. 'Covid-19 pandemic: trafficking in persons considerations in internal displacement contexts', Global Protection Cluster, March 2020, https://www.globalprotectioncluster.org/wp-content/uploads/GPC-Task-Team-on-Anti-COVID-guidance_final_SM.pdf.
46. Stefania Giannini and Anne-Birgitte Albrectsen, 'Covid-19 school closures around the world will hit girls hardest', UNESCO, 31 March 2020, https://en.unesco.org/news/covid-19-school-closures-around-world-will-hit-girls-hardest.
47. 'UNICEF executive director Henriette Fore's remarks at a press conference on new updated guidance on school-related public health measures in the context of Covid-19', UNICEF, 15 September 2020, https://www.unicef.org/press-releases/unicef-executive-director-henrietta-fore-remarks-press-conference-new-updated.
48. 'The other impact of Covid-19: human trafficking cases are on the rise', Blue Dragon, 29 July 2020, https://www.bluedragon.org/latest-news/the-other-impact-of-covid-19-human-trafficking-cases-are-on-the-rise/.
49. 'Landlords coercing tenants unable to pay rent to provide sex: sex trafficking or not?', Polaris, 6 May 2020, https://polarisproject.org/blog/2020/05/landlords-coercing-tenants-unable-to-pay-rent-to-provide-sex-sex-trafficking-or-not/.
50. 'Covid-19 and child, early and forced marriage: an agenda

for action', Girls Not Brides, April 2020, https://www.girlsnotbrides.org/wp-content/uploads/2020/04/COVID-19-and-child-early-and-forced-marriage.pdf.
51. 'New UNFPA projections predict calamitous impact on women's health as Covid-19 pandemic continues', UNFPA, 28 April 2020, https://www.unfpa.org/press/new-unfpa-projections-predict-calamitous-impact-womens-health-covid-19-pandemic-continues.
52. Global Initiative Against Transnational Organized Crime, Civil Society Observatory of Illicit Economies in Eastern and Southern Africa, *Risk Bulletin*, 11, August–September 2020, https://globalinitiative.net/wp-content/uploads/2020/09/ESA-RB11.pdf.
53. Ingrid Gercama and Sanne Derks, 'Coronavirus: a devil's bargain for Dutch sex workers', Deutsche Welle, 11 June 2020, https://www.dw.com/en/coronavirus-a-devils-bargain-for-dutch-sex-workers/a-53744562.
54. Syamantak Ghosh, 'Covid-19: sex workers suffer during social distancing in India', Deutsche Welle, 13 April 2020, https://www.dw.com/en/covid-19-sex-workers-suffer-duringsocial-distancingin-india/a-53106907.
55. Kate Martyr, 'Coronavirus in Germany: how a Romanian sex worker is affected by prostitution ban', Deutsche Welle, 7 August 2020, https://www.dw.com/en/coronavirus-in-germany-how-a-romanian-sex-worker-is-affected-by-prostitution-ban/a-54484061.

## 5. BUSINESS AS USUAL

1. Drug trafficking is still the largest source of profit for organised crime. One would need to make seizures of two-thirds of all drugs to make the business go bust—and law enforcement agencies are nowhere close to that. These are conservative fig-

ures, as profits can be much higher. See David Nutt, *Drugs without the Hot Air: Making sense of legal and illegal drugs*, Cambridge: UIT, 2020, p. 328. An estimated 10% to 20% of drugs are currently seized, depending on the type, place and market.

2. Cocaine production has increased year-on-year over this period. Heroin production also increased, with a spike in 2017 and then some declines thereafter.
3. Juan Carlos Garzón Vergara, 'La erradicación forzada no ha aumentado, pero los cultivadores la están pasando mal', Fundación Ideas para la Paz, 19 May 2020, http://staging.ideaspaz.org/publications/posts/1838.
4. Cecilia Anesi, Giulio Rubino, Nathan Jaccard, Antonio Baquero, Lilia Saúl Rodríguez and Aubrey Belford, 'What lockdown? World's cocaine traffickers sniff at movement restrictions', OCCRP, 20 May 2020, https://www.occrp.org/en/coronavirus/what-lockdown-worlds-cocaine-traffickers-sniff-at-movement-restrictions.
5. Redacción Pares, 'Pandemia afectaría producción y distribución de drogas', Fundación Pares, 8 May 2020, https://pares.com.co/2020/05/08/coronavirus-afectaria-produccion-y-distribucion-de-cocaina/.
6. UNODC, *World Drug Report 2020*, Booklet 3, June 2020, pp. 25–26, https://wdr.unodc.org/wdr2020/field/WDR20_Booklet_3.pdf.
7. Deborah Bonello, 'Coronavirus is leading to shortages of fentanyl and meth', Vice, 19 March 2020, https://www.vice.com/en_us/article/wxek4m/coronavirus-is-leading-to-shortages-of-fentanyl-and-meth; and León Krauze, 'El coronavirus está perjudicando al narco y hay una oportunidad de acorralar a los cartels', *Washington Post*, 15 June 2020, https://www.washingtonpost.com/es/post-opinion/2020/06/04/el-coronavirus-esta-perjudicando-al-narco-y-hay-una-oportunidad-de-acorralar-los-carteles/.

8. For such claims, see Parker Asmann 'US chemicals help fuel Mexico drug production: report', InSight Crime, 11 September 2020, https://www.insightcrime.org/news/brief/us-chemicals-help-fuel-mexico-drug-production/; Cam Simpson, Michael Smith and Nacha Cattan, 'Heroin's hidden ingredient is a chemical made by U.S. companies', *Bloomberg Businessweek*, 26 August 2020, https://www.bloomberg.com/news/features/2020-08-26/u-s-drug-crisis-is-made-in-mexico-with-american-raw-materials.
9. 'México aumenta incautaciones de fentanilo, niega producción', AP News, 18 September 2020, https://apnews.com/cdd2c266371bb9f104499aab1a17f7d3.
10. 'Covid-19 and the drug supply chain: from production and trafficking to use', UNODC, Research Brief, 2020, p. 17, https://www.unodc.org/documents/data-and-analysis/covid/Covid-19-and-drug-supply-chain-Mai2020.pdf.
11. Global Initiative Against Transnational Organized Crime, Civil Society Observatory of Illicit Economies in Eastern and Southern Africa, 'Is Afghanistan a new source for methamphetamines in East and southern Africa?' *Risk Bulletin*, 12, September–October 2020.
12. Personal communication with Brazilian prosecutors and journalists, May–June 2020, https://globalinitiative.net/wp-content/uploads/2020/10/GI-TOC-ESAObs-RB12.pdf.
13. Andrew Doyle and Ray Rigamonti, 'Coronavirus: monitoring passenger jet activity through the hibernation phase', CIRIUM, accessed 22 May 2020, https://www.cirium.com/thoughtcloud/coronavirus-monitoring-passenger-jet-activity-through-the-hibernation-phase/.
14. This argument is spelled out in greater detail in Jason Eligh, 'Crisis and opportunity: impacts of the coronavirus pandemic on illicit drug markets', Global Initiative Against Transnational Organized Crime, Policy Brief, May 2020, pp. 11–13,

https://globalinitiative.net/wp-content/uploads/2020/05/Crisis-and-Opportunity-Jason-Eligh-GITOC.pdf.

15. Personal communication from law enforcement officers engaged in interdiction at the Maritime Analysis and Operations Centre, Lisbon, September 2019. A figure of 65% is used by Ivan Briscoe, 'What makes countries vulnerable to transnational organised crime', NOREF, September 2011, https://noref.no/content/download/166249/687580/version/2/Briscoe_NOREF_Vulnerability%20to%20organised%20crime.pdf.
16. This conclusion is based on GI interviews. See Eligh, 'Crisis and opportunity', pp. 11–13.
17. Eligh, 'Crisis and opportunity', pp. 11–13.
18. *EU Drug Markets: Impact of Covid-19*, Lisbon and The Hague: European Monitoring Centre for Drugs and Drug Addiction and Europol, May 2020, p.10, https://www.emcdda.europa.eu/publications/joint-publications/eu-drug-markets-impact-of-covid-19_en.
19. Eligh, 'Crisis and opportunity', pp. 11–12.
20. Sam Morgan, 'Keep on trucking: EU deploys "green lanes" to unclog freight', Euractiv, 23 March 2020, https://www.euractiv.com/section/transport/news/keep-on-trucking-eu-deploys-green-lanes-to-unclog-freight/.
21. In mid-April 2020, the UK Border Force discovered 14 kg of cocaine hidden within boxes of face masks that were sent across the English Channel.
22. *EU Drug Markets: Impact of Covid-19*, p. 9.
23. *EU Drug Markets: Impact of Covid-19*, p. 9.
24. Alicia Liliana Méndez, 'Las incautaciones de cocaína se incrementaron en un 8 por ciento', *El Tiempo* (Bogota), 3 July 2020, https://www.eltiempo.com/justicia/conflicto-y-narcotrafico/incautaciones-de-cocaina-han-crecido-en-2020-un-8-por-ciento-514142.

25. Late 2019 and the first six months of 2020 have seen considerable political conflict in Bissau as a new political elite have taken power after an election, the results of which have been contested. The Bissau-Guinean military, which has long played a key role in facilitating the trafficking of cocaine through the country, appears to be once again assertive.
26. Personal communication, April 2020.
27. See Mark Shaw and A. Gomes, 'Breaking the vicious cycle: cocaine politics in Guinea-Bissau', Global Initiative Against Transnational Organized Crime, Policy Brief, May 2020, https://globalinitiative.net/wp-content/uploads/2020/05/Guinea-Bissau_Policy-Brief_Final2.pdf.
28. *CBP Enforcement Statistics Fiscal Year 2020*, https://www.cbp.gov/newsroom/stats/cbp-enforcement-statistics.
29. *EU Drug Markets: Impact of Covid-19*.
30. The fact that the survey is 'expert opinion' means of course that it is much less reliable than, for example, a comprehensive drug user survey. But some of the experts consulted would have had access to user data from the ground.
31. These included the Netherlands and Belgium, both important transit countries for shipments of the drug arriving in containers; significant seizures occurred here.
32. Austria, Belgium, Czechia, Finland, Hungary, Latvia, the Netherlands and Sweden. *EU Drug Markets: Impact of Covid-19*, pp. 16–17.
33. *EU Drug Markets: Impact of Covid-19*, p. 14.
34. *EU Drug Markets: Impact of Covid-19*, pp. 21–23.
35. As an illustration of the difficulties of gathering data on drug prices and availability, there are some contradictions in the various reports. For example, government experts from Czechia reported to the European authorities that, across all drug types, there had been no change in price or availability. UNODC suggested that its field reporting showed that

in Czechia 'heroin has disappeared from the street-level market'.

36. *EU Drug Markets: Impact of Covid-19*, p. 26.
37. 'Covid-19 and the drug supply chain: from production and trafficking to use', UNODC, Research Brief, 2020, p. 34. There were major drug seizures in several cities in the region, including Cairo and Tangier, and no major changes in drug availability.
38. 'Covid-19 and the drug supply chain: from production and trafficking to use', UNODC, Research Brief, p. 33.
39. *EU Drug Markets: Impact of Covid-19*, p. 33.
40. 'Covid-19 and the drug supply chain: from production and trafficking to use', UNODC, Research Brief, pp. 33–34.
41. Max Daly, 'Drug dealers are dressing up as delivery drivers, joggers and nurses to sell heroin during lockdown', Vice, 7 April 2020, https://www.vice.com/en_uk/article/n7jgyg/drug-dealers-crack-heroin-coronavirus-lockdown.
42. Tammy Ayres and Craig Ancrum, 'PPE and contactless delivery: drug dealers reveal how they are adapting to coronavirus', *The Conversation*, 21 May 2020, https://theconversation.com/ppe-and-contactless-delivery-drug-dealers-reveal-how-they-are-adapting-to-coronavirus-138952.
43. 'Covid-19 and drugs: drug supply via darknet markets', EMCDDA, May 2020, https://www.emcdda.europa.eu/system/files/publications/13042/EMCDDA-report_Covid19-darknet-final.pdf.
44. AR Winstock, EL Davies, G Gilchrist, A Zhuparris, JA Ferris, LJ Maier and MJ Barratt, *Global Drug Survey: Special edition on Covid-19*, 2 June 2020, https://www.globaldrugsurvey.com/wp-content/themes/globaldrugsurvey/assets/GDS_COVID-19-GLOBAL_Interim_Report-2020.pdf.
45. Navjeevan Gopal, 'Explained: how Covid-19 is helping Punjab's war on drugs', *The Indian Express*, 27 June 2020,

https://indianexpress.com/article/explained/punjab-drug-addiction-amid-coronavirus-pandemic-6477060/.

46. Eligh, 'Crisis and opportunity', p. 6.
47. Comments made during the virtual launch in May 2020 of the report of the Global Commission on Drugs, *Enforcing Drug Laws: Refocusing on organized crime elites*.

## 6. CRIMINAL COMMODITIES

1. Brandon Prins, 'Piracy is on the rise, and coronavirus could make it worse', World Economic Forum, 15 May 2020, https://www.weforum.org/agenda/2020/05/global-sea-piracy-coronavirus-covid19/.
2. Lucy Martin, 'Coronavirus: piracy incidents double across Asia during pandemic', BBC, 17 July 2020, https://www.bbc.com/news/business-53426890.
3. Kevin Drew, 'Amid a pandemic, the Jolly Roger flies high', U.S. News, 30 July 2020, https://www.usnews.com/news/best-countries/articles/2020-07-30/world-sees-upswing-of-maritime-piracy-amid-coronavirus-pandemic.
4. Theo Locherer, 'Surge of piracy amid coronavirus outbreak', *Global Risk Insights*, 4 October 2020, https://globalriskinsights.com/2020/10/surge-of-piracy-amid-coronavirus-outbreak/.
5. United States Department of State, Security Alert: US Embassy Mexico City, 17 June 2020, https://mx.usembassy.gov/security-alert-u-s-embassy-mexico-city-mexico-06-17-2020/.
6. Alex Kimani, 'Oil piracy has spiked during Covid pandemic', *Oil Price*, 18 August 2020, https://oilprice.com/Geopolitics/International/Oil-Piracy-Has-Spiked-During-Covid-Pandemic.html.
7. Kirk Semple, 'Piracy surges in Gulf of Mexico prompting US warning', *New York Times*, 18 June 2020, https://www.nytimes.

com/2020/06/18/world/americas/gulf-mexico-pirates-ships.html.

8. Kimani, 'Oil piracy has spiked during Covid pandemic'.
9. 'Pirates are kidnapping more seafarers off West Africa, IMB reports', ICCWBO, 14 September 2020, https://iccwbo.org/media-wall/news-speeches/imb-piracy-report-2020/.
10. Locherer, 'Surge of piracy amid coronavirus outbreak'.
11. Eugenio Cusumano and Stefano Ruzza, 'Security privatization at sea: piracy and the commercialization of vessel protection', *International Relations*, 32, 1, 2018, pp. 80–103, https://journals.sagepub.com/doi/pdf/10.1177/0047117817731804.
12. Livia Wagner, 'Organized crime and illegally mined gold in Latin America', Global Initiative Against Transnational Organized Crime, April 2016, https://globalinitiative.net/wp-content/uploads/2016/03/Organized-Crime-and-Illegally-Mined-Gold-in-Latin-America.pdf.
13. Presentation of Adriana Abdenur at the Global Initiative Network Virtual Group Discussion on Environmental Crime, 29 April 2020.
14. Marcena Hunter, 'Pulling at golden webs: combatting criminal consortia in the African artisanal and small-scale gold mining and trade sector', ENACT Africa, April 2019, https://enactafrica.org/research/research-papers/pulling-at-golden-webs-combating-criminal-consortia-in-the-african-artisanal-and-small-scale-gold-mining-and-trade-sector.
15. 'Money laundering/terrorist financing risks and vulnerabilities associated with gold', Financial Action Task Force and Asia-Pacific Group on Money Laundering, July 2015, https://www.fatf-gafi.org/media/fatf/documents/reports/ML-TF-risks-vulnerabilities-associated-with-gold.pdf.
16. Alan Martin and Joanne Lebert, 'Covid-19 and ASM: illicit traders cashing in on vulnerable miners in conflict prone

areas', IMPACT, 10 April 2020, https://www.planetgold.org/covid-19-asm-illicit-traders-cashing-vulnerable-miners-conflict-prone-areas.

17. Sam Jones and Valentina Romei, 'Pandemic makes world's billionaires—and their advisors—richer', *Financial Times*, 24 October 2020, https://www.ft.com/content/ab30d301-351b-4387-b212-12fed904324b.
18. Quoted in Martin and Lebert, 'Covid-19 and ASM'.
19. 'How smuggled DRC gold passes through Entebbe', *Daily Monitor*, 24 July 2020, https://www.monitor.co.ug/uganda/special-reports/how-smuggled-drc-gold-passes-through-entebbe-1908854.
20. Martin and Lebert, 'Covid-19 and ASM'.
21. Nicholas Bariyo and Joe Parkinson, 'Under cover of coronavirus lockdown, a booming trade in conflict gold', *Wall Street Journal*, 9 July 2020, https://www.wsj.com/articles/under-cover-of-coronavirus-lockdown-a-booming-trade-in-conflict-gold-11594285200.
22. Interview with head of security for a large mining company, October 2020.
23. Fernando Carvalho, 'Mining industry and sustainable development: time for change', *Food and Energy Security*, 6, 2, 2017, https://onlinelibrary.wiley.com/doi/epdf/10.1002/fes3.109.
24. 'SA lockdown: fears rise for illegal miners hiding underground', Reuters, 29 April 2020, https://www.dailymaverick.co.za/article/2020-04-29-fears-rise-for-illegal-south-african-miners-hiding-underground-in-virus-lockdown/.
25. 'Nine illegal miners killed in South Africa', Africanews, 1 February 2020, https://www.africanews.com/2020/02/01/nine-illegal-miners-killed-in-south-africa-police/.
26. Mia Lindeque, '2 zama zamas killed, 6 injured in shooting in Florida', EWN, 19 June 2020, https://www.msn.com/en-za/news/national/2-zama-zamas-killed-6-injured-in-shooting-in-florida/ar-BB15HsnH.

27. Global Initiative Against Transnational Organized Crime, Civil Society Observatory of Illicit Economies in Eastern and Southern Africa, 'Gold and guns: audacious armed robberies of gold smelting facilities in South Africa', *Risk Bulletin*, 13, October–November 2020.
28. Interviews with illegal gold-mining experts in Peru in March 2020 during the 5th National Congress of Specialized Prosecutors in Environmental Matters of Peru and 1st International Congress on Environmental Crimes.
29. 'Defending tomorrow: the climate crisis and the threats against land and environmental defenders', Global Witness, July 2020, https://www.globalwitness.org/en/campaigns/environmental-activists/defending-tomorrow/.
30. There is a depressing drumbeat of such cases. As we finished this chapter, Fikile Ntshangase, a leading member of the Mfolozi Community Environment Organisation, was assassinated in South Africa's KwaZulu-Natal province. She had been opposing the expansion of a mine in her area.
31. Aramís Castro and Clarys Cárdenas, 'Crimen e impunidad en Madre de Dios: el cuarto asesinato de un líder ambiental en pandemia' [Crime and impunity in Madre de Dios: the fourth murder of an environmental leader in a pandemic], *Ojo Publico*, 13 September 2020, https://ojo-publico.com/2087/madre-de-dios-el-cuarto-asesinato-de-un-lider-ambiental-en-pandemia?fbclid=IwAR1z2GW11qbuipQBBktUudeGZS9BQib2lqcsPwLXBGr6YHuF2Y2z0YNBAes.
32. Juliane Kippenberg, 'Global gold supply chains just got riskier', London Bullion Market Association Virtual Summit blog, 23 September 2020, https://www.lbmaresponsiblesourcingsummit2020.com/post/manage-your-blog-from-your-live-site; 'Violent abuses in illegal gold mines', Human Rights Watch, Venezuela, 4 February 2020, https://www.hrw.org/news/2020/02/04/venezuela-violent-abuses-illegal-gold-mines.

33. 'Violent abuses in illegal gold mines', Human Rights Watch, Venezuela.
34. 'Findings on the worst forms of child labor', US Department of Labor, September 2020, https://www.dol.gov/agencies/ilab/resources/reports/child-labor/findings.
35. Wagner, 'Organized crime and illegally mined gold in Latin America'.
36. Livia Wagner and Thi Hoang, 'Aggravating circumstances: how coronavirus impacts human trafficking', Global Initiative Against Transnational Organized Crime, May 2020, https://globalinitiative.net/wp-content/uploads/2020/06/Aggravating-circumstances-How-coronavirus-impacts-human-trafficking-GITOC-1.pdf.
37. 'Minería ilegal en Amazonía peruana frena pero aún vive incluso con cuarentena', *Gestión Perú*, 8 July 2020, https://gestion.pe/peru/mineria-ilegal-en-amazonia-peruana-frena-pero-aun-vive-incluso-con-cuarentena-noticia/.
38. Terrence McCoy and Heloísa Traiano, 'In the Amazon, the coronavirus fuels an illegal gold rush--and an environmental crisis', *Washington Post*, 4 September 2020, https://www.washingtonpost.com/world/the_americas/in-the-amazon-the-coronavirus-fuels-an-illegal-gold-rush—and-an-environmental-crisis/2020/09/03/0a4c62e6-e624-11ea-970a-64c73a1c2392_story.html.
39. Approximately 143,000 square kilometres (55,000 square miles) of Indigenous land overlaps with active mining concessions (concessions in which exploration or exploitation are under way) and known illegal mining areas—much of it in Venezuela, Brazil and Colombia. The remaining 302,000 square kilometres (117,000 square miles) of Indigenous land overlaps with concessions that have been demarcated but not allocated or where mining operations have not yet started.
40. Kippenberg, 'Global gold supply chains just got riskier'.

41. Francesca García Delgado, 'Madre de Dios: la minería ilegal de oro no da tregua en época de pandemia' [Madre de Dios: illegal gold mining does not give truce in times of pandemic], *El Comercio*, 2 June 2020, https://elcomercio.pe/peru/madre-de-dios/coronavirus-en-peru-madre-de-dios-la-mineria-ilegal-de-oro-no-da-tregua-en-epoca-de-pandemia-informe-noticia/.
42. 'Minam evaluará en Madre de Dios lucha contra coronavirus y la minería ilegal' [Minam will evaluate the fight against coronavirus and illegal mining in Madre de Dios], Andina, 27 August 2020, https://andina.pe/agencia/noticia-minam-evaluara-madre-dios-lucha-contra-coronavirus-y-mineria-ilegal-811551.aspx.
43. See Sostenible, Aumenta la minería illegal en los Farallones de Cali durante la cuarentena, [Illegal mining increases in the Farallones de Cali during the quarantine], 5 November 2020, https://sostenibilidad.semana.com/impacto/articulo/coronavirus-en-colombia-aumenta-la-mineria-ilegal-en-los-farallones-de-cali-durante-la-cuarentena/50807.
44. 'Nuevo proyecto de ley contra la extracción ilícita de minerals', Hablemos de minería, 22 July 2020, http://hablemosdemineria.com/2020/07/nuevo-proyecto-ley-la-extraccion-ilicita-minerales/.

## 7. WILDLIFE'S REVENGE?

1. Tommy Tsan-Yuk Lam et al., 'Identifying SARS-Cov-2-related coronaviruses in Malayan pangolins', *Nature*, 583, 26 March 2020, https://www.nature.com/articles/s41586–020–2169–0.pdf.
2. The connection between wildlife markets and the spread of zoonotic diseases is not of course new. In the case of the Severe Acute Respiratory Syndrome (SARS) outbreak of 2003, which

had similar symptoms to Covid-19 and is also a coronavirus, the palm civet was identified as the likely intermediary (with Chinese horseshoe bats being the likely original source). Palm civets had been sold at the time in live-animal markets in Guangdong, China's most populous province.

3. A survey of consumers' past habits suggested a significant market for wildlife at such markets, with just under 10% of respondents in a survey of consumers in Vietnam, Thailand, Myanmar and Hong Kong SAR reporting that they, or someone they knew, had made such a purchase in the past twelve months. Live birds were the most commonly purchased item (46%), followed by snakes (34%), bats (23%), civets (20%), pangolins (19%) and turtles (15%).
4. Traffickers in Mexico, for example, are enjoying the spoils of a fairly new and lucrative trade in the bladder of the totoaba fish, which is found only in the Gulf of California and is sold almost exclusively to consumers in Asian markets. See more here: https://www.insightcrime.org/news/brief/how-mexican-crime-groups-profit-from-illegal-fish-bladder-trade/.
5. See Aron White, 'Chinese government policy on wildlife trade: what has changed, what has not and why it matters', RUSI Commentary, 13 July 2020, https://rusi.org/commentary/chinese-government-policy-wildlife-trade-what-has-changed-what-has-not-and-why-it-matters?page=37.
6. Scott Neuman, 'U.S. pressures China to close wet markets thought to be source of Covid-19', NPR, 23 April 2020, https://www.npr.org/sections/coronavirus-live-updates/2020/04/23/842178010/u-s-pressures-china-to-close-wet-markets-thought-to-be-source-of-covid-19?t=1597072882128.
7. The use of the term 'wet market' in China itself caused some confusion. The term is from Hong Kong English and is used to describe outdoor vegetable, fruit, meat and seafood stores, which have slippery concrete floors from food waste and

washing water. Contrary to what was sometimes assumed, the 'wet' did not refer to the blood of newly killed animals.

8. 'Smoke and Mirrors: China's complicity in the global illegal pangolin trade', Environmental Investigation Agency, October 2020, https://eia-international.org/wp-content/uploads/EIA-Smoke-and-Mirrors-2020-FINAL.pdf.
9. White, 'Chinese government policy on wildlife trade'.
10. Wufei Yu, 'Coronavirus: revenge of the pangolins?', *New York Times*, 5 March 2020, https://www.nytimes.com/2020/03/05/opinion/coronavirus-china-pangolins.html.
11. There is strong support among most ordinary Asian people for the closure of illegal markets selling wildlife: a post-Covid-19 survey in five countries (although excluding China) suggested that 94% of respondents were supportive of illegal market closures to prevent similar viral outbreaks to that of the coronavirus.
12. It is important to be aware that zoonotic disease risks are equally relevant for the legal wildlife trade—SARS likely emerged from legal (and, from a conservation perspective, harmless) farming of a wild animal species in China. But illegal trade practices undermine health control measures, so they are an added risk.
13. Rebecca Wong, 'The role of reputation in the illegal purchase of protected wildlife in China', *Deviant Behavior*, 2016, http://dx.doi.org/10.1080/01639625.2016.1248716.
14. Christian Shepherd and Qianer Liu, 'Will Covid-19 tame China's wildlife trade?', *Financial Times Magazine*, 30 July 2020, https://www.ft.com/content/55b2f73f-c05f-4faf-ba89-1af0c082644b.
15. In several markets in particular, some important shifts in consumer culture seem to have occurred. In Vietnam, which is an important market for wildlife products, 31% of respondents reported that they have completely stopped the habit,

and another 10% pledged to consume less. It should be noted too that 8% of respondents in the survey cited above suggested that they were likely or very likely to continue to buy wildlife products, including small but important numbers who indicated that they would likely consume more (in Vietnam that figure was 4%). These respondents reported that they expected to obtain illegal wildlife products through either trusted traders or from overseas suppliers.

16. Personal communication, June 2020.
17. Discussions with Global Initiative members, July 2020.
18. Department of Environment, Forestry and Fisheries, press release: 'Rhino poaching decreases by more than half in first half of 2020', 31 July 2020, https://www.environment.gov.za/mediarelease/rhinopoachingdecreases.
19. At the time of writing, data on rhino poaching for the fourth quarter of 2020 had not yet been released.
20. Ayat S. Karokaro, 'Trafficking of thousands of songbirds highlights rampant trade in Indonesia', Mongabay, 3 July 2020, https://news.mongabay.com/2020/07/trafficking-of-thousands-of-songbirds-highlights-rampant-trade-in-indonesia/; and Elizabeth Claire Alberts, 'Authorities seize record 26 tons of illegal shark fins in Hong Kong', Mongabay, 7 May 2020, https://news.mongabay.com/2020/05/authorities-seize-record-26-tons-of-illegal-shark-fins-in-hong-kong/.
21. Chris Dalby, 'Coronavirus has not slowed looting of Latin America's maritime species,', InSight Crime, 24 June 2020, https://www.insightcrime.org/news/brief/coronavirus-trafficking-maritime-biodiversity/.
22. 'Coronavirus hace que se incremente el tráfico ilegal de fauna silvestre en América Latina', Conexion Capital, 23 May 2020, https://conexioncapital.co/coronavirus-hace-que-se-incremente-el-trafico-ilegal-de-fauna-silvestre-en-america-latina/.

23. Dalby, 'Coronavirus has not slowed looting of Latin America's maritime species'.
24. Personal communication, August 2020.
25. Interviews with participants in the abalone trade, Cape Town, August 2020; 'Empty shells: abalone poaching and trade from southern Africa', TRAFFIC, 18 September 2018, https://www.traffic.org/publications/reports/empty-shells/.
26. Interviews with participants in the abalone trade, Cape Town, August 2020.
27. 'Reported wildlife poaching in India more than doubles during Covid-19 lockdown', TRAFFIC, 3 June 2020, https://www.traffic.org/publications/reports/reported-wildlife-poaching-in-india-more-than-doubles-during-covid-19-lockdown/.
28. We are grateful to our colleague Alastair Nelson for this information.
29. Anna Gross et al., 'Global deforestation accelerates during pandemic', *Financial Times*, 9 August 2020, https://www.ft.com/content/b72e3969-522c-4e83-b431-c0b498754b2d.
30. Deborah Bonello, 'Illegal logging in Chihuahua is now Mexico cartel territory', InSight Crime, 10 January 2020, https://www.insightcrime.org/news/analysis/illegal-logging-chihuahua-mexico-cartel/.
31. Deborah Bonello, "How Drug Cartels Moved into Illegal Logging in Mexico," InSight Crime, September 18 2019, https://www.insightcrime.org/investigations/drug-cartels-illegal-logging-mexico/.
32. Peter Lindsay et al., 'Conserving Africa's wildlife and wildlands through the Covid-19 crisis and beyond', *Nature Ecology and Evolution*, 4, 2020, https://doi.org/10.1038/s41559-020-1275-6.
33. See, for example, Nathan Bennett et al., 'The Covid-19 pandemic, small-scale fisheries and coastal fishing communities',

*Coastal Management*, 48, 4, 2020, https://www.tandfonline.com/doi/full/10.1080/08920753.2020.1766937; on Brazil, see Eduardo Campos Lima, 'In Covid's shadow, illegal fishing flourishes', *Hakai Magazine*, 8 July 2020, https://www.hakaimagazine.com/news/in-covids-shadow-illegal-fishing-flourishes/.

34. 'Satellite data indicate illegal fishing surged in Philippines during Covid-19 lockdown', EcoWatch, 8 June 2020, https://www.ecowatch.com/illegal-fishing-philippines-2646162839.html.
35. Peter Lindsay et al., 'Conserving Africa's wildlife and wildlands through the Covid-19 crisis and beyond'.
36. There are many legitimate reasons for this that do not belong in this chapter but relate to the human cost and consequences of the drug trade.
37. Fabio Zuker, 'Next pandemic? Amazon deforestation may spark new diseases', Reuters, 19 October 2020, https://www.reuters.com/article/us-brazil-disease-amazon-deforestation-t-idUSKBN2741IF.
38. Scanlon made the argument in several forums; see https://www.linkedin.com/pulse/fresh-look-global-wildlife-trade-law-can-cites-help-scanlon-ao/.

## 8. IT'S VIRTUAL

1. Martha Mendoza and Jim Gomez, 'Big child webcam sex bust reveals rising abuse', Associated Press, 10 May 2017, https://www.spokesman.com/stories/2017/may/09/big-child-webcam-sex-bust-reveals-rising-abuse/.
2. Corinne Redfern, 'Coronavirus locks down the Philippines, but children face threat of online abuse', Fuller Project, 27 March 2020, https://fullerproject.org/story/coronavirus-locks-down-the-philippines-but-children-face-threat-of-online-abuse/.

3. 'Webcam child sex tourism—becoming sweetie: a novel approach to stopping the global rise of webcam child sex tourism', Terre des Hommes, no date, https://www.tdh.ch/en/projects/sweetie-how-stop-webcam-child-sex-tourism.
4. 'Online sexual exploitation of children in the Philippines: analysis and recommendations for governments, industry and civil society', International Justice Mission, May 2020, https://www.ijm.org/documents/Final-Public-Full-Report-5_20_2020.pdf.
5. 'Safe online', End Violence Against Children, no date, https://www.end-violence.org/safe-online.
6. 'Exploiting isolation: offenders and victims of online child sexual abuse during the Covid-19 pandemic', Europol, 19 June 2020, https://www.europol.europa.eu/publications-documents/exploiting-isolation-offenders-and-victims-of-online-child-sexual-abuse-during-covid-19-pandemic.
7. Louise Donovan and Corinne Redfern, 'Online child abuse flourishes as investigators struggle with workload during pandemic', *The Telegraph*, 27 April 2020, https://www.telegraph.co.uk/global-health/science-and-disease/online-child-exploitation-flourishes-investigators-struggle/.
8. 'Millions of attempts to access child sexual abuse online during lockdown', Internet Watch Foundation, 20 May 2020, https://www.iwf.org.uk/news/millions-of-attempts-to-access-child-sexual-abuse-online-during-lockdown.
9. Michelle Drouin, Brandon T. McDaniel, Jessica Pater and Tammy Toscos, 'How parents and their children used social media and technology at the beginning of the Covid-19 pandemic and associations with anxiety', *Cyberpsychology, Behavior and Social Networking*, published online 27 July 2020 ahead of print, https://www.liebertpub.com/doi/full/10.1089/cyber.2020.0284.
10. Elizabeth Dwoskin and Nitasha Tiku, 'Facebook sent home

thousands of human moderators due to the coronavirus: now the algorithms are in charge', *Washington Post*, 24 March 2020, https://www.washingtonpost.com/technology/2020/03/23/facebook-moderators-coronavirus/.

11. 'School closings due to Covid-19 present potential for increased risk of child exploitation', FBI, 23 March 2020, https://www.fbi.gov/news/pressrel/press-releases/school-closings-due-to-covid-19-present-potential-for-increased-risk-of-child-exploitation/layout_view.
12. George Nikolaidis, 'One in five children suffers one or another form of sexual abuse or victimization during their childhood', Council of Europe, interview and transcript, no date, https://www.coe.int/en/web/portal/covid-19-one-in-five-children-suffers-one-or-another-form-of-sexual-abuse-or-victimisation-during-their-childhood.
13. Lucia Bird, Thi Hoang, Julia Stanyard, Summer Walker and Simone Haysom, 'Transformative technologies: how digital is changing the landscape of organised crime', Global Initiative, June 2020, https://globalinitiative.net/cyber-tech-organized-crime/.
14. 'The economic impact of cybercrime: no slowing down', CSIS and McAfee, February 2018, https://www.mcafee.com/enterprise/en-us/forms/gated-form.html?docID=5fee1c652573999d75e4388122bf72f5&tag=ec&eid=18TL_ECGLQ1_CT_WW&elqCampaignId=23163.
15. Deepen Desai, '30,000 percent increase in Covid-19 themed attacks', Zscaler, 23 April 2020, https://www.zscaler.com/blogs/research/30000-percent-increase-covid-19-themed-attacks.
16. Rob Lefferts, 'Microsoft shares new threat intelligence, security guidance during global crisis', Microsoft, 8 April 2020, https://www.microsoft.com/security/blog/2020/04/08/microsoft-shares-new-threat-intelligence-security-guidance-during-global-crisis/.

17. Samantha Schwartz, 'Malicious domains are floating around the cloud: here's the threat to companies', CIO Dive, 4 May 2020, https://www.ciodive.com/news/malicious-domains-coronavirus-cloud/577220/?mc_cid=3edb85eadd&mc_eid=94d6c1fd2d.
18. 'Facebook's algorithm: a major threat to public health', Avaaz, 19 August 2020, https://avaazimages.avaaz.org/facebook_threat_health.pdf.
19. Ashkan Vila, David Bryant and Limor Kessem 'Trickbot campaigns targeting users via Department of Labor FMLA spam', Security Intelligence, 30 April 2020, https://securityintelligence.com/posts/trickbot-campaigns-targeting-users-via-department-of-labor-fmla-spam/.
20. Anastasia Austin, 'Latin America under threat of cybercrime amid coronavirus', InSight Crime, 10 April 2020, https://www.insightcrime.org/news/analysis/threat-cyber-crime-coronavirus/.
21. Samantha Schwartz, 'Coronavirus-related cyberattacks are like a kicked "hornet's nest"', CIO Dive, 12 May 2020, https://www.ciodive.com/news/coronavirus-related-cyber-attacks-are-like-a-kicked-hornets-nest/577701/?mc_cid=3edb85eadd&mc_eid=94d6c1fd2d.
22. 'Unit 42, 2020 Unit 42 IoT threat report', Palo Alto Networks, 10 March 2020, https://unit42.paloaltonetworks.com/iot-threat-report-2020/.
23. Jonathan Greig, 'Microsoft catches cybercriminals adding malware to "John Wick 3", "Contagion" torrents', *Tech Republic*, 1 May 2020, https://www.techrepublic.com/article/microsoft-catches-cybercriminals-adding-malware-to-john-wick-3-contagion-torrents/.
24. Samuel Woodhams, 'Covid-19 digital rights tracker', Top 10 VPN, 20 March 2020, https://www.top10vpn.com/research/investigations/covid-19-digital-rights-tracker/.

25. Philip Virgo, 'Lockdown has transformed the scale and nature of cybercrime', *Computer Weekly*, 8 September 2020, https://www.computerweekly.com/blog/When-IT-Meets-Politics/Tackling-the-Post-Covid-Cybercrime-Pandemic.
26. 'French newspaper Le Figaro exposes 7.4 billion users' records', *CISO Mag*, 4 May 2020, https://cisomag.eccouncil.org/french-newspaper-le-figaro-exposes-7-4-bn-users-records/.
27. Lawrence Abrams, 'Hackers say they stole millions of credit cards from Banco BCR', Bleeping Computer, 1 May 2020, https://www.bleepingcomputer.com/news/security/hackers-say-they-stole-millions-of-credit-cards-from-banco-bcr/.
28. Scott Ikeda, 'Half a million Zoom accounts compromised by credential stuffing, sold on dark web', *CPO Magazine*, 27 April 2020, https://www.cpomagazine.com/cyber-security/half-a-million-zoom-accounts-compromised-by-credential-stuffing-sold-on-dark-web/.
29. Catalin Cimpanu, 'Details of 44m Pakistani mobile users leaked online, part of bigger 115 cache', Zero Day, 6 May 2020, https://www.zdnet.com/article/details-of-44m-pakistani-mobile-users-leaked-online-part-of-bigger-115m-cache.
30. Linda Tucci, 'Economic recession to spur "dramatic increase" in cybercrime', SearchCIO, 4 February 2009, https://searchcio.techtarget.com/blog/TotalCIO/Economic-recession-to-spur-dramatic-increase-in-cybercrime.
31. Mathew J. Schwartz, 'Cybercrime-as-a-service economy: stronger than ever', BankInfoSecurity, 14 September 2016, https://www.bankinfosecurity.com/cybercrime-as-a-service-economy-stronger-than-ever-a-9396.
32. Lawrence Abrams, 'Ransomware gangs to stop attacking health orgs during pandemic', Bleeping Computer, 18 March 2020, https://www.bleepingcomputer.com/news/security/ransomware-gangs-to-stop-attacking-health-orgs-during-pandemic/.

33. Rob Lefferts, 'Microsoft shares new threat intelligence, security guidance during global crisis', Microsoft, 8 April 2020, https://www.microsoft.com/security/blog/2020/04/08/microsoft-shares-new-threat-intelligence-security-guidance-during-global-crisis/.
34. 'Interpol report shows alarming rate of cyberattacks during Covid-19', INTERPOL, 4 August 2020, https://www.interpol.int/en/News-and-Events/News/2020/INTERPOL-report-shows-alarming-rate-of-cyberattacks-during-Covid-19.
35. 'Fighting a Covid-19 surge in cybercrime', Oxford Business Group, 7 August 2020, https://oxfordbusinessgroup.com/news/fighting-covid-19-surge-cybercrime.
36. Ryan Gallagher, 'Hackers target WHO by posing as think tank, broadcaster', Bloomberg, 7 May 2020, https://www.bloomberg.com/news/articles/2020-05-07/hackers-target-who-by-posing-as-think-tank-broadcaster.
37. 'Ransomware groups continue to target healthcare, critical services; here's how to reduce risk', Microsoft, 28 April 2020, https://www.microsoft.com/security/blog/2020/04/28/ransomware-groups-continue-to-target-healthcare-critical-services-heres-how-to-reduce-risk.
38. Helene Fouquet, 'Paris hospitals target of failed cyber-attack, authority says', Bloomberg, 23 March 2020, https://www.bloomberg.com/news/articles/2020-03-23/paris-hospitals-target-of-failed-cyber-attack-authority-says.
39. Jonathan Greig, 'Ransomware attack on Colorado hospital highlights fears of more healthcare hostage situations', *TechRepublic*, 4 May 2020, https://www.techrepublic.com/article/ransomware-attack-on-colorado-hospital-highlights-fears-of-more-healthcare-hostage-situations/.
40. 'Coronavirus: cyber-attacks hit hospital construction companies', BBC, 13 May 2020, https://www.bbc.com/news/technology-52646808.

41. 'Europe's largest private hospital operator Fresnius hit by ransomware', *Krebs on Security*, 6 May 2020, https://krebsonsecurity.com/2020/05/europes-largest-private-hospital-operator-fresenius-hit-by-ransomware.
42. Melissa Eddy and Nicole Periroth, 'Cyber attack suspected in German woman's death', *New York Times*, 18 September 2020, https://www.nytimes.com/2020/09/18/world/europe/cyber-attack-germany-ransomeware-death.html.
43. Kevin Collier, 'Major hospital system hit with cyberattack, potentially largest in US history', NBC News, 28 September 2020, https://www.nbcnews.com/tech/security/cyberattack-hits-major-u-s-hospital-system-n1241254.
44. Phil Taylor, 'Covid-19 themed cyber attacks hit healthcare bodies', *Pharmaphorum*, 15 April 2020, https://pharmaphorum.com/news/covid-19-themed-cyberattacks-hit-healthcare-bodies.
45. Alex Coop, 'York University cyber-attack looks like ransomware, says security expert', *IT World Canada*, 6 May 2020, https://www.itworldcanada.com/article/york-university-cyber-attack-looks-like-ransomware-says-security-expert.
46. Dan Sabbagh, 'Hackers accessed vaccine documents in cyber-attack on EMA', *The Guardian*, 9 December 2020, https://www.theguardian.com/world/2020/dec/09/hackers-accessed-vaccine-documents-in-cyber-attack-on-ema.
47. Tod Wiesel, 'Keep an eye on North Korean cybercrime as Covid-19 spreads', *The Diplomat*, 18 March 2020, https://thediplomat.com/2020/03/keep-an-eye-on-north-korean-cybercrime-as-covid-19-spreads/.
48. David E. Sanger and Sharon LaFraniere, 'Cyberattacks discovered on vaccine distribution operations', *New York Times*, 3 December 2020, https://www.nytimes.com/2020/12/03/us/politics/vaccine-cyberattacks.html.
49. Gordon Corera, 'Coronavirus: cyber-spies hunt Covid-19

research, US and UK warn', BBC, 5 May 2020, https://www.bbc.com/news/technology-52551023.
50. Nick Statt, 'US government accuses Chinese "cyber actors" of trying to steal Covid-19 vaccine research', The Verge, 13 May 2020, https://www.theverge.com/2020/5/13/21257341/us-government-coronavirus-vaccine-china-theft-spy-accuses-fbi-cisa.
51. Scott Henderson, Gabby Roncone, Sarah Jones, John Hultquist and Ben Read, 'Vietnamese threat actors APT32 targeting Wuhan government and Chinese Ministry of Emergency Management in latest example of Covid-19 related espionage', FireEye, 22 April 2020, https://www.fireeye.com/blog/threat-research/2020/04/apt32-targeting-chinese-government-in-covid-19-related-espionage.html.
52. Wasim Ahmed, Joseph Downing, Marc Tuters and Peter Knight, 'Four experts investigate how the 5G coronavirus conspiracy theory began', *The Conversation*, 11 June 2020, https://theconversation.com/four-experts-investigate-how-the-5g-coronavirus-conspiracy-theory-began-139137.
53. Nic Fildes, Mark Di Stefano and Hannah Murphy, 'How a 5G coronavirus conspiracy spread across Europe', *Financial Times*, 16 April 2020, https://www.ft.com/content/1eeedb71-d9dc-4b13-9b45-fcb7898ae9e1.
54. Corinne Reichert, '5G coronavirus conspiracy theory leads to 77 mobile towers burned in UK, report says', CNET, 7 May 2020, https://www.cnet.com/health/5g-coronavirus-conspiracy-theory-sees-77-mobile-towers-burned-report-says/.
55. Mike Schuler, 'Suspecting cyber attack, MSC reports network outage', gCaptain, 10 April 2020, https://gcaptain.com/msc-reports-network-outage-cyber-attack-cannot-be-ruled-out.
56. Alicia Hope, 'Toll Group's operations shut down by yet another ransomware attack', *CPO Magazine*, 14 May 2020,

https://www.cpomagazine.com/cyber-security/toll-groups-operations-shut-down-by-yet-another-ransomware-attack.
57. 'Massive fraud against state unemployment insurance programmes', United States Secret Service, 14 May 2020, https://www.documentcloud.org/documents/6891584-GIOC-Alert-20–027-I-State-Unemployment-Fraud-002.html.
58. 'Threat actor dossier: scattered canary', Agari, 2019, https://www.agari.com/cyber-intelligence-research/whitepapers/scattered-canary.pdf.
59. Mike Baker, 'Feds suspect vast fraud network is targeting US unemployment schemes', *New York Times*, 16 May 2020, https://www.nytimes.com/2020/05/16/us/coronavirus-unemployment-fraud-secret-service-washington.html?referringSource=articleShare.
60. GAO, 'Data protection: actions taken by Equifax and federal agencies in response to the 2017 breach', August 2018, https://www.warren.senate.gov/imo/media/doc/2018.09.06%20GAO%20Equifax%20report.pdf.
61. 'Coronavirus aid resumes after scammers clone state website', Deutsche Welle, 17 April 2020, https://www.dw.com/en/germany-coronavirus-aid-resumes-after-scammers-clone-state-website/a-53168539.
62. Summer Walker, 'Cyber-insecurities? A guide to the UN cybercrime debate', Global Initiative Against Transnational Organized Crime, March 2019, https://globalinitiative.net/wp-content/uploads/2019/03/TGIATOC-Report-Cybercrime-in-the-UN-01Mar1510-Web.pdf.
63. Simone Haysom, 'In search of cyber-enabled disruption', Global Initiative Against Transnational Organized Crime, February 2019, https://globalinitiative.net/wp-content/uploads/2019/02/TGIATOC-FinalSynthesis-Web.pdf.
64. 'Cybercrime and Covid-19: Risks and responses', UNODC,

14 April 2020, https://www.unodc.org/documents/Advocacy-Section/UNODC_-_CYBERCRIME_AND_COVID19_-_Risks_and_Responses_v1.2_-_14-04-2020_-_CMLS-COVID19-CYBER1_-_UNCLASSIFIED_BRANDED.pdf.

65. Nick Statt, 'Major tech platforms say they're "jointly combating fraud and misinformation" about Covid-19', The Verge, 16 March 2020, https://www.theverge.com/2020/3/16/21182726/coronavirus-covid-19-facebook-google-twitter-youtube-joint-effort-misinformation-fraud.
66. Jim Waterson, 'Tech firms criticized for "lack of answers" on Covid-19 disinformation', *The Guardian*, 30 April 2020, https://www.theguardian.com/world/2020/apr/30/tech-firms-criticised-for-lack-of-answers-on-covid-19-disinformation.
67. 'Domains of danger: how website speculators and registrars trade internet safety for profit', Digital Citizens Alliance, August 2020, https://www.digitalcitizensalliance.org/clientuploads/directory/Reports/DCA-DOMAINS-OF-DANGER.pdf.
68. Brian Monroe, 'In pandemic fraud, cyber fusillades, more criminals choosing crypto to buy virtual weapons, get paid after successful attacks: FinCEN', Association of Certified Financial Crime Specialists, 15 May 2020, https://www.acfcs.org/in-pandemic-fraud-cyber-fusillades-more-criminals-choosing-crypto-to-buy-virtual-weapons-get-paid-after-successful-attacks-fincen.
69. Cecilia Kang, Jack Nicas and David McCabe, 'Amazon, Apple, Facebook and Google prepare for their "Big Tobacco moment"', *New York Times*, 29 July 2020, https://www.nytimes.com/2020/07/28/technology/amazon-apple-facebook-google-antitrust-hearing.html.
70. Jim Waterson, 'Influencers among "key distributors" of coro-

navirus misinformation', *The Guardian*, 8 April 2020, https://www.theguardian.com/media/2020/apr/08/influencers-being-key-distributors-of-coronavirus-fake-news.

## 9. THE FISH ROTS FROM THE HEAD

1. 'Timeline: WHO's Covid-19 response' (dated 11 March 2020), WHO, accessed 25 October 2020, https://www.who.int/emergencies/diseases/novel-coronavirus-2019/interactive-timeline#!.
2. Keith Bradsher, 'China dominates medical supplies, in this outbreak and the next', *New York Times*, 5 July 2020, https://www.nytimes.com/2020/07/05/business/china-medical-supplies.html.
3. Taisei Hoyama and Rintaro Hosokawa, 'Reliance on Chinese protective gear soars in pandemic's wake', *Nikkei Asia*, 24 August 2020, https://asia.nikkei.com/Spotlight/Coronavirus/Reliance-on-Chinese-protective-gear-soars-in-pandemic-s-wake.
4. OECD and EUIPO, *Mapping the Real Routes of Trade in Fake Goods*, Paris: OECD Publishing, 2017, https://read.oecd-ilibrary.org/governance/mapping-the-real-routes-of-trade-in-fake-goods_9789264278349-en#page5.
5. OECD, *Trends in Trade in Counterfeit and Pirated Goods*, Paris: OECD Publishing, 2019, https://read.oecd-ilibrary.org/trade/trends-in-trade-in-counterfeit-and-pirated-goods_fc47e382-en#page1.
6. OECD and EUIPO, *Trade in Counterfeit Pharmaceutical Products*, Paris: OECD Publishing, 2020, https://www.oecd-ilibrary.org/sites/a7c7e054-en/index.html?itemId=/content/publication/a7c7e054-en.
7. 'Crime and contagion: the impact of a pandemic on organised crime', Global Initiative Against Transnational Organized

Crime, March 2020, https://globalinitiative.net/wp-content/uploads/2020/03/GI-TOC-Crime-and-Contagion-The-impact-of-a-pandemic-on-organized-crime-1.pdf.

8. OECD, *Trends in Trade in Counterfeit and Pirated Goods*.
9. UNCTAD, *World Investment Report 2019*, ch. 4: Special Economic Zones, 2020, https://unctad.org/system/files/official-document/WIR2019_CH4.pdf.
10. OECD, *Governance Frameworks to Counter Illicit Trade*, Paris, Paris: OECD Publishing, 2018, https://read.oecd-ilibrary.org/governance/governance-frameworks-to-counter-illicit-trade_9789264291652-en#page16.
11. OECD and EUIPO, *Trade in Counterfeit Pharmaceutical Products*.
12. Frank M. Snowden, *Epidemics and Society: From the Black Death to the present*, New Haven: Yale University Press, 2020
13. Carly Silver, 'How ancient cure-alls paved the way for drug regulation', *The Atlantic*, 10 January 2017, https://www.theatlantic.com/health/archive/2017/01/how-ancient-cure-alls-paved-the-way-for-drug-regulation/512594/.
14. 'Reality check, coronavirus: what misinformation has spread in Africa?', BBC, 24 April 2020, https://www.bbc.com/news/world-africa-51710617.
15. Malavika Vyawahare, 'Madagascar's president promotes unproven herbal cure for Covid-19', Mongabay, 20 April 2020, https://news.mongabay.com/2020/04/madagascars-president-promotes-unproven-herbal-cure-for-covid-19/.
16. Anna Merlan, 'World leaders are hyping bogus Covid cures', Vice, 13 August 2020, https://www.vice.com/en/article/889eva/world-leaders-are-hyping-bogus-covid-cures.
17. Pratik Jakhar, 'Covid-19: China pushes traditional remedies amid outbreak', BBC, 28 June 2020, https://www.bbc.com/news/world-asia-53094603.
18. Julia Carrie Wong, 'Hydroxychloroquine: how an unproved drug became Trump's coronavirus "miracle cure"', *The*

*Guardian*, 7 April 2020, https://www.theguardian.com/world/2020/apr/06/hydroxychloroquine-trump-coronavirus-drug.

19. 'Concern as counterfeit medicine floods market', *Daily Monitor*, 14 May 2020, https://www.monitor.co.ug/News/National/Concern-counterfeit-medicine-floods-market/688334-5552280-6ojulpz/index.html.
20. Sam Piranty, 'Coronavirus fuels a surge in fake medicines', BBC, 9 April 2020, https://www.bbc.com/news/health-52201077.
21. María Silvia Trigo, Anatoly Kurmanaev and José María León Cabrera, 'With officials' backing, dubious virus remedies surge in Latin America', *New York Times*, 22 August 2020, https://www.nytimes.com/2020/07/23/world/americas/chlorine-coronavirus-bolivia-latin-america.html.
22. Ernesto Londoño, 'Bolsonaro hails anti-malarial pill even as he fights coronavirus', *New York Times*, 8 July 2020, https://www.nytimes.com/2020/07/08/world/americas/brazil-bolsonaro-covid-coronavirus.html.
23. Tom Porter and Qayyah Moynihan, 'Bolivia's senate approved "miracle mineral solution"—a toxic bleach with no medical use—as a treatment for Covid-19', *Business Insider*, 16 July 2020, https://www.businessinsider.com/bolivian-senate-approves-toxic-bleach-as-covid-19-treatment-2020–7?r=US&IR=T.
24. Trigo, Kurmanaev and Cabrera, 'With officials' backing, dubious virus remedies surge in Latin America'.
25. Patricia J. García, 'Corruption in global health: the open secret', *The Lancet*, 27 November 2019, https://www.thelancet.com/journals/lancet/article/PIIS0140-6736(19)32527-9/fulltext.
26. Rachel Tansey, 'The creeping privatisation of healthcare: problematic EU policies and the corporate lobby push',

Corporate Europe Observatory, 2 June 2017, https://corporateeurope.org/en/power-lobbies/2017/06/creeping-privatisation-healthcare.

27. Taryn Vian, 'Anti-corruption, transparency and accountability in health: concepts, frameworks and approaches', *Global Health Action*, 13, 1: Anti-corruption, transparency and accountability, 2020, https://www.tandfonline.com/doi/full/10.1080/16549716.2019.1694744.
28. Karen Hussmann, 'Health sector corruption: practical recommendations for donors', *U4*, 10, 2020, https://www.u4.no/publications/health-sector-corruption.pdf.
29. Donald M. Berwick and Andrew D. Hackbarth, 'Eliminating waste in US healthcare', *Journal of the American Medical Association*, 307, 14, April 2011, https://pubmed.ncbi.nlm.nih.gov/22419800/.
30. Lisa O'Carroll, 'Sierra Leone investigates alleged misuse of emergency Ebola funds', *The Guardian*, 17 February 2015, https://www.theguardian.com/world/2015/feb/17/sierra-leone-investigates-alleged-misuse-of-emergency-ebola-funds.
31. Parker Asmann, 'Guatemala elites exploited health sector to pocket millions: prosecutors', InSight Crime, 23 July 2019, https://www.insightcrime.org/news/brief/guatemala-elites-exploited-health-sector-pocket-millions/.
32. 'Parallel contagion: is mafia entrepreneurship exploiting the pandemic?', Global Initiative Against Transnational Organized Crime, April 2020, https://globalinitiative.net/wp-content/uploads/2020/04/Italian-Connection-v7.pdf.
33. 'Parallel contagion II: how has mafia entrepreneurship exploited the pandemic?', Global Initiative Against Transnational Organized Crime, 11 June 2020, https://globalinitiative.net/analysis/parallel-contagion-mafia-covid/.
34. Miles Johnson, 'How the mafia infiltrated Italy's hospitals and laundered the profits globally', *Financial Times*, 9 July

2020, https://www.ft.com/content/8850581c-176e-4c5c-8b38-debb26b35c14.

35. Christoph B. Schiltz, 'Frau Merkel, bleiben Sie standhaft!' [Stay firm, Mrs Merkel!], *Die Welt*, 8 April 2020, https://www.welt.de/debatte/kommentare/article207146171/Debatte-um-Corona-Bonds-Frau-Merkel-bleiben-Sie-standhaft.html.
36. 'Coronavirus: secrecy surrounds India PM Narendra Modi's "$1bn" Covid-19 fund', BBC, 30 June 2020, https://www.bbc.com/news/world-asia-india-53151308.
37. Renato Alves, 'Coronavirus corruption a new headache for Brazilian governors', *Brazilian Report*, 30 September 2020, https://brazilian.report/power/2020/09/30/coronavirus-corruption-a-new-headache-for-brazilian-governors/.
38. Gram Slattery and Ricardo Brito, 'The ventilators never came: how graft hammered Brazil's Covid-19 response', Reuters, 25 September 2020, https://uk.reuters.com/article/us-health-coronavirus-brazil-corruption-idUKKCN26G1EW.
39. 'Another disease plagues Brazil's Covid fight: corruption', France24, 26 August 2020, https://www.france24.com/en/20200826-another-disease-plagues-brazil-covid-fight-corruption.
40. 'Brazil senator caught hiding money "between buttocks"', Deutsche Welle, 15 October 2020, https://www.dw.com/en/brazil-senator-caught-hiding-money-between-buttocks/a-55291992.
41. Joan Suazo and Daniela Castro, 'Mr. HispanoPreneur™: The man behind Honduras' $47 million coronavirus disaster', OCCRP, 16 October 2020, https://www.occrp.org/en/coronavirus/mr-hispanopreneurtm-the-man-behind-honduras-47-million-dollar-coronavirus-disaster.
42. Adriana Homolova and Dada Lyndell, 'Europe's Covid-19

spending spree unmasked', OCCRP, 21 October 2020, https://www.occrp.org/en/members/28-ccwatch/cc-watch-indepth/13286-europe-s-covid-19-spending-spree-unmasked.

43. George Monbiot, 'The government's secretive Covid contracts are heaping misery on Britain', *The Guardian*, 21 October 2020, https://www.theguardian.com/commentisfree/2020/oct/21/government-covid-contracts-britain-nhs-corporate-executives-test-and-trace.
44. Simon Murphy and Sarah Marsh, 'UK government urged to justify £108m contact-tracing deal with Serco', *The Guardian*, 11 August 2020, https://www.theguardian.com/business/2020/aug/11/uk-government-serco-contact-tracing-contract-leaked-memo.
45. Benjamin Mueller and Jane Bradley, 'England's "world beating" system to track the virus is anything but', *New York Times*, 17 June 2020, https://www.nytimes.com/2020/06/17/world/europe/uk-contact-tracing-coronavirus.html.
46. Mark Harris and David Pegg, '£45m deal for NHS masks collapses amid fraud claims', *The Guardian*, 3 November 2020, https://www.theguardian.com/society/2020/nov/03/45m-deal-for-nhs-masks-collapses-amid-claims?CMP=share_btn_tw.
47. Ana Poenariu, 'The convict and coronavirus: Romania's million-mask mess', OCCRP, 15 April 2020, https://www.occrp.org/en/coronavirus/convict-and-coronavirus-romanias-million-mask-mess.
48. Global Initiative Against Transnational Organized Crime, podcast: 'The impact: coronavirus and organised crime', Episode 10: 'Covid and corruption', Part 1, June 2020.
49. 'Connecting the business and human rights and anti-corruption agendas' (A/HRC/44/43), United Nations Human Rights Council, 17 June 2020, https://www.ohchr.org/

Documents/Issues/Business/A_HRC_44_43_Advance EditedVersion.pdf.
50. Sarah Repucci and Amy Slipowitz, 'Democracy under lockdown: the impact of Covid-19 on the global struggle for freedom', Freedom House, 2020, https://freedomhouse.org/report/special-report/2020/democracy-under-lockdown.
51. 'The pandemic has eroded democracy and respect for human rights', *The Economist*, 17 October 2020, https://www.economist.com/international/2020/10/17/the-pandemic-has-eroded-democracy-and-respect-for-human-rights.
52. 'RSF addresses Human Rights Council on pandemic-linked press freedom violations', Reporters Without Borders, 15 September 2020, https://rsf.org/en/news/rsf-addresses-human-rights-council-pandemic-linked-press-freedom-violations.
53. Jason Leopold, 'The FBI has limited public records requests during the coronavirus pandemic', Buzzfeed News, 17 March 2020, https://www.buzzfeednews.com/article/jasonleopold/fbi-limitng-foia-during-coronavirus-covid19.
54. Homolova and Lyndell, 'Europe's Covid-19 spending spree unmasked'.
55. Jodi Vittori, 'Corruption vulnerabilities in the US response to the coronavirus', Carnegie Endowment for International Peace, 20 March 2020, https://carnegieendowment.org/2020/03/20/corruption-vulnerabilities-in-u.s.-response-to-coronavirus-pub-81336.
56. Sarah Chayes, 'Look out, corruption ahead', *The Atlantic*, 17 April 2020, https://www.theatlantic.com/ideas/archive/2020/04/course-relief-money-will-be-ill-spent/610126/.

## 10. COVID AND PUNISHMENT

1. Yasantha Naidoo and Nivashni Nair, '16 police stations close in two days as Covid-19 continues to spread', *The Herald* (Port

Elizabeth), 1 July 2020, https://www.heraldlive.co.za/news/2020-07-01-16-police-stations-close-in-two-days-as-covid-19-continues-to-spread/.

2. GI-TOC carried out interviews or discussions with a cross-section of police managers, serving and retired, who expressed this view.
3. Personal communication with our colleague Jason Eligh, August 2020.
4. 'Más refuerzos para la seguridad de la población', *El Peruano*, 29 July 2020, https://elperuano.pe/noticia/100322-mas-refuerzos-para-la-seguridad-de-la-poblacion; Peter Watson, 'Perú refuerza su Policía Nacional ante la reanudación de las actividades económicas tras el Covid', Infodefensa, 21 July 2020, https://www.infodefensa.com/latam/2020/07/21/noticia-refuerza-policia-nacional-reanudacion-actividades-economicas-covid.html.
5. John Stogner, Bryan Lee Miller and Kyle McLean, 'Police stress, mental health and resiliency during the Covid-19 pandemic', *American Journal of Criminal Justice*, 45, 2020, p. 721.
6. Quentin Ariès and Michael Birnbaum, 'Covid-19 surge in Belgium leads to shortage of doctors, teachers and police', *Washington Post*, 24 October 2020, https://www.washingtonpost.com/world/europe/belgium-covid-hospitals-schools/2020/10/23/85358010-14a9-11eb-a258-614acf2b906d_story.html.
7. Personal communication and Global Initiative daily monitoring reports, March–September 2020.
8. See Stogner, Miller and McLean, 'Police stress, mental health and resiliency during the Covid-19 pandemic', p. 721.
9. Victor Maphosa, 'Zimbabwe: cops accused of soliciting Covid-19 bribes', *The Herald* (Harare), 7 April 2020, https://allafrica.com/stories/202004070417.html.
10. This was in the state of Illinois. Dean C Alexander and Niyazi

Ekici, 'Survey: Covid-19's impact on LE operations', *POLICE1*, 24 July 2020, https://www.police1.com/coronavirus-covid-19/articles/survey-covid-19s-impact-on-le-operations-JmGm4beDhdAHhrE5/.

11. Stogner, Miller and McLean, 'Police stress, mental health and resiliency during the Covid-19 pandemic', p. 722.
12. Personal communication with our colleague Jason Eligh, August 2020.
13. 'Impact of Covid-19 on port control units and selected border customs points worldwide and shifts in trafficking', RHIPTO Norwegian Center for Global Analyses, 17 April 2020.
14. Yosuke Onchi, 'South Korea shuts parliament and courts as coronavirus swells', *Nikkei Asia*, 25 February 2020, https://asia.nikkei.com/Spotlight/Coronavirus/South-Korea-shuts-parliament-and-courts-as-coronavirus-swells.
15. Galih Gumelar, 'Indonesian courts to go virtual during Covid-19', *Jakarta Post*, 21 April 2020, https://www.thejakartapost.com/news/2020/04/20/indonesian-courts-to-go-virtual-during-covid-19.html/.
16. Global Initiative Against Transnational Organized Crime, Civil Society Observatory of Illicit Economies in Eastern and Southern Africa, 'Kenyan gang members facing increased police extortion', *Risk Bulletin*, 9, June–July 2020, https://globalinitiative.net/analysis/esaobs-risk-bulletin-9/.
17. Gumelar, 'Indonesian courts to go virtual during Covid-19'.
18. UK House of Commons Justice Select Committee, 'How the coronavirus impacted the justice system', 5 August 2020, https://houseofcommons.shorthandstories.com/justice-coronavirus-impact-on-probation-prisons-courts-legal-professions/index.html.
19. 'Slovak journalist murder trial hearings postponed over coronavirus moves', Reuters, 12 March 2020, https://uk.reuters.

com/article/uk-health-coronavirus-slovakia-trial/slovak-journalist-murder-trial-hearings-postponed-over-coronavirus-moves-idUKKBN20Z1VJ.

20. 'Swiss court postpones Liberia war crimes trial over coronavirus', Swissinfo, 18 March 2020, https://www.swissinfo.ch/eng/international-justice-_swiss-court-postpones-liberia-war-crimes-trial-over-coronavirus-/45625234; 'Swiss court sets November trial date for ex-ULIMO commander, Alieu Kosiah', *Front Page Africa*, press release, 25 August 2020, https://frontpageafricaonline.com/liberia-war-crimes-trial/swiss-court-sets-november-trial-date-for-ex-ulimo-commander-alieu-kosiah/.
21. 'Slovak tycoon Kocner cleared of murder of journalist and fiancée', BBC, 2 September 2020, https://www.bbc.co.uk/news/world-europe-54010733; Miroslava German Sirotnikova, 'Slovak businessman and associate found not guilty of ordering murder of journalist', *Balkan Insight*, 3 September 2020, https://balkaninsight.com/2020/09/03/slovak-businessman-and-associate-found-not-guilty-of-ordering-murder-of-journalist/.
22. Gumelar, 'Indonesian courts to go virtual during Covid-19'.
23. Nathaniel Janowitz, 'Mexico Just Postponed the Legalization of Weed to 2021 Due to COVID', Vice, 10 December 2020, https://www.vice.com/en/article/y3gbvy/mexico-just-postponed-the-legalization-of-weed-to-2021due-to-covid.
24. 'Covid-19 preparedness and responses in prisons', UNODC, Position Paper, 31 March 2020, p. 2.
25. Brazilian Ministry of Justice and Public Security, 'Depen atualiza dados sobre a população carcerária do Brasil', 14 February 2020, https://www.gov.br/mj/pt-br/assuntos/noticias/depen-lanca-paineis-dinamicos-para-consulta-do-infopen-2019. The number is for June 2019. There is no data reported for 2020.

26. Brazilian National Council of Justice, 'Covid-19 no sistema prisional', 28 September 2020, https://www.cnj.jus.br/wp-content/uploads/2020/09/Monitoramento-Semanal-Covid-19-Info-30.09.20.pdf.
27. Brazilian National Council of Justice, 'Covid-19 no sistema prisional'.
28. Brazilian National Council of Justice, 'CNJ renova Recomendação n° 62 por mais 90 dias e divulga novos dados', 12 June 2020, https://www.cnj.jus.br/cnj-renova-recomendacao-n-62-por-mais-90-dias-e-divulga-novos-dados/.
29. Tiago Angelo, 'Brasil é denunciado na ONU e OEA por avanço do coronavírus nos presídios', *ConJur*, 23 June 2020 https://www.conjur.com.br/2020-jun-23/brasil-denunciado-onu-avanco-coronavirus-presidios.
30. Penal Reform International, 'Coronavirus: healthcare and human rights of people in prison', Briefing Note, 16 March 2020, p. 2.
31. Penal Reform International, 'Coronavirus: healthcare and human rights of people in prison', p. 11.
32. Brazilian National Council of Justice, Recommendation 62/2020, 17 March 2020, https://www.cnj.jus.br/wp-content/uploads/2020/03/62-Recomenda%C3%A7%C3%A3o.pdf.
33. André Richter, 'CNJ aprova restrição para soltura de presos por covid-19', Agência Brasil, 22 September 2020, https://agenciabrasil.ebc.com.br/justica/noticia/2020–09/cnj-aprova-restricao-para-soltura-de-presos-por-covid-19.
34. See Isadora Peron, 'CNJ: 32,5 mil presos foram colocados em liberdade devido à pandemia', *Valor Econômico*, 12 June 2020, https://valor.globo.com/brasil/noticia/2020/06/12/cnj-325-mil-presos-foram-colocados-em-liberdade-devido-pandemia.ghtml. The number covers the period from

17 March until mid-June 2020. The figure includes 19 Brazilian states and excludes data from the states of Acre, Amapá, Ceará, Espírito Santo and Rio de Janeiro, where it was not possible to quantify the number of people released.

35. Manuel Marraco, 'España puso en libertad a 4.356 presos para frenar la propagación del coronavirus en las cárceles', *El Mundo España*, 18 June 2020, https://www.elmundo.es/espana/2020/06/18/5eeb4fb8fc6c831f1d8b45f9.html.
36. Cain Burdeau, 'Europe released 128,000 prisoners to prevent virus outbreaks', Courthouse News Service, 18 June 2020, https://www.courthousenews.com/europe-released-128000-prisoners-to-prevent-virus-outbreaks/.
37. Marraco, 'España puso en libertad a 4.356 presos para frenar la propagación del coronavirus en las cárceles'.
38. Burdeau, 'Europe released 128,000 prisoners to prevent virus outbreaks'.
39. UK Ministry of Justice, 'HM Prison and Probation Service Covid-19 official statistics data to 7 August 2020', 14 August 2020, https://assets.publishing.service.gov.uk/government/uploads/system/uploads/attachment_data/file/909207/HMPPS_Covid19_WE_07082020_Pub_Doc.pdf.
40. The Iranian and Afghan numbers are quoted in Vanda Felbab-Brown, 'How Covid-19 is changing law enforcement practices by police and by criminal groups', Brookings Institution, 7 April 2020, https://www.brookings.edu/blog/order-from-chaos/2020/04/07/how-covid-19-is-changing-law-enforcement-practices-by-police-and-by-criminal-groups/.
41. The country's prison system has a stated total capacity of 80,763, making the current number of prisoners (113,031) an overpopulation of 40%.
42. South Africa's 243 correctional facilities have a capacity for 118,572 beds but are currently experiencing an overpopula-

tion rate of almost 23%, with 145,376 inmates. Peter Dube, 'Covid-19: South Africa releases 7,000 inmates to decongest prisons', *Nation*, 18 July 2020, https://nation.africa/kenya/news/africa/covid-19-south-africa-releases-7-000-inmates-to-decongest-prisons-1900922.

43. 'Announced release of detainees in justice system due to Covid-19', Human Rights Watch, 15 March–22 May 2020, https://www.hrw.org/sites/default/files/media_2020/05/announced_releases_detainees_covid19_1.pdf.
44. 'Announced release of detainees in justice system due to Covid-19', Human Rights Watch, 15 March—22 May 2020.
45. 'Covid-19 prisoner releases too few, too slow', Human Rights Watch, 27 May 2020, https://www.hrw.org/news/2020/05/27/covid-19-prisoner-releases-too-few-too-slow.
46. 'Egyptian journalist Mohamed Monir dies after contracting Covid-19 in pretrial detention', Committee to Protect Journalists, 13 July 2020, https://cpj.org/2020/07/egyptian-journalist-mohamed-monir-dies-after-contracting-covid-19-in-pretrial-detention/.
47. Sergio Nazarro, Lyes Tagziria and Ruggero Scaturro, 'Lockdown in lock-up: Italy's prison system has been plunged into crisis by the pandemic—and by the mafia', Global Initiative Against Transnational Organized Crime, https://globalinitiative.net/italy-prisons-covid/.
48. Liana Milella and Salvo Palazzolo, 'Mafiosi e trafficanti, in 376 fuori dal carcere per l'emergenza virus', *La Repubblica*, 3 May 2020, www.repubblica.it/cronaca/2020/05/03/news/mafiosi_e_trafficanti_in_376_fuori_dal_carcere_per_l_emergenza_virus-255528216/; Olga Bibus, '376 boss scarcerati, ai domiciliari nei loro territori: la lista riservata pubblicata da Repubblica', *Open*, 6 May 2020, www.open.online/2020/05/06/376-boss-scarcerati-ai-domiciliari-nei-loro-territori-la-lista-riservata-pubblicata-da-repubblica/.

49. Article 41(bis) of the Prison Administration Act is a provision used against high-profile criminals imprisoned for mafia-type association and activities, serious drug trafficking, homicides and terrorism.
50. Sergio Nazzaro, Lyes Tagziria and Ruggero Scaturo, "Lockdown in lock-up: Italy's prison system has been plunged into crisis by the pandemic", Global Initiative Against Transnational Organized Crime, 20 May 2020, https://globalinitiative.net/analysis/italy-prisons-covid/.
51. Giuseppe Pipitone, 'Coronavirus, approvato il decreto di Bonafede per far tornare dentro i mafiosi: "Rivalutare ok ai domiciliari per emergenza sanitaria in 15 giorni. Anche prima se ci sono penitenziari o reparti adeguati"', *Il Fatto Quotidiano*, 9 May 2020, https://www.ilfattoquotidiano.it/2020/05/09/coronavirus-approvato-il-decreto-di-bonafede-per-far-tornare-dentro-i-mafiosi-rivalutare-ok-ai-domiciliari-per-emergenza-sanitaria-in-15-giorni-anche-prima-se-ci-sono-penitenziari-o-reparti-adegu/5796988/.
52. 'Coronavirus, ancora ai domiciliari 112 boss (su 223) scarcerati durante l'emergenza. Bonafede: "Condizioni sono state rivalutate dai giudici"', *Il Fatto Quotidiano*, 3 September 2020, https://www.ilfattoquotidiano.it/2020/09/03/coronavirus-ancora-ai-domiciliari-112-boss-su-223-scarcerati-durante-lemergenza-bonafede-condizioni-sono-state-rivalutate-dai-giudici/5919242/.
53. In India, for example, a breathless media report noted that police rearrested 50 former inmates for a range of offences from robbery to burglary and that the prison releases had led to a 'surge' in crime. See Ajay Kumar and Chayyanika Nigam, 'Coronavirus: released on parole, criminals get back in action, crime surges', *India Today*, 19 July 2020, https://www.indiatoday.in/mail-today/story/coronavirus-released-on-parole-criminals-get-back-action-crime-surges-1702067-2020-07-19.

54. See the city data presented in Emily Badger and Quoctrung Bui, 'The pandemic has hindered many of the best ideas for reducing violence', *New York Times*, 6 October 2020, https://www.nytimes.com/interactive/2020/10/06/upshot/crime-pandemic-cities.html.

## 11. GANGLAND RULES

1. See the video report at https://www.bbc.com/news/av/world-africa-52205727.
2. Peta Thornycroft, 'Unprecedented truce in notorious South African slums as gangs join forces to hand out coronavirus aid', *Daily Telegraph*, 12 April 2020, https://www.telegraph.co.uk/news/2020/04/12/unprecedented-truce-notorious-south-african-slums-gangs-join/.
3. 'Cape Town now ranks as the 8th most violent city in the world', *BusinessTech*, 11 June 2020, https://businesstech.co.za/news/lifestyle/407087/cape-town-now-ranks-as-the-8th-most-violent-city-in-the-world/.
4. Interview, Cape Town, 9 April 2020.
5. Discussions with a variety of gang bosses and members in South Africa, April–June 2020. Local law enforcement was not fooled, however, saying publicly that the truce, despite the reports, was of little value.
6. 'Gangs' is really shorthand for a spectrum of criminal formations with mafia-like characteristics: clear territorial control, distinctive names and symbols, and a criminal culture which connects them to members, and often leaders, who are in prison. In almost all cases, the link between prisons and the streets is a fluid one, with gang leaders behind bars still exerting great influence. In every case, gangs threaten, corrupt and seek to undermine and control state institutions, particularly those concerned with security and justice.

7. Steven Dudley, 'Covid-19: gangs, statemaking, threats and opportunities', InSight Crime, 7 October 2020, https://www.insightcrime.org/news/analysis/covid-19-gangs-statemaking-opportunities/.
8. This is a consistent theme running through multiple case studies. See Felia Allum and Stan Gilmour (eds.), *Handbook of Organised Crime and Politics*, Cheltenham: Edgar Elgar, 2019.
9. Christopher Woody, '400 murders a day: 10 reasons why Latin America is the world's most violent place', *Business Insider*, 10 September 2019, www.businessinsider.com/latin-america-is-the-worlds-most-violent-region-crime-2019-9?r=US&IR=T.
10. Maurizio Catino, *Mafia Organizations: The visible hand of criminal enterprise*, Cambridge: Cambridge University Press, 2019, p. 274.
11. Ricardo Moraes, Debora Moreira and Rodrigo Viga Gaier, 'Gangs call curfews as coronavirus hits Rio favelas', Reuters, 24 March 2020, https://www.reuters.com/article/us-health-coronavirus-brazil-favelas-fea-idUSKBN21B3EV; Bom Dia Rio, 'Coronavírus: traficantes e milicianos impõem toque de recolher em comunidades do Rio', *G1*, 23 March 2020, https://g1.globo.com/rj/rio-de-janeiro/noticia/2020/03/23/coronavirus-traficantes-e-milicianos-impoem-toque-de-recolher-em-comunidades-do-rio.ghtml; Catia Seabra and Júlia Barbon, 'Tráfico e milícia ordem toque de recolher em favelas do Rio por causa do coronavírus', *Folha de São Paulo*, 25 March 2020, https://www1.folha.uol.com.br/cotidiano/2020/03/trafico-e-milicia-ordenam-toque-de-recolher-em-favelas-do-rio-por-causa-do-coronavirus.shtml.
12. Moraes, Moreira and Gaier, 'Gangs call curfews as coronavirus hits Rio favelas'. A YouTube video of one message can be found at https://youtu.be/45TC-iadFFo.
13. Kevin Sieff, Susannah George and Kareem Fahim, 'Now

joining the fight against coronavirus: the world's armed rebels, drug cartels and gangs', *Washington Post*, 14 April 2020, https://www.washingtonpost.com/world/the_americas/coronavirus-taliban-ms-13-drug-cartels-gangs/2020/04/13/83aa07ac-79c2-11ea-a311-adb1344719a9_story.html.

14. Gaëlle Rivard Piché, 'In El Salvador, criminal gangs are enforcing virus-related restrictions: here's why', *Washington Post*, 1 June 2020, https://www.washingtonpost.com/politics/2020/06/01/el-salvador-criminal-gangs-are-enforcing-coronavirus-curfews-heres-why/.
15. Raphael Bruce, Alexsandros Cavgias and Luis Meloni, 'Filling the void? Organised crime and Covid-19 in Rio de Janeiro', Social Science Research Network, 21 August 2020, https://papers.ssrn.com/sol3/papers.cfm?abstract_id=3678840.
16. Luis Fajardo, 'Coronavirus: Latin American crime gangs adapt to pandemic', BBC, 21 April 2020, https://www.bbc.com/news/world-latin-america-52367898.
17. 'Indonesian police's plan to use gangs to uphold Covid-19 protocols causes concern', *Straits Times*, 15 September, 2020, https://www.straitstimes.com/asia/se-asia/indonesian-polices-plan-to-involve-gangs-to-uphold-covid-19-health-protocols-causes.
18. 'Indonesian police's plan to use gangs to uphold Covid-19 protocols causes concern'.
19. John Sullivan, Robert Bunker and Juan Ricardo Gómez Hecht, 'Third generation gangs strategic note no. 23: El Salvadoran gangs (maras) enforce domestic quarantine/stay at home orders (cuarentena domiciliar)', in John Sullivan and Robert Bunker (eds.), *Covid-19, Gangs, and Conflict: A Small Wars Journal–El Centro reader*, Bethesda, MD: Small Wars Foundation, 2020, p. 15.
20. For a critique of this, see Cecília Olliveira, Carlos Nhanga

and Yuri Eiras, 'O malabarismo da grande imprensa para omitir os nomes da facções coloca cidadãos em risco', *The Intercept*, 11 August 2020, https://theintercept.com/2020/08/11/imprensa-rio-faccoes-milicias-trafico/.

21. Vincent Barone, 'El Chapo's daughter, Mexican cartels distribute coronavirus aid packages', *New York Post*, 17 April 2020, https://nypost.com/2020/04/17/el-chapos-daughter-and-mexican-cartels-distribute-coronavirus-relief/.
22. For a useful summary of the trail and the level of violence linked to Guzmán and the Sinaloa cartel, see https://www.pbs.org/newshour/show/the-shocking-violence-that-characterized-the-reign-of-el-chapo.
23. Robert Bunker and John Sullivan, 'Mexican cartel strategic note no. 29: an overview of cartel activities related to Covid-19 humanitarian response', in Sullivan and Bunker (eds.), *Covid-19, Gangs, and Conflict: A Small Wars Journal–El Centro reader*, Bethesda, MD: Small Wars Foundation, 2020, pp. 23–47.
24. 'Mexican president tells gangs to stop handing out coronavirus aid', Al Jazeera, 21 April 2020, https://www.aljazeera.com/news/2020/4/21/mexico-president-tells-gangs-to-stop-handing-out-coronavirus-aid.
25. Personal communication, April 2020.
26. In El Salvador the two largest Barrio 18 factions suspended collection of street taxes while MS-13 continued them. See Sullivan, Bunker and Hecht, 'Third generation gangs strategic note no. 23: El Salvadoran gangs (maras) enforce domestic quarantine/stay at home orders (cuarentena domiciliar)', pp. 11–22.
27. Personal communication with local business representatives, September 2020.
28. Anita Prado and Guilherme Peixoto, 'Milícia obriga reabertura de comércio da Zona Oeste e Região Metropolitana do

Rio para manter cobrança de taxas', *G1*, 17 April 2020, http://g1.globo.com/rj/rio-de-janeiro/noticia/2020/04/17/milicia-obriga-reabertura-do-comercio-para-recolher-taxa-em-comunidades-do-rj.ghtml.

29. Julia Stanyard, 'Gangs in lockdown: impact of Covid-19 restrictions on gangs in East and southern Africa', Global Initiative Against Transnational Organized Crime, November 2020, https://globalinitiative.net/analysis/gangs-in-lockdown-za/.
30. Stanyard, 'Gangs in lockdown'.
31. Stanyard, 'Gangs in lockdown'.
32. Based on interviews conducted by our colleague Antônio Sampaio. It is likely that they took over at least some of the drug-trafficking operations. But the implications are unclear. The CV may, for instance, prioritise shipments to Rio rather than European clients. But then again it is not very clear if the local CV members are closely linked to—or even commanded by—Rio's CV leadership.
33. 'Polícia Federal no AM deflagra operação contra tráfico internacional de drogas', *G1*, 24 August 2020, https://g1.globo.com/am/amazonas/noticia/2020/08/24/policia-federal-no-am-deflagra-operacao-contra-trafico-internacional-de-drogas.ghtml.
34. Global Initiative interviews with gang members in Cape Town, May 2020.
35. Mary Beth Sheridan, 'Violent criminal groups are eroding Mexico's authority and claiming more territory', *Washington Post*, 29 October 2020, https://www.washingtonpost.com/graphics/2020/world/mexico-losing-control/mexico-violence-drug-cartels-zacatecas/.
36. Fajardo, 'Coronavirus: Latin American crime gangs adapt to pandemic'.

## 12. WHO'S GOING TO PAY?

1. Nina Siegal, 'Where have 140 million Dutch tulips gone? Crushed by the coronavirus', *New York Times*, 12 April 2020, https://www.nytimes.com/2020/04/12/world/europe/netherlands-tulips-coronavirus.html.
2. 'How Covid-19 is disrupting the lives of flower farmers in Kenya', *Marie Claire*, 26 May 2020, https://www.marieclaire.co.uk/reports/as-covid-19-devastates-the-global-flower-trade-kenyan-flower-farmers-are-adversely-affected-698444.
3. Gloria Mwaniga, 'How a Kenyan flower producer bloomed through Covid-19', World Bank International Finance Corporation, September 2020, https://www.ifc.org/wps/wcm/connect/news_ext_content/ifc_external_corporate_site/news+and+events/news/insights/i15-kenya-flowers.
4. Gonzalo Solano, 'Ecuador's blooming flower industry feels pandemic's punch', *Washington Post*, 28 August 2020, https://www.washingtonpost.com/world/the_americas/ecuadors-blooming-flower-industry-feels-pandemics-punch/2020/08/28/86ecdcea-e944-11ea-bf44-0d31c85838a5_story.html.
5. Gita Gopinath, 'A long, uneven and uncertain ascent', International Monetary Fund, 13 October 2020, https://blogs.imf.org/2020/10/13/a-long-uneven-and-uncertain-ascent/.
6. Lora Jones, Daniele Palumbo and David Brown, 'Coronavirus: a visual guide to the economic impact', BBC, 29 June 2020, https://www.bbc.com/news/business-51706225.
7. 'The pandemic is plunging millions back into extreme poverty', *The Economist*, 26 September 2020, https://www.economist.com/international/2020/09/26/the-pandemic-is-plunging-millions-back-into-extreme-poverty.
8. Vicente Nunes, 'Fraudes continuam a todo vapor no pagamento do auxílio emergencial de R$ 600', *Correio Braziliense*,

4 July 2020, https://blogs.correiobraziliense.com.br/vicente/fraudes-continuam-a-todo-vapor-no-pagamento-do-auxilio-emergencial-de-r-600/.

9. Guy Chazan, 'Germany cracks down on coronavirus aid fraud', *Financial Times*, 19 April 2020, https://www.ft.com/content/c2123b10-2fa5-4fe7-9422-44de8541f527.
10. Gene Marks, 'Thanks to the Covid bailout, the stories of small business fraud keep rolling in', *The Guardian*, 24 September 2020, https://www.theguardian.com/business/2020/sep/24/small-business-fraud-stories.
11. 'Man pleads guilty to Covid-19 fraud involving paycheck protection program', United States Attorney's Office, Eastern District of Virginia, 25 August 2020, https://www.justice.gov/usao-edva/pr/man-pleads-guilty-covid-19-fraud-involving-paycheck-protection-program.
12. 'BEC attacks surge as fraudsters eye pandemic opportunity', PYMNTS, 6 July 2020, https://www.pymnts.com/news/b2b-payments/2020/data-corporate-fraud-pandemic-bec/.
13. Jessica Silver-Greenberg, David Enrich, Jesse Drucker and Stacy Cowley, 'Large, troubled companies got bailout money in small-business loan program', *New York Times*, 26 April 2020, https://www.nytimes.com/2020/04/26/business/coronavirus-small-business-loans-large-companies.html.
14. Stephanie Ruhle, Jonathan Allen and Michael Cappetta, 'How private jet owners got a subsidy from coronavirus relief funds', NBC News, 28 May 2020, https://www.nbcnews.com/politics/politics-news/how-private-jet-owners-got-subsidy-coronavirus-relief-funds-n1217061.
15. Greg Iacurci, 'Americans lost $77 million to Covid-19 fraud—and that's just the "tip of the iceberg"', CNBC, 7 July 2020, https://www.cnbc.com/2020/07/07/covid-19-fraud-has-cost-americans-at-least-77-million.html.
16. Mark Henricks and Daphne Foreman, 'After the Covid-19

deluge, a bankruptcy tidal wave?', *Forbes*, 23 September 2020, https://www.forbes.com/sites/advisor/2020/09/23/after-the-covid-19-deluge-a-bankruptcy-tidal-wave/#34ae3bce4aba.

17. Silver-Greenberg, Enrich, Drucker and Cowley, 'Large, troubled companies got bailout money in small-business loan program'.
18. 'The impact of Covid-19 on organised crime', UNODC, 2020, https://www.unodc.org/documents/data-and-analysis/covid/RB_COVID_organized_crime_july13_web.pdf.
19. UNODC, E4J University module series: Organised crime, Module 4: Infiltration of organised crime in business and government, n.d., https://www.unodc.org/e4j/en/organized-crime/module-4/key-issues/loansharking.html.
20. 'A parallel contagion: is mafia entrepreneurship exploiting the pandemic?', Global Initiative Against Transnational Organized Crime, April 2020, https://globalinitiative.net/wp-content/uploads/2020/04/Italian-Connection-v7.pdf.
21. 'Gli affair della criminalità organizzata a Milano ai tempi dell'epidemia di coronavirus', Rai News, 12 June 2020, https://www.rainews.it/dl/rainews/media/Gli-affari-della-criminalita-organizzata-a-Milano-ai-tempi-epidemia-di-coronavirus-9c8f5064-dbf1-40ad-9621-cbad098f9ca3.html.
22. Global Initiative Against Transnational Organized Crime, podcast: 'The impact: coronavirus and organised crime, Episode no. 12, https://globalinitiative.net/analysis/a-pandemic-and-organized-crime/.
23. Robert Saviano, 'Why the mafia are taking care of everyone's business', *The Guardian*, 25 April 2020, https://www.theguardian.com/world/2020/apr/25/why-mafia-taking-care-of-everyones-business-in-pandemic.
24. Marco Le Moglie and Giuseppe Sorrenti, 'Revealing "Mafia Inc."? Financial crisis, organised crime and the birth of new

enterprises', Working Paper no. 251, University of Zurich, Department of Economics, December 2019, http://www.econ.uzh.ch/static/wp/econwp251.pdf.

25. Melissa Barra, 'Faced with the Covid-19 crisis, the Italian mafia sees business opportunities', France24, 2 May 2020, https://www.france24.com/en/20200502-faced-with-the-covid-19-crisis-the-italian-mafia-sees-business-opportunities.
26. 'Trade shows signs of rebound from Covid-19, recovery still uncertain', World Trade Organization, 6 October 2020, https://www.wto.org/english/news_e/pres20_e/pr862_e.htm#:~:text=The%20WTO%20now%20forecasts%20a,in%202021%20(Chart%201).
27. Anthony Faiola, 'The virus that shut down the world', *Washington Post*, 26 June 2020, https://www.washingtonpost.com/graphics/2020/world/coronavirus-pandemic-globalization/.
28. Kumutha Ramanathan, 'Oil prices fall as Covid-19 cases spike', Yahoo Finance, 29 September 2020, https://uk.finance.yahoo.com/news/oil-prices-fall-as-covid-cases-spike-085017570.html.
29. Ruth Olurounbi, 'Nigeria dangerously exposed to oil crash', *Petroleum Economist*, 24 March 2020, https://www.petroleum-economist.com/articles/politics-economics/africa/2020/nigeria-dangerously-exposed-to-oil-crash.
30. Yinka Adegoke, 'African economies are being burdened with commodities-linked debt even as prices tumble', *Quartz*, 16 March 2020, https://qz.com/africa/1818645/african-economies-burdened-with-commodities-debt-as-prices-tumble/.
31. 'A tale of two continents: fighting inequality in Africa', Oxfam, September 2019, https://www-cdn.oxfam.org/s3fs-public/file_attachments/bp-tale-of-two-continents-fighting-inequality-africa-030919-en.pdf.

32. Jubilee Debt Campaign, 'G20 must cancel debt to stop coronavirus "third wave" devastating developing countries', Media briefing for G20 finance ministers' meeting on 15 April 2020, https://oi-files-d8-prod.s3.eu-west-2.amazonaws.com/s3fs-public/2020-04/Debt%20media%20briefing%20ahead%20of%20G20.pdf.
33. Rajeev Syal, 'Drug money saved banks in global crisis, claims UN advisor', *The Guardian*, 13 December 2009, https://www.theguardian.com/global/2009/dec/13/drug-money-banks-saved-un-cfief-claims.
34. Larry Elliott, 'China's economy was first in to Covid crisis—and is first out', *The Guardian*, 19 October 2020, https://www.theguardian.com/world/2020/oct/19/china-economy-covid-crisis-beijing.
35. Maria Abi-Habib, 'How China got Sri Lanka to cough up a port', *New York Times*, 25 June 2020, https://www.nytimes.com/2018/06/25/world/asia/china-sri-lanka-port.html.
36. Fabien Pacory, 'The BRI and the free trade zones strategy', *Asia-Pacific Circle*, 23 January 2019, https://asiapacificcircle.org/asia-pacific-insights-trends/fabien-pacory-bri-free-trade-zones-strategy/.
37. OECD, *Governance Frameworks to Counter Illicit Trade*, Paris: OECD Publishing, 2018, https://read.oecd-ilibrary.org/governance/governance-frameworks-to-counter-illicit-trade_9789264291652-en#page16.
38. OECD and EUIPO, *Trade in Counterfeit Goods and Free Trade Zones: Evidence from recent trends*, Paris: OECD Publishing, 2018, https://read.oecd-ilibrary.org/trade/trade-in-counterfeit-goods-and-free-trade-zones_9789264289550-en#page4.
39. Ferigo Foscari et al., 'Covid-19: Italy expands Golden Power review of foreign investments', White & Case, 10 April 2020, https://www.whitecase.com/publications/alert/covid-19-italy-expands-golden-power-review-foreign-investments#:~:

text=23%20of%202020%20(the%20'Decree,into%20 law%20by%20Law%20No.

40. Amber Milne, 'UK under fire for suggesting coronavirus "great leveller"', Reuters, 9 April 2020, https://in.reuters.com/article/us-health-coronavirus-leveller-trfn/uk-under-fire-for-suggesting-coronavirus-great-leveller-idUSKCN21R30P.
41. Marcelle Sussman Fischler, 'As summer nears, the Hamptons face a "feeding frenzy"', *New York Times*, 13 May 2020, https://www.nytimes.com/2020/05/13/realestate/virus-rentals-hamptons.html.
42. Dominic-Madori Davis, 'Billionaires chartering superyachts for months at a time to ride out the coronavirus pandemic', *Business Insider*, 27 March 2020, https://www.businessinsider.com/billionaires-escaping-to-chartered-superyachts-amid-coronavirus-2020-3?r=US&IR=T.
43. Chuck Collins, Omar Ocampo and Sophia Paslaski, 'Billionaire bonanza 2020: wealth windfalls, tumbling taxes and pandemic profiteers', Institute for Policy Studies, 2020, https://ips-dc.org/wp-content/uploads/2020/04/Billionaire-Bonanza-2020.pdf.
44. Rupert Neate, 'Billionaires' wealth rises to $10.2 trillion amid Covid crisis', *The Guardian*, 7 October 2020, https://www.theguardian.com/business/2020/oct/07/covid-19-crisis-boosts-the-fortunes-of-worlds-billionaires.
45. Ruchi Gupta, 'How much does Jeff Bezos make a second?', *Market Realist*, September 2020, https://marketrealist.com/p/how-much-does-jeff-bezos-make-a-second/.
46. Tatiana Walk-Morris, 'E-commerce sales spiked nearly 93% in May', *Retail Dive*, 15 June 2020, https://www.retaildive.com/news/e-commerce-sales-spiked-nearly-93-in-may/579725/.
47. Alana Semuels, 'Many companies won't survive the pan-

demic: Amazon will emerge stronger than ever', *Time*, 28 July 2020, https://time.com/5870826/amazon-coronavirus-jeff-bezos-congress/.

48. Jack Nicas, 'He has 17,700 bottles of hand sanitizer and nowhere to sell them', *New York Times*, 14 March 2020, https://www.nytimes.com/2020/03/14/technology/coronavirus-purell-wipes-amazon-sellers.html.
49. Cameron Faulkner and Jacob Kastrenakes, 'Amazon says it'll spend $4 billion or more dealing with Covid-19', The Verge, 30 April 2020, https://www.theverge.com/2020/4/30/21243112/amazon-q1-2020-earnings-covid-19-coronavirus-jeff-bezos.
50. Megan Henney, 'Amazon paid tax rate of 1.2% on $13B in profits last year', Fox Business, 6 February 2020, https://www.foxbusiness.com/money/amazon-federal-income-taxes-2019.
51. Petr Jansky and Miroslav Palansky, 'Estimating the scale of profit shifting and tax revenue losses related to foreign direct investment', *International Tax and Public Finance*, 26, 2019, https://link.springer.com/article/10.1007/s10797-019-09547-8.
52. David L. Carden, 'To pay for the pandemic, dry out the tax havens', *Foreign Policy*, 16 July 2020, https://foreignpolicy.com/2020/07/16/tax-havens-apple-costs-pandemic/.
53. Oliver Bullough, *Moneyland: Why thieves and crooks now rule the world and how to take it back*, London: Profile Books, 2018.
54. Olga B. Jonas, 'Pandemic risk', World Bank, October 2013, https://openknowledge.worldbank.org/bitstream/handle/10986/16343/WDR14_bp_Pandemic_Risk_Jonas.pdf?sequence=1&isAllowed=y.
55. See https://missingprofits.world.
56. Douglas Dalby, 'Campaigners slam "toothless" Covid-19 bailout bans on tax haven companies', OCCRP, 29 June

2020, https://www.icij.org/investigations/panama-papers/campaigners-slam-toothless-covid-19-bailout-bans-on-tax-haven-companies/.
57. Jason Leopold et al., 'The FinCen files', BuzzFeed News, 20 September 2020, https://www.buzzfeednews.com/article/jasonleopold/fincen-files-financial-scandal-criminal-networks.
58. Gabriel Moberg, Suspicious activities: How dirty money is moved around the financial system, Global Initiative Against Transnational Organized Crime, 10 November 2020, https://globalinitiative.net/analysis/suspicious-activities-how-dirty-money-is-moved-around-the-financial-system/
59. Mark Bou Mansour, 'Bail, or bailout? Tax experts publish 5-step test for Covid-19 business bailouts', Tax Justice Network, 23 April 2020, https://www.taxjustice.net/2020/04/23/bail-or-bailout-tax-experts-publish-5-step-test-for-covid19-business-bailouts/.

## 13. PREVENTION, TREATMENT AND CURE

1. Rym Momtaz, 'Emmanuel Macron on coronavirus: "We're at war"', Politico, 16 March 2020, https://www.politico.eu/article/emmanuel-macron-on-coronavirus-were-at-war/.
2. Haley Ott, 'Fight against coronavirus in Africa is an "existential war for the continent"', CBS News, 1 April 2020, https://www.cbsnews.com/news/coronavirus-africa-fight-is-an-existential-war-for-the-continent/.
3. Kevin Rawlinson, '"This enemy can be deadly": Boris Johnson invokes wartime language', *The Guardian*, 17 March 2020, https://www.theguardian.com/world/2020/mar/17/enemy-deadly-boris-johnson-invokes-wartime-language-coronavirus.
4. Remarks by President Trump, Vice President Pence and members of the Coronavirus Task Force in press briefing, 22 March

2020, https://www.whitehouse.gov/briefings-statements/remarks-president-trump-vice-president-pence-members-coronavirus-task-force-press-briefing-8/.

5. Julia Buxton, 'Drugs and development: the great disconnect', Policy Report 2, Swansea University Global Drug Policy Observatory, 2015, https://www.swansea.ac.uk/media/Drugs-and-Development-The-Great-Disconnect.pdf.
6. Tuesday Reitano, Sasha Jesperson and Lucia Bird, *War on Crime: Militarised responses to organised crime*, London: Palgrave, 2017.
7. Speech to the 50th Session of the UN Commission on Narcotic Drugs (CND), Vienna, 12 March 2007. The phrase on Afghanistan is from a presentation of UNODC's report on opium poppy cultivation in the country in 2007.
8. Giuseppe Pipitone, 'Spain, a safe haven for mafias in a mafia-free country. Under the shadow of the Kremlin', *Il Fatto Quotidiano*, March 2017, https://www.ilfattoquotidiano.it/longform/mafia-and-organized-crime-in-europe/focus/spain/.
9. Andy Ross et al., 'A review of strategies for intervening early to prevent or reduce youth crime and anti-social behaviour', UK Department for Education Research Report, 2011, https://assets.publishing.service.gov.uk/government/uploads/system/uploads/attachment_data/file/182548/DFE-RR111.pdf.
10. Emily Badger and Quoctrung Bui, 'The pandemic has hindered many of the best ideas for reducing violence', *New York Times*, 6 October 2020, https://www.nytimes.com/interactive/2020/10/06/upshot/crime-pandemic-cities.html.
11. Count the costs: wasting billions and undermining economies', Transform Drug Policy Foundation, n.d., https://transformdrugs.org/product/count-the-costs-wasting-billions-and-undermining-economies/.

12. Rashawn Ray, 'What does "defund the police" mean and does it have merit?', Brookings Institution, 19 June 2020, https://www.brookings.edu/blog/fixgov/2020/06/19/what-does-defund-the-police-mean-and-does-it-have-merit/.
13. Summer Walker, 'Reforming the response paradigm: what does Black Lives Matter tell us about tackling organized crime', Global Initiative Against Transnational Organized Crime, September 2020, https://globalinitiative.net/wp-content/uploads/2020/09/Reforming-the-response-paradigm-What-does-Black-Lives-Matter-tell-us-about-tackling-organized-crime.pdf.
14. Walter Kemp, 'Protecting communities: responding to the impact of urban drug markets', Global Initiative Against Transnational Organized Crime, July 2020, https://globalinitiative.net/analysis/urban-drug-markets/.

# ACKNOWLEDGEMENTS

As managers of a dynamic and growing organisation, it is not easy for us to find the time to write a book. But we felt this was an important contribution that had to be made at an epochal period in history. The pandemic has caused widespread harm and enormous loss of life; its impact on the illicit economy is only one component, but it is one that is likely to have far-reaching implications, which we feel need to be captured and understood. We hoped we have helped with that and, in doing so, will in some small way possibly alleviate suffering down the line.

We by no means did this alone. We also have to thank all of the staff at the Global Initiative Against Transnational Organized Crime, a tremendous group of committed, talented and hard-working professionals. A number contributed directly to the research on which this book is based, and we would like to cite them by name: Lucia Bird, Ana Castro, Jason Eligh, Siria Gastélum Félix, Joyce Kimani, Prem Mahadevan, Jack Meegan-Vickers, Mariana Mora Gomez, Alastair Nelson, Ana Paula Oliveira, Julian Rademeyer, Antônio Sampaio, Ruggero Scaturro, Julia Stanyard, Lyes Tagziria, Andreia

Teixeira, Ian Tennant, Livia Wagner and Summer Walker. Everyone in the organisation contributed, not least by gracefully helping us find the time and headspace to write, and humouring us while we did so.

In addition, we relied upon the various networks from which our organisation benefits: the Network of Experts, a distinguished, 500-strong group of professionals who stand at the front line of the fight against organised crime all over the globe; and our field network of researchers, analysts and community liaisons who face genuine threats to their lives from organised crime and corrupt officials, yet find the courage to share their experiences all the same.

We would like to offer our sincere thanks to Michael Dwyer and the team at Hurst Publishers, for supporting this book when it was an optimistic proposal, for patiently putting up with a few deadline slips, and then ushering it through publication with the utmost professionalism. We are very proud and humbled to be part of the Hurst catalogue, which always distinguishes itself with its incomparable list of relevant, carefully researched and important analytical publications.

Special thanks to Deborah Bonello and Alex Goodwin, who read, critiqued, edited and helped us to restructure the work. It is infinitely better because of their input. As for Alex in particular, we might not have made it over the finish line without him, his encouraging good cheer and talented wordsmithing.

Tuesday Reitano would like to dedicate this book to her cousin, Eitan Silkoff, a talented violinist and wonderful soul, who fell victim to organised crime during Covid.

He passed away in September, to the grief of all of our family. I thank my co-author and long-time co-conspirator, Mark Shaw, who is a deep and true friend who simply makes everything better. I am so glad that we finally had a chance to write a book together. I also want to add a special word of thanks to my best friend, Jenny Brace, who always champions the vulnerable, and fights on the side of what is right and good, no matter what. Thanks as always to my parents, Nigel and Helen, and my brother Edward, for all they have done to support me throughout my life. And from the bottom of my heart I thank my family—Carlo, Giorgio and Valentina—who really don't care what I'm writing about anymore but are nonetheless understanding and supportive. I love them all so much, and I'm sorry for the time I steal from them and the stress I inject into their lives while doing it.

Mark Shaw is deeply conscious of how much time the Global Initiative takes away from his family. Before the pandemic, it was weeks of travel, replaced during the pandemic by hours in my study, alternately writing and shouting down the phone. So a huge thank-you to Brigitte, Hannah and Nick, who good-naturedly put up with it all—with grace and love. They are a constant reminder that there is more to the world than crime. Also a thank-you to my parents, Fred and Joan, for a lifetime of support. Tuesday Reitano has been an important, dedicated and long-time collaborator on all things criminal—not least of all, on this book. A deeply grateful thank-you.

# INDEX

Note: Page number followed by "*n*" refers to notes; "*f*" refers to figures; "*t*" refers to tables.


abalone (marine snail), 105–6, 112
academic year cancellation, 60
acetic anhydride, 69, 70
Adhanom Ghebreyesus, Tedros, 98, 133, 149
Afghanistan
  methamphetamine production, 70
  migrants, 17
  opium poppy production, 69–70
  prisoners, release of, 162
Africa
  Covid-19 hotspots, 12
  debt rise, 195
  e-commerce boom, 22
  medical misinformation, 136–7
  wildlife trade, 101–2
African Union, 205
airlines, commercial
  drug trafficking in, 65–6
  flights per day, 13
  flights suspension, 2, 4, 11–13
  growth rate, 31–2, 47
  illicit goods movement on, 32
  wildlife trafficking in, 101–2
Albania, 29
alcohol, 8, 20, 21
Algeria, 55
Amazon (company), 199
Amazon basin, 91, 93–5
Amazonas (Brazilian state), 144, 182–3
Amnesty International, 15

amphetamine, 75, 76, 79
Andean Amazon Monitoring Project, 94
Angola, 108, 195
Annan, Kofi, 42
anti-Covid measures. *See* government's anti-Covid measures
Argentina, 12, 21, 110, 201
artisanal gold mining, 86–8, 91–2, 96
Asia
  forest exploitation, 108
  migrant crisis, 48
  piracy attacks in Asian waters, 83–4, 85
  wet markets, 97–100
  wildlife trafficking, 4, 105–6
asylum seeking, 50–2
Australia, 45, 205

bailouts, 189, 190, 191
Baja California (Mexico), 107
Bank of England, 201
bankruptcy, 15, 189, 191–2
BBC (British Broadcasting Corporation), 138, 169
BEC (Business email compromise), 22–3, 128–9
Belgium, 73, 148, 153, 201
Belt and Road Initiative (China), 196
Bezos, Jeff, 199
  Amazon (company), 199
Bitcoin, 33–4
Black Death, 9–10
black markets. *See* illicit markets
'blanked sailings', 72
'blood diamonds', 40
Bolivia, 67, 93, 95
  chlorine dioxide legalizing bill, 138
Bolsonaro, Jair, 12, 94, 138, 144
bonded labour, 57–8
Bonura, Francesco, 165
border closures, 2, 13, 17, 46, 49–52
  human smuggling during, 54–6
  wildlife trade, effects on, 101–2
Borsellino, Paolo, 28
Bosnia and Herzegovina, 54
Brazil, 12, 29, 110
  criminal governance, 174–6, 178
  drug seizure (2019), 45
  extortion threats, 181
  financial frauds, 190
  funds misappropriation, 144
  gangs lockdowns imposition, 174–5

gangs' violence along northern drug routes, 182
illegal gold mining, 85, 93–4, 95
prison system, 159–61
virus infection on police personnel, 153
British Virgin Islands, 146
Brno University Hospital (Czech Republic), 124
Broad, Steve, 101
Brown and Burk (pharmaceutical company), 138
Bukele, Nayib, 175
Bulgaria, 76
Bunker, Robert, 179
bushmeat poaching, 107–8
Business email compromise (BEC), 22–3, 128–9

Camorra (Italian mafia), 141, 166
Canada, 50, 125
cannabis, 19–20, 75, 76, 79
Cape Town (South Africa), 78–9
extortion economies, growth of, 181
gangland truce in, 169–70, 182
car sales, 47
Catino, Maurizio, 174
Central America
cheap mobile-phone technology, spread of, 33
extortion in, 37
human smuggling in, 36
Chapo 701 (firm), 178–9
Charming Kitten (cybercriminal group), 124
Chayes, Sarah, 149
Chiapas (Mexico), 52–3
Chihuahua (Mexico), 109
child labour, 61–2
child marriages, 61
child pornography, 24, 116–17, 119
Child sexual abuse material (CSAM), 24, 115, 116
children smuggling, 36
children
behavior surveillance reduction, 117
in gangs recruitment, 61
online sexual exploitation, 24, 115–18
sexual exploitation, 24, 60, 92–3
social media usage rate, 117
'webcam child sex tourism', 115–16
China, 44
anti-wildlife trafficking campaigns, 100–1

Belt and Road Initiative, 196
chemical precursors shipments from, 68, 72
companies illicit manufacturing, 16–17
criminal governance, 173
flight suspension to/from, 12
foreign direct investment, 196
Huanan Seafood Wholesale Market, 97, 98
illegal fishing, 110
illegal wildlife products, demands for, 38, 97, 98
as leading surgical masks manufacturer, 134
PPE exports, 134
Shanghai trade fall, 13
spread of Covid-19, 11
US accusation and conspiracy theories, 126–7
virus identification and transmission, 1
wet markets, 97–100, 111, 246–7*n*7
White Paper on Traditional Chinese Medicine, 137
wholesale food markets, closure of, 1
cigarettes smuggling, 21, 183–4
CITES (Convention on International Trade in Endangered Species of Wild Fauna and Flora), 111–12
Ciudad Juárez (Mexico), 53
civil society
investment on, as preventive measures 213–14
pandemic action, 8
Clark, Helen, 81
Cobham, Alex, 202–3
coca bush, 67, 68, 71
cocaine, 18, 19, 35, 39, 75, 79
crops eradication programmes, 67
production and challenges, 67–8, 71, 235*n*2
seizures of, 45, 72
trafficking, 73–4
Cold War, 27, 28, 29, 40, 41
Colombia, 12, 29
cocaine production and challenges, 67–8, 71
cocaine seizures, 73
Congress mining bill, 95
illicit gold trade, 85, 93
prisoners, release of, 162
Comando Vermelho (CV), 182–3, 278*n*32
commercial airlines. *See* airlines, commercial
Congo, Democratic Republic of (DRC), 108, 138

illicit gold mining, 86–8, 95
contact-tracing apps, 121–2
*Contagion* (movie), 121
Conte, Giuseppe, 12
'Corona-Antivirus' email scam, 22–3, 120–1
corruption, 213
in Covid-19 relief fund, 144
in health sectors, 139–42
Cosa Nostra (mafia), 165, 166
Costa Rica, 21, 121, 122
Costa, Antonio Maria, 4–5, 196, 208
Costantino, Fabio, 165
Council of Europe, 161
counterfeiters, 18, 134–5
counterfeiting and pirating, 18, 22, 34, 134–6, 138
medicines, 135–6, 138
court systems, 156–9, 167
courts shut down, 156
virtual hearings, 157–8, 167
Covid-19 (novel coronavirus)
affects vulnerable groups, 25
barriers and restrictions, 47–8
conspiracy theories, 126–7
contact-tracing efforts, 121–2
criminal operations, impact on, 38–9
debt cancellation claims, 195–6
economic and social activity collapse, 2–3, 9, 13
EU drug markets, impacts on, 75–80, 75*f*
foreign direct investment, 194–7
and global policy approach rethinking, 81–2
impacts on crime, 3–6
as pandemic, 2
pornography, impacts on, 23–4, 116–7, 119
port protocols changes, 155
preventions and cures misinformation, 136–9
and refugee resettlement, 52–4
relief fund, 142–7, 200–1
rich-poor inequality, 198–9
and school closure, 60, 61, 177
small businesses bankruptcy, 191–2
sports, impact on, 16
spread of, 1–2, 3, 11–12
tenders and contracts, 141–2, 144–7
transmission and symptoms, 1, 97
vaccine race, 125, 126

war metaphor, 205–9
Western hemisphere
articles on, 11
and wildlife trade opinion survey (Mar 2020), 100, 246*n*3
*see also* airlines, commercial; border closures; criminal justice system; cybercrimes; drug trafficking/industry; drugs; economy; gold mining, illegal (and trade); government's anti-Covid measures; wildlife trade, illegal (animals and products trade)
CovidLock (app), 121
criminal economy, 39–41, 106–7
criminal governance, 169–77
in slums, 25–6, 174–5
criminal justice system
court system, 156–9, 167
jails and prisons, 159–64
criminal operations, 38–9
criminal markets. *See* illicit markets
cryptocurrencies, 33–4, 129, 130
CSAM (Child sexual abuse material), 24, 115, 116
curfew. *See* lockdowns/curfews
cyberattacks
on education sector, 125–6, 125*f*
on health institutes, 124–5, 126
on logistics and transport companies, 127
on medical research institutes, 125–6, 125*f*
on unemployment system, 127–9
*see also* cybercrimes
cybercrimes, 22–4, 118–32, 152
contact-tracing efforts, 121–2
coronavirus-themed attacks, 119–22, 119*f*, 123–4
cybercriminals domain names registration, 120, 119*f*
data breaches, 122, 124, 128
as easy business, 123
global GDP of, 119
illegal streaming, 121
law enforcement counter-cybercrime, 129–30
malware encounters Report (Apr 2020), 125–6, 125*f*
multi-jurisdictional nature of, 129–30

online disinformation on public figures, 130
online sexual exploitation, 23–4, 115–18
ransomware delivery methods, 120–1
ransomware gangs moral behavior, 123
second wave of, 123–7
strategy shifting, 124
two schools of, 118–19
*see also* cyberattacks; cyberspace
cyberspace
commercial activity growth, 21–2, 32
encrypted communication technologies, 32–3
insecurity of, 129–32
Cyprus, 50–1

*Daily Telegraph* (newspaper), 169
Dar es Salaam (Tanzania), 182
dark web, 32, 116, 122
drug markets, 20, 79
data breaches, 122, 124, 128
deforestation, illegal, 38, 108–10, 111
and illegal gold mining, 93–4
democratisation, wave of, 40
Denmark, 201
'deviant globalization', 30–1
domestic abuses, 59
child labour, 61–2
child marriages, 61
forced labour, 57–9
forced marriages, 59, 60–1
labour exploitation, 92–3
sexual exploitation, 24, 60, 92–3, 115–18
doorstep scammers, 19
drug mules, 65–6, 210
travel suspension affects, 65–6
drug trafficking/industry, 18, 19–20, 65–6, 234–5*n*1
by air, 65–6, 72
darknet drug markets, 20, 79
EMCDDA–Europol report (Apr 2020), 75–7, 75*f*
global policy approach rethinking, 81–2
production before pandemic, 67
by sea, 71–3, 82
seizures of, 45, 72–4
travel suspension affects, 65–6
drugs
business in 1970s, 35
control global annual expenditure, 211

cultivation and production, 67–72
online drug retailing, 20, 79
party drugs, 19–20, 79
price changes during (Covid-19), 75–7, 75*f*, 78–80
seizures of, 45, 72–4
shaped regional political economy, 39
UN convention discussion on, 43
'war on drugs', 208
*see also* synthetic drugs
drugs dealers
adaptability, 18–20, 78–9, 80–2
criminal governance, 175–6
disguises as essential workers, 20, 79
drug distribution strategies, 78–9
*see also* drug trafficking/industry; drugs
drugs trade, 19–20, 35–6
dealer's adaptability, 18–20, 78–9, 80–2
*see also* drug trafficking/industry
Dubai, 34

East Africa, 39, 70
Ebola epidemic (2014), 140
E-commerce, 22–4, 199
economy, illegal, 7, 45, 212
academic studies on, 29–30
anti-Covid measures and, 15–17
growth through online, 21–4
mining economy, 86–9, 90
economy
billionaires wealth, rise of, 198–9
collapse of, 2–3, 9, 13, 187–9, 194
criminal economy, 39–41, 106–7, 183–5
extortion economy growth, 181
growth of (1990s), 28, 29
loan-sharking (usury), 192–4
night-time economy, 62
oil economy, 13
pandemic relief fund, 13, 142–7, 200–1
rich-poor inequality, 198
small businesses bankruptcy, 191–2
tax avoidance, 199–200, 201
ECOWAS (Economic Community of West African States), 54

Ecstasy (MDMA, Methylene-dioxymethamphetamine), 19, 75, 76
Ecuador, 187
El Salvador, 175, 277*n*26
elephant poaching, 103–4
11 September 2001 terrorist attacks, 43
Eligh, Jason, 80
Elmed Medical Systems (firm), 145
EMCDDA. *See* European Monitoring Centre for Drugs and Drug Addiction (EMCDDA)
EncroChat (app), 33
English Channel (sea route), 55–6
environmental crimes
  deforestation, illegal, 38, 93–4, 108–10, 111
  fishing, illegal, 110
  marine environment, collapse of, 110
  wildlife conservation, 110–13
Equifax data breach (2017), 128
Escobar, Pablo, 35
Europe
  asylum application, fall of, 51
  Black Death, 9–10
  cannabis consumption, 20
  Covid-19, first wave of, 12
  drug price changes during (Covid-19), 75–7, 75*f*
  drug seizures in, 73
  drugs dealers adaptability, 18–20
  health infrastructure cyberattacks, 124–5, 126
  human smuggling, 49
  'migration crisis' (2014 and 2016), 36, 45–6, 48, 49
  online drug retailing, 79
  police brutality (in curfew) videos, 15
  prisoners, release of, 161–2
European Medicines Agency, 126
European Monitoring Centre for Drugs and Drug Addiction (EMCDDA), 20, 79
  EMCDDA–Europol report (Apr 2020), 75–7, 75*f*
European Union (EU), 50, 51, 142, 162
  Covid-related procurement, 146–7
  EU-Turkey summit (Nov 2015), 51–2
Europol, 24, 49, 75, 116, 118

drug seizures report (May 2020), 72, 73
EMCDDA–Europol report (Apr 2020), 75–7, 75*f*
extortion, 37, 56, 181

Facebook, 117, 120, 184
Falcone (Giovanni) assassination, 27–8, 42, 214
FBI (Federal Bureau of Investigation), 118, 148
fentanyl (synthetic drug), 20, 35–6, 68, 79
Filippone, Rocco Santo, 165
Financial Action Task Force, 34
financial crisis (2008), 3, 31, 196
financial system (global), 194–8
foreign direct investment security risks, 196–7
frauds, 190–1
*Financial Times*, 87
FinCEN leak, 201–2
fishing, illegal, 110
flight drug-courier business (mules), 65–6
flight suspension. *See* airlines, commercial
flower industry, 187–9
*Forbes* (magazine), 192
forced displacement, 48
forced marriages, 59, 60–1
foreign direct investment, 196–7
forest exploitation, 108–10
41-bis regime (Italy), 165
France, 75, 76, 77, 99, 201
hospital systems, cyberattacks on, 124
police brutality in curfew, 15
prisoners, release of, 162
free trade zones (FTZs), 196–7
Freedom House (think tank), 147
Fresnius, 124–5
front line workers, 60, 205–6
fuel smuggling, 39
funds misappropriation, 143–7

gangs
abalone trade, 105–6
children and girls recruitment in, 61
and communities relationship, 172
criminal economies expansion through violence, 183–5
criminal governance and infection rates, 175–6

definition, 274*n*6
food distribution, 21, 177, 178–9
gangs lockdowns imposition, 174–5, 177
'government functions' role, 169–77
illegal alcohol and cigarette trade, 183–4
as market suppliers, 20–1
money and food parcels distributing strategy, 177–80
moral behavior, 123
South Africa gangland truce, 169–70, 171–2, 174, 180, 182
as state, 183–5
territory concept, 171–2, 175–6
violence as survival key, 172
violence expansion during lockdowns, 180–3
GCC (Gulf Cooperation Council), 57, 58
GDP, 47, 119, 195
cybercrimes, 119
fall of, 2–3
Germany, 45, 125, 126
business enterprise crime (BEC) in, 128
'ghost payrolls', 141
Glenny, Misha, 29
*McMafia*, 29–30
Global Initiative Against Transnational Organized Crime, 3–4
Global Witness, 91
globalisation, 31–2, 41
Goetz, Alain, 87
gold laundering, 86
gold mining, artisanal, 86–8, 91–2, 96
gold mining, illegal (and trade), 38, 85–96, 244*n*39
armed attacks on gold-smelting facilities, 90
deforestation and, 93–4
gold price, rise of, 87–8
governments response to, 94–5
illegal miners (*zama zamas*), 88–90
indigenous groups, threats to, 91–2, 94
licensing illegal miners, 91
licit vs. illicit mining, 91–2
mafia struggle to control over, 90–3
Operation Mercury (2019), 93
regulation and license, 90–2
sexual and labour exploitation in, 92–3

spreads under (Covid-19), 93–6
government's anti-Covid measures, 12–15
emergency financial measures, 13, 189, 190–1
nightlife entertainment closure, 15–16, 62
pandemic relief fund, 13, 142–7, 200–1
prisoners, release of, 160–4, 163*t*, 167–8
social distancing measures, 2, 13, 19, 151, 154, 160
travel restrictions, 2, 4, 11–13, 63, 65–6, 96, 101–2
*see also* border closures
Gratteri, Nicola, 193
Greece, 52
*Guardian, The* (newspaper), 51
Guatemala, 141
Guinea-Bissau, 39, 73–4, 238*n*25
drug trafficking in, 39, 73–4
Gulf Cartel, 179
Gulf Cooperation Council (GCC), 57, 58
Gulf of Aden, 83, 208
Gulf of Guinea, 84–5
Gulf of Mexico, 84
Guterres, António, 49
Guzmán, Alejandrina, 178
Guzmán, Joaquín 'El Chapo', 21

Harirud River, 17
health sectors, 111–12
corruption in, 139–42
counterfeiting and pirating health products, 18, 22, 34, 134–6, 138
Covid-19 relief fund, 13, 142–7, 200–1
cyberattacks on, 124–5, 126
fake pharmaceuticals, operation against, 18–19
health care access as human rights, 147
health workers as 'front line', 205–6
health-care assets, privatisation of, 139–42
mafia penetration in, 141
medical misinformation, 136–9
heroin, 20, 39, 69, 75, 235*n*2
poppy production, 35–6
price rise, 78
seizure of (Sep 2019), 45
homicides, 167–8, 171–2
in Cape Town, 169
Honduras, 14–15, 144–5

Hong Kong SAR, 100
 illegal wildlife products, seizures of, 104
Hope, Alejandro, 185
HSBC money laundering (2012), 33
Huanan Seafood Wholesale Market (Wuhan), 97, 98
Human Rights Watch, 92
human rights
 and anti-corruption relations, 147–9
 health care access as, 147
 media rights, violation of, 148
human smugglers, 36–7, 46, 54–7
 challenges of, 54–7
human smuggling, 17, 36–7, 46, 48–9
 into human trafficking, 57
 organised criminal smugglers, 36–7
 smuggling routes, 48–9, 54–6
human trafficking, 24, 25, 37, 46, 48, 57–63
 forced labour, 57, 58–9
 global report (2019), 37
 labour contract fraud, 57–8
 travel suspension effects on, 55
 victims as bonded servitude, 37
 victims of, 57–63
Hungary, 49–50
hydroxychloroquine (antimalarial drug), 137–8

identity theft, 128
illegal gold mining. *See* gold mining, illegal (and trade)
illegal miners (*zama zamas*), 88–90
illegal wildlife trade. *See* wildlife trade, illegal (animals and products trade)
illegal, unreported and unregulated fishing (IUU), 110
*Illicit* (Naím), 29
illicit markets, 3–4, 6, 40, 43, 45, 46
 growth of, 5–6, 34–9
 term definition, 6–7
 organised crime and, 3, 5–6
 pandemic shaped, 7, 8–9
 during early 1990s, 30–1
 Asian middle class as driver of, 30–1
 globalisation and technology effects on, 31–4
 drug markets, 20, 79, 75–80, 75*f*

preventive measures for, 212–13
see also gold mining, illegal (and trade); wildlife trade, illegal (animals and products trade)
illicit narcotics, 3, 45
see also drugs
illicit trade
books on, 29
counterfeit medicines, 18, 22, 134–5
gold price rise and, 87–8
'special economic zones' proliferation, 135–6
see also illicit markets
ILO (International Labour Organization), 57
IMF (International Monetary Fund), 2, 189
IMPACT (civil society organization), 87
India, 38, 57, 58, 273*n*53
drug and chemical precursor production and shipment, 72
'PM Cares Fund', 143
prisoners, release of, 162
Indonesia, 57, 104, 110, 162
gang–government 'overlap', 176–7
Indonesian Market Traders Association, 176–7
Indonesian Supreme Court, 156, 157
InSight Crime, 104
Institute for Policy Studies (United States), 198
Inter-American Commission on Human Rights, 159–60
International Civil Aviation Organization, 31
International Labour Organization (ILO), 57
International Monetary Fund (IMF), 2, 189
International Organization for Migration (IOM), 37, 54
Internet Watch Foundation, 117
internet
criminal expansion, role in, 21, 31, 32
e-commerce boom, 22–3
online drug retailing, 20, 79
platform for illegal advertising and sales, 32, 38, 112
porn sites visitors, rise of, 23
users growth rate, 21–3, 32
see also cybercrimes; cyberspace
INTERPOL, 18, 44, 55, 118

fake pharmaceuticals, operation against, 18–19
IOM (International Organization for Migration), 37, 54
Iran, 11, 126, 162
border control and virus transmission, 17
Irish Prison Service, 160
Italian mafias, 28–9
health sector and funeral services penetration, 141–2
loan-sharking, 193–4
mafiosi, release of, 164–6
migration of, 30
'Ndrangheta boss arrest, 16, 165
Italy, 41, 42
criminal governance, 173
Falcone and Borsellino assassination, 27–8
foreign investment risks, 197
lockdown, 12, 13
mafiosi, release of, 164–6
Ministry of Justice, 165, 166
Palermo bombing (23 May 1992), 27–8
prisoners, release of, 162
rescue on Mediterranean sea, 50
state of emergency declaration, 11–12
subprime financial crisis (2007) assessment, 194
Ituri (Congo), 87

jails and prisons, 159–64
mafiosi, release of, 164–6
pre-trial detention, review of, 160–1
prisoners, release of, 160–4, 163*t*, 167–8
*see also* criminal justice system
Jalisco New Generation Cartel (Mexico), 135, 179
Japan, 41, 125, 173
Johannesburg (South Africa), 90
Johnson, Boris, 205
*Journal of the American Medical Association*, 140

'kafala' sponsorship system, 58
Kenya Wildlife Service, 107–8
Kenya, 18, 38–9, 61, 208
counterfeit hand sanitisers distribution, 18
flowers exports, 187
kids recruitment in gangs, 61

kidnapping (virtual) ransom scams, 61–2
gang violence, rise of, 181
wildlife trafficking reports, 105
Korea, 126
Kosiah, Alieu, 158
Krastev, Ivan, 7–8
Kruger National Park (South Africa), 102, 103
Kuciak (Ján) murder trial, 157, 158

La Pampa, 93, 94
labour exploitation, 57–63
bonded labour, 57–8
child labour, 61–2
forced labour, 57, 58–9
in gold mines, 92–3
labour contract fraud, 57–8
*Lancet, The* (journal), 139
Latin America
against chemical precursors shipment, 68
cocaine production and challenges, 67–8
gangs 'criminal governance', 171, 173–6
gangs food distribution, 178–9
gangs lockdowns imposition, 174–5, 177
illegal logging, 108–9
medical misinformation, 138
virus infection on police personnel, 153
wildlife trafficking in, 104–5
law enforcement agencies, 4, 13, 16, 24, 100, 105, 110, 116, 129–30, 151, 155, 166
cooperation between states, 44
improvement policy, 211, 213
*Le Figaro* (newspaper), 122
Libya, 41, 50, 55
civil war (2011), 41
human smugglers, 55
loan-sharking (usury), 192–4
lockdowns/curfews, 1–2, 6, 49, 101–2
and domestic abuse, 59
first wave of, 53
and forest exploitation, 108–10
gangs lockdowns imposition, 174–5, 177
gangs violence expansion during, 180–3
human rights abuses and, 14–15
illicit manufacturing, 16–17

military and police brutalities, 14–15
and online e-commerce boom, 22–3
online sexual exploitation, 23–4, 115–18
police front-end role during, 151–4
porn sites visitors rise during, 23–4
strict lockdown (Mar-May), 16
*see also* border closures; cybercrimes; gold mining, illegal (and trade); wildlife trade, illegal (animals and products trade)
logging, illegal, 108–9
London, 34
López Obrador, Andrés Manuel, 13, 179
Lopez, Axel G., 145
Los Durango, 179
Los Viagras, 179
lottery scams, 61–2
Lukashenko, Alexander, 137

Macron, Emmanuel, 205
Madre de Dios (Peru), 94, 95
mafias
anti-mafia magistrates assassination (Italy), 27–8
food parcels distribution, 21, 177
loan-sharking, 193–4
local mafias into global networks, 27, 30
academic studies on, 28–30
gold mining control, 90–3
health sector penetration, 141
*see also* gangs; Italian mafias
Magufuli, John, 137
Malaysia, 45
forced labour practices during pandemic, 58–9
Malta, 51
Mandetta, Luiz Henrique, 176
Manenberg (Cape Town), 21
marijuana, 74
marine wildlife trafficking, 105–7
maritime drug trafficking, 71–3, 82, 83
*see also* shipping
masks, 18, 134
3M masks, 146
shortage of, 152
Matamoros (Mexico), 53
*McMafia* (Glenny), 29–30
Medellín Cartel, 35
medical misinformation, 136–9

Mediterranean Sea, 37, 50, 208
Mediterranean Shipping Company, 127
Merkel, Angela, 142
methamphetamine (synthetic drug), 20, 45, 67, 76, 79
  production booming, 70
  seizures of, 74
  supply and shipment issues, 68–9
Mexican cartels, 36, 178–9
  on chemical precursors, 68–9
  migrants kidnapping and extortion involvement, 56–7
Mexico, 12
  anti-migrant sentiment in, 52–3
  counterfeit medicines supply, 135
  criminal governance in, 173, 174
  drug-trafficking groups territory control, 185
  'El Chapo's provisions', 178–9
  fentanyl and methamphetamines seizure, 69
  heroin poppy production in, 35–6
  illegal logging in, 109
  mafia and gangs food parcels distribution, 21, 177, 178–9
  marijuana legalisation bill, 159
  maritime threats, 84
  turtles seizure of, 107
  wildlife trafficking in, 104–5, 107, 246*n*4
Microsoft, 120, 121, 124
migrant workers
  abuse and exploitation against, 56–9
  into forced labour, 57–9
  kidnapping, 56
  in nightlife industry, 62
migration crisis, 48–54
  and human smuggling, 54–7
migration, illegal, 36–7
migration
  anti-migrant sentiment, 52–3
  disappearance and death, 36–7
  during pandemic, 47–54
  growth rate, 47
  politicians on migrants, 49
Milan (Italy), 193
Mixed Migration Centre, 54
mobile phones, 32–3
Modi, Narendra, 143
  'PM Cares Fund', 143

money laundering, 33–4
gold usage in, 86
Monir, Mohamed, 164
moratorium policy, 189
Morrison, Scott, 205
MS-13 (gang), 175
Myanmar, 100
Naím, Moisés, 29
*Illicit*, 29

Nairobi (Kenya), 18
Nakuru (Kenya), 181–2
National Council of Justice (Brazil), 159, 160–1
National Crime Agency, 45
National Forestry and Grasslands Administration, 99
National Health Commission (China), 137
National Penitentiary Department (Brazil), 159
*Nature Ecology and Evolution* (journal), 110
'Ndrangheta (mafia), 165, 166
Nepal (India), 108
Netherlands, 127, 160
flower industry, collapse of, 187
*New York Times*, 210
New York, 12
Nigeria, 14, 29, 195
lockdown, 14
Scattered Canary unemployment insurance fraud, 127–8
drug traffickers, 65, 66, 82
nightlife entertainment closure, 15–16, 62
Nixon, Richard, 208
North America, 12, 48, 79
North Korea, 126
North Rhine–Westphalia (NRW), 128–9
Northern Family (Familia do Norte, FDN), 182–3
Norway, 76, 162

Oaxaca (Mexico), 105, 107
oil prices, 13, 195
online drug retailing, 20, 79
online scams. *See* cybercrimes
online sexual exploitation, 23–4, 115–18
drivers of, 116
Operation Black Cross, 141
Operation Mercury (2019), 93
opium poppy production, 69–70
Orbán, Viktor, 49–50
Organisation for Economic Cooperation and Development (OECD), 134–5, 136, 197
organised crime

challenges for, 41–4
counterfeiting virus-mitigating products, 18, 22, 34, 134–6, 138
disease language for, 208–9
and flesh trade, 24
legal goods shortages and, 20–1
in 1990s, 27–31
police response to, 154–6, 166–7
prevention, treatment and cure for, 210–15
rise of, 4–5
and shipping industry, 17–21
similarities between pandemic and, 207
states offerings to, 20–1
studies on, 3–4
technology usage, 31–4
term definition, 6
victims of, 25–6
*see also* cybercrimes; gold mining, illegal (and trade); human smuggling; human trafficking; illicit markets; wildlife trade, illegal (animals and products trade)
Organized Crime and Corruption Reporting Project (OCCRP), 145–6, 148

Pacheco, Roberto, 92
Pakistan, 57, 58
Palermo bombing (23 May 1992), 27–8
Palermo Protocol (Dec 2000), 42–3
Panama Papers, 34
Panama, 21
pandemic relief funding, 142–7, 200–1
pandemic. *See* Covid-19 (novel coronavirus)
pangolin, 97, 98, 99, 112
Paraguay, 21
party drugs, 19–20, 79
*see also* cocaine; synthetic drugs
Paycheck Protection Program (PPP), 191
Penal Reform International, 160
perlemoen. *See* abalone (marine snail)
personal protective equipment (PPE), 18, 20, 58, 59, 133, 134, 145, 147, 152
Peru, 12, 91
cocaine production, 67, 71
Covid-19 misinformation, 138–9

illegal gold mining, 85, 91, 94–5
indigenous leaders assassination, 91–2
Ministry of Environment, 95
sexual and labour exploitation in, 92–3
virus infection on police personnel, 153
pharmaceutical industry, 136
counterfeiting medicines and health products, 18, 22, 34, 134–6, 138
*see also* health sectors
Philippines, 57, 110, 115
phishing scams, 119–20, 121
piracy attacks, 83–5
on ships and oil infrastructure, 84
pirates, 208
kidnapping-for-ransom, 84–5
poaching, 38, 101, 102
bushmeat, 107–8
elephant, 103–4
rhino, 38, 102–3, 103*f*, 112, 208
*see also* wildlife trade, illegal (animals and products trade)
Poland, 42, 201
Polaris, 60
police stations, closure of, 151–2
police
brutality during lockdown, 14, 15
domestic violence rise and, response to, 154
front-end role during lockdowns, 151–4
organised crime, response to, 154–6, 166–7
virus infection on, 152–3
Pompeo, Mike, 98
Pornhub (website), 23–4
pornography, 23–4, 116–17, 119
site visitors, rise of, 23
PPE (personal protective equipment), 18, 20, 58, 59, 133, 134, 145, 147, 152
Prime Minister's Citizen Assistance and Relief in Emergency Situations Fund ('PM Cares Fund') (India), 143
prisons. *See* jails and prisons
private philanthropy, 200–1
prostitution, 60, 61, 63, 210
public health systems. *See* health sectors
public procurement, 142–7
Puerto Rico, 121
Punjab (India), 80

Rajoelina, Andry, 137
Ramaphosa, Cyril, 12
refugee camps, 52–4
refugee crisis (2013), 45–6
  *see also* migration crisis
Reporters Without Borders, 148
rhino poaching, 38, 102–3, 103*f*, 112
  war on poachers, 208
rhinos, 38, 100, 102
Rio de Janeiro (Brazil), 144, 174–5
  extortion threats, 181
  *favelas*, 21
Rohingya refugees, 56
Romania, 146–7
Rotterdam Port, 73
Russia, 29, 30, 44, 78, 173

Santos, Edmar, 144
SARS (Severe Acute Respiratory Syndrome), 245–6*n*2, 247*n*12
SARS-CoV-2. *See* Covid-19 (novel coronavirus)
Saviano, Robert, 194
Scanlon, John, 112
Scaramella, Amedeo, 193
'Scattered Canary' (Nigerian criminal group), 127–8
school closures, 60, 61, 177
sea
  drug trafficking by, 71–3, 82, 83
  piracy attacks, 83–5
Self.inc (website), 22
Serbia, 50
sex workers, 24, 25, 62–3
shark fins, 104
Shining Path (guerrilla group), 91
shipping, 17–18
  customs reduction and smuggling, 17–18, 155
  global shipping community, 83
Sierra Leone, 140
Singapore Strait, 83
social distancing measures, 2, 13, 19, 151, 154, 160
social media
  public figures, false rumours on, 130
  *see also* internet
Somalia, 29, 85
  charcoal smuggling, 38
  pirates, 83
Sonko, Mike, 137
South Africa, 12, 29
  alcohol banning, 81
  Cape Flats police operations reports, 153
  doorstep scammers, 19
  drugs dealers distribution strategies, 78–9

extortion economies, growth of, 181
gangland truce in, 169–70, 171–2, 174, 180, 182
gangs 'government functions' role, 169–70, 172
gangs as market suppliers, 20–1
gangs challenges in abalone trade, 105–6
gangs illegal alcohol and cigarette trade, 183–4
heroin, price rise of, 78
illegal gold miners crisis, 88–90
illegal gold mining, 88–90, 95
lockdown, 12, 89, 90, 169
military brutalities (in curfew), 15
moratorium on alcohol and tobacco (and legal goods), 20
police stations closure, 151
prisoners, release of, 162–3, 271–2*n*42
rhino poaching in, 102–3, 103*f*
virus transmission, 12
South America, 12
South China Sea, 83
South Korea, 156
South Sudan, 86
Spain, 11, 76, 77, 162
sports, cessation of, 16
Sri Lanka, 196
states
convention against organized crime, 43–4
and crime, ties between, 39–41
gangs as, 183–5
opportunities creation for organised crime, 20–1
refugee crisis, response to, 46
subsidies offerings, 13
*see also* government's anti-Covid measures
Stock, Jürgen, 55
Sullivan, John, 179
Suspicious Activity Reports (SARs), 202
Sweden, 76
Swiss Federal Criminal Court, 158
Switzerland, 19
synthetic drugs, 35–6, 39
fentanyl, 20, 35–6, 68, 79
methamphetamine, 20, 45, 67, 68–9, 70, 74, 76
price changes, 75, 75*f*, 76–7
Syria/Syrian, 36, 53
refugees, 50, 51–2

Taliban, 70

tax havens, 200, 201, 203
TCM (Traditional Chinese Medicine), 99, 137
technology, 21–2, 31, 32–4
Thailand, 11, 24, 100
tiger trade, 102
timber mafias, 109
tobacco, 20
Toll Group (firm), 127
Top Glove (firm), 58–9
totoaba fish bladders, 104, 107, 246*n*4
Traditional Chinese Medicine (TCM), 99, 137
transactional sex, 60
'transnational organised crime', 27–31, 46
  academic studies on, 28–30
  early 1990s, 27–31
  global assessment (2010), 30
  rise of networks, 30
  *see also* organised crime
Transparency International, 140
travel suspension, 63, 96
  air travel, 2, 4, 11–13
  maritime, 50–2
  *see also* border closures
Triads (Chinese mafia), 28, 193
Trickbot Trojan campaign, 120–1
Trudeau, Justin, 50
Trump, Donald, 11, 14
  Covid-19 misinformation, 137–8
  South Carolina rally (Feb 2020), 49
  war metaphor, use of, 205
Tuchman, Barbara, 9–10
Turkey, 51
  EU-Turkey summit (Nov 2015), 51–2
  prisoners, release of, 161–2, 164
turtles, 104–5, 107

Uganda, 14, 86
UN Human Rights Commission, 148
UN Security Council, 40
  ministerial conference (Naples, Nov 1994), 42
unemployment crisis, 2, 13, 58, 187, 189
  insurance fraud, 127–8
UNESCO (United Nations Educational, Scientific and Cultural Organization), 60
UNHCR (United Nations High Commissioner for Refugees), 52
United Arab Emirates, 58
United Kingdom (UK)
  aggressive tax avoidance, 201

attacks on 5G towers, 127
Border Force, 18, 237*n*21
child pornography, 117
Covid-19 as 'great leveller', 198
drugs smuggling, 18
English Channel as migrant smugglers route, 55–6
'furlough fraud', 191
heroin seizure (Sep 2019), 45
Intelligence and Security Committee of Parliament, 34
medical research institutes cyberattacks, 125
National Health Service, 59
Police forces on drugs dealers, 20, 78
prison population fall, 162
public procurement decisions, 146
virtual court system, 157
United Nations (UN), 60, 159
global poverty estimation, 189
Global Strategy and Plan on Drugs, 81
United Nations Convention Against Transnational Organized Crime (UNTOC), 42–4, 113, 214
United Nations Educational, Scientific and Cultural Organization (UNESCO), 60
United Nations High Commissioner for Refugees (UNHCR), 52
United Nations Office on Drugs and Crime (UNODC), 5, 30, 55, 77, 130
human smuggling report (2010), 48–9
human trafficking global report (2019), 37
opium harvest monitoring, 70
*World Drug Report* (2020), 35
United Nations Population Fund, 61
United States (US), 41, 42
accusation on China, 126–7
BEC scams, 23, 128
border closure and rules, 49
Canada-US border closure, 50
children smuggling in southern border, 36

cocaine seizure (Jun 2019), 45
'Corona-Antivirus' email scam, 23, 120–1
COVID-19's effects on police, 153
cyber-attacks on health sectors, 124, 125, 126
e-commerce boom, 199
11 September 2001 terrorist attacks, 43
Federal Trade Commission, 191
FinCEN leak, 201–2
Food and Drug Administration, 139
global 'war on terrorism', 42
negative oil prices, 195
New York Police Department, 153
opioid crisis, 35
pre-trial detention, review of, 160
Scattered Canary unemployment insurance fraud, 127–8
'war on drugs', 208
University of Oxford, 131
UNODC. *See* United Nations Office on Drugs and Crime (UNODC)
UNTOC (United Nations Convention Against Transnational Organized Crime), 42–4, 113, 214
US Customs and Border Patrol (CBP), 74
US Department of Labor, 92, 120
US Secret Service, 127
US State Department, 84

vaccine race, 125, 126
Venezuela, 68, 92, 94
ventilators, 144, 145
Ventrici, Francesco, 165
Vetere, Eduardo, 41–2
Vietnam, 38, 100, 102, 247–8*n*15
Vory (Russian mafia), 28

war
and crime function, 40–1
definition, 206
metaphor, 205–9
*Washington Post*, 175
'webcam child sex tourism', 115–16
websites
coronavirus-related domain names purchase, 22, 120, 119*f*
state´s official site mimic fraud, 128–9
growth rate, 32

*see also* cybercrimes
West Africa, 30, 39
 Ebola epidemic (2014), 140
 human smuggling in, 54–5
Western Europe, 11
wet markets, 97–100, 111, 246–7*n*7
 closing down idea, 99–100
 internal resistance to closing, 99
 resistance to, 98–9
WhatsApp, 33, 79, 178
White, Aron, 99
WHO (World Health Organization), 2, 18–19, 120, 124, 133, 138, 147
wildlife trade, illegal (animals and products trade), 37–8, 97–108, 111–13, 247*n*11
 Asian middle class role in, 30–1
 consumer attitudes, 100–1
 Covid-19 and wildlife trade opinion survey (Mar 2020), 100, 246*n*3
 criminals adaptability during pandemic, 105–6
 demand for, 4, 37–8
 internet advertising and sales, 32, 38, 112
 lockdowns and border closures, 101–2
 public health dimension of, 111–12
 regulation of, 99–100
 seizures of, 104
 trust deficit in, 100
 wildlife conservation efforts, 110–13
wildlife trafficking, 97–8, 101–8, 111–13
 anti-wildlife trafficking campaigns, 100–1
 commercial airlines suspension and, 101–2
 lockdowns and border closures, 101–2
 marine wildlife trafficking, 105–7
 *see also* wildlife trade, illegal (animals and products trade)
Williams, Phil, 41
Win Billion Investment Group (Win BIG), 146
Witzel, Wilson, 144
women
 forced marriages, 59, 60–1
 in nightlife criminal industries, 62
 in opium poppy-growing, 70
 sexual exploitation, 24, 60, 92–3, 115–18
work from home, 13, 23, 51, 117, 121

World Bank, 189
  2013 report, 201
World Health Organization (WHO), 2, 18–19, 120, 124, 133, 138, 147
Wuhan (China), 1
  wild animals trade, 97
  Huanan Seafood Wholesale Market, 97, 98

Yakuza (Japanese mafia), 16, 28, 193
York University (Toronto, Canada), 126

Zagaria, Pasquale, 165–6
*zama zamas*. *See* illegal miners (*zama zamas*)
Zambia, 108
Zimbabwe, 154